The Media

THE CREDIBILITY OF INSTITUTIONS, POLICIES AND LEADERSHIP
A Series funded by the Hewlett Foundation
Kenneth W. Thompson, *Series Editor*

The Media

The Credibility of Institutions, Policies and Leadership
Volume 5

Edited by
Kenneth W. Thompson

University Press of America
Lanham • New York • London

Copyright © 1985 by

University Press of America,™ Inc.

4720 Boston Way
Lanham, MD 20706

3 Henrietta Street
London WC2E 8LU England

Co-published by arrangement with
The White Burkett Miller Center of Public Affairs,
The University of Virginia

Library of Congress Cataloging in Publication Data
Main entry under title:

The Media.

(The Credibility of institutions, policies and
leadership ; v. 5)
    1. Presidents—United States—Press conferences—
Addresses, essays, lectures. 2. Mass media—Political
aspects—United States—Addresses, essays, lectures.
I. Thompson, Kenneth W., 1921-   . II. Series.
JK518.M43   1985   353.03'5   84-29086
ISBN 0-8191-4442-8 (alk. paper)
ISBN 0-8191-4443-6 (pbk. : alk. paper)

Table of Contents

V. Conclusion

Preface

Having first examined the credibility of ideas and approaches to politics and foreign policy, we turn in Part Two to a survey of leading institutions in American society. To select them confronts those who are organizing such a series with their first problem. To analyze and evaluate them presents a second concern. To seek out the professional competence for such inquiries is a third but not the final choice to be faced.

Inevitably the choice of the leading institutions in American society engenders controversy. We have chosen to begin with the media as an increasingly powerful force in American life. Its influence seems clear in almost every dimension of contemporary politics and society. We expect to continue in our studies with the church and the state. To exclude the economic institutions and the private sector from any list of primary institutions would be unacceptable. Yet other institutions of no less significance cry for discussion including the family, the schools and the membership of intermediary institutions that ease and foster society's coping with its social and economic problems including a host of voluntary organizations.

Yet those who would advance the understanding of the leading institutions in American life and public attitudes and responses to them must begin where access is possible. The Miller Center's dominant emphasis on the American presidency leads naturally to a discussion of the media. Studies of the presidency cannot be made other than in the context of an understanding of the American political system and the state. Inquiries that throw a strong light on the public sector display alongside it the workings of the private sector and a vast array of interrelationships. The church stands apart from the public and private sectors but its importance for them both arises from its proclaiming many of the values that inspire the standards society has embraced.

Through such reasoning, we have chosen for consideration a group of institutions which make up the subject matter of Part Two.

I

The Media:
Power and Responsibility

INTRODUCTION

The power of the mass media would appear to be self-evident in the 1980s. In the summer of 1984, some 80 million Americans viewed the Olympics televised from Los Angeles. Following the Democratic Convention in July of 1984 which was marked by exceptional political oratory viewed by an audience of 40–50 million, a surge in the popularity of the Mondale-Ferraro candidacy moved them to within a few points of President Reagan. For both party conventions the impact before they met of television relentlessly recording the results of primary elections from January to June has weakened the role of the political parties and removed the possibility of a genuinely deliberative convention. Few can argue against the proposition that the media has become the message and, to quote Sander Vanocur, that television had supplanted the political process.

In one sense, television has brought the people closer to the cherished dream of democratic thinkers from Thomas Jefferson to Thomas Dewey. More people than ever before are within reach of being able to appropriate the cultural and intellectual treasures of the western world. Television brings the best in music, theater and dance into Everyman's living room. Not only the evening news transmitted instantaneously as history unfolds but public affairs discussions have become common fare. Investigative reporters stand watch over the classical standard that political leaders must be "purer than Caeser's wife." Observers ask if Watergate or ending the war with Vietnam would have occured without television let alone the defeat of McCarthyism. An audience beginning with pre-schoolers and ending with senior citizens can all enjoy the fruits of innovative educational programs. Television as the most revolutionary of all forms of communication reaches everyone.

Yet despite all its power, or perhaps because of it, the media stirs anxiety and alarm which in recent years has swept across American society. Established institutions and practices are threatened by the power of television: the local congregation by network evangelists, the political party by spot political commercials, issue-oriented candidates by politicians skilled in one liners tailored for ten to thirty-second capsules, serious commentary by scandal and sensationalism, good news by bad news, and education by entertainment.

Moreover, the suspicion persists that television reporting slants the news. Conservatives charge that Ivy League liberals and leftists dominate the media. Liberals worry about the power of giant corporations that pay for broadcasting through expensive advertising. Television is either too liberal or too conservative, as the case may be, for half of its listening audience. The high cost of producing television's best programs invites the conspiratorial theory that "he who pays the piper calls the tune."

A somewhat different version of such a theory is expressed in the indictment of television put forward by those who say it brings victory or defeat to rivals in a political race. By televising the results of voting in the east or midwest, television influences voters in the west who have not gone to the polls. It favors glamorous movie stars or celebrated military men over experienced political leaders better able to govern. How often are we not told that Lincoln or Washington, neither of whose appearances were captivating, would probably have failed politically in a television age.

The media sees itself in an adversarial, confrontational stance *vis-à-vis* newsmakers. Its foremost claim is that newsmen are continuously in search of the truth. By implication, those who are the subjects of reporting seek to conceal or obscure at least part of the truth. The task of a newsman is to ferret out what newsmakers seek to hide. Thus the relationship between newsmakers and news reporters is often conflictual. Tensions exist. Helen Thomas and the White House reporters view the struggle from one vantage point while Jody Powell and most press secretaries, whether for presidents or other public or private leaders, see the competition from the other end of the telescope. In an ideal world, the relationship might be a cooperative one of giving and sharing. In the real world, skepticism and mild distrust are often present.

Honesty requires that we say that the net effect and long-term influence of the media remain something of a question. The public's concern centers on whether the media's investigatory skills are matched by a sense of responsibility. Sometimes those who gain most notice and attention in the media appear to be willing to discover a story whatever the costs. Some reporters ride rough-shod over the personal lives and reputations of dedicated leaders. Truth is subordinated to the unquenchable thirst to be the first to disclose a scandal. The restricted coverage possible in relatively short news reports puts a premium on simplification even if the story throws a dark shadow over a long and unblemished professional career.

The media rests its case on the first amendment but especially where national security is involved the need for freedom with responsibility is apparent. The public knows all too little about the assumptions and commitments of those who proclaim they speak the truth. If disclosures of wrong doing by public servants are a responsibility of the media shouldn't the public also have the right to know when news reports are based on faulty evidence? Is there a rule for the media equivalent to the constraint on freedom of speech contained in the judgment that no one can cry fire in a crowded theater?

Those who are contributors to the present volume are mainly professionals in one sector or the other of news interpreting or reporting. Their professional experience, however, has prepared them not to defend the media in any blanket sense but to help others understand its workings. No one of these observers considers all the questions which have been posed regarding the media. Taken together they illuminate some of the shadowy corners in the debate over the good and the bad aspects of television and investigative reporting.

What remains is the need for an authoritative and comprehensive inquiry into the responsibility of the media. It would be our hope that whoever undertakes this monumental task would find that the pages of this little volume provide useful background and fruitful source material.

II

The Media
And Politics

The President and Communications: The Media and the Political Process
SANDER VANOCUR

NARRATOR: We have tried in organizing the Miller Center Forums to draw from as broad a constituency of university and community leaders as we could. This isn't the first time that Sander Vanocur has had an appeal for a wide ranging group. When he was an undergraduate at Northwestern University, professors invited him to be a member of each graduate seminar. He continued to display precociousness at the London School of Economics where he gravitated toward one of the great teachers of political science, a man who invariably turned out to be the center of intellectual excitement, namely Martin Wight whose slender little book, fifty-seven pages I believe, on power politics, reissued after his death by his students in a 300 page edition based on his notes, remains a classic in the field of international politics. From the London School of Economics where he was a student as well as a British correspondent for CBS News, Sandy went to NBC News where he served in various capacities from 1957–1971. That was a time when, following the gradual disappearance of some of the early great figures like Edward R. Murrow and Elmer Davis from radio news, a lot of us came to depend upon Sander Vanocur as White House correspondent for NBC, as the *Today Show* host, and subsequently from 1971–1977, Senior Correspondent of the National Public Affairs Center for the TV division of Public Broadcasting Service. He was a columnist for the *Washington Post* from 1975–1977. He is now Vice President in charge of Special Reporting Units of ABC News. He has served, as it were, on the night shift as consultant to outside groups such as the Center for the Study of Democratic Institutions where he had a close, and complicated relationship with Mr. Robert Hutchins, the founder of that important Center.

He was Professor of Communications at Duke University. It's a great personal honor and privilege to introduce Sander who will speak on the President and the Media in the Political Process.

MR. VANOCUR: Thank you Ken. Had it not been for Ken I might have gravitated at Northwestern to the history department and historians like Ray Billington. I mention that because most of my training has been as a political scientist, whether I was studying with Ken, Hans Morgenthau, or Charles Hyneman, or just covering politics. I wish in some ways I had devoted more time to history because now as a political scientist, a part-time one, I am forced to try to read the journal of the American Political Science Association for which I am not equipped because it's all written in mathematical symbols.

The reason I state this is that I want to offer some tentative observations, and they are tentative. I'm not being modest about it—I agree with John Kenneth Galbraith that modesty is a highly overrated virtue—but I'm offering these things in a tentative way because I don't think I have the proper historical background to know if things were worse or better in other times in terms of the press in this country. For example, George Reedy throws out the proposition that the political life of this country was better when newspapers were tied intimately to one party or another. I don't know enough for example about the role of the press in elections, though I know something about the role of the Hearsts, the Pulitzers and Horace Greeley. I don't know for example, how billboards were used or handbills were used at the turn of the century.

All I really know basically is what I have been doing for the last twenty years, which is television. And the proposition which I want to lay before you is that I think television is coming very close to becoming either *the* major part—which it is already—of the political process or it is in danger, or we are in danger, of it becoming the political process itself. And, as I am now fifty-one years of age and about to enter that period of life when I repeat myself, I'd like to read you something I wrote at the *Washington Post* which still stands up as I worry about this process. It's about President Carter as he was going to take over as President of the United States. It's datelined January 16, 1977:

> Jimmy Carter will succumb to a virus when he stands
> before the east front of the Capitol to take the oath of

office as President of the United States. The virus which is of recent origin is commonly called Presidential Television. It is known to have two strains, domestic and foreign. There's no known cure for either. The foreign variety is the more virulent of the two. It's characterized by a restlessness which usually surfaces after the first few months in office which can only be relieved by jet travel, airport receptions, motorcades, banquets, toasts, and full and frank exchanges of views. Greatest comfort is provided by the patient's progress being continuously monitored by live television cameras until the virus has run its course which usually occurs somewhere in the vicinity of Andrews Air Force Base outside of Washington. . . .

And I went on talking about Eisenhower, Nixon and so forth — and Kennedy who began the process. A month later after President Carter did the speech on energy wearing a cardigan and sitting in front of a fireplace and a Gilbert Stuart portrait of Washington I wrote:

Watching President Carter's first fireside chat on television the other night I was reminded of Oscar Levant's description of Hollywood, "You have to sweep away the surface tinsel to get to the real tinsel underneath."

I said that Mr. Carter's not a simple man; he's about as simple as Cardinal Richelieu, and I begin to think he makes John F. Kennedy look like Jack Armstrong, the all-American boy, when it comes to understanding and manipulating television. I concluded by saying that, "at the risk of sounding dyspeptic I would suggest that President Carter dispense with all these attempts at contrivance, and that includes his plans for radio call-in sessions. This is not governing; it is tinsel television and radio designed to create symbols that may in time become in his own mind gratifying substitutes for decision and action."

The reason I wrote that is that over the years I have tried to keep track of what passes for power in Washington. When I arrived there in 1960, power to me was represented by people who wouldn't talk to me or kept their names out of the paper, men like Richard Russell, Clinton Anderson, a man named Al Thomas, who I will talk about in a minute and George Mahon. In other words power holders were the people you never saw mentioned in the paper or interviewed on *Meet the Press*. That was the secret of their power. In 1962, I mentioned to Larry O'Brien one night that I'd seen Al Thomas at the White House and asked what he was doing. He said that he was assuring President Kennedy that if a recession threatened, he, Albert Thomas, could pump about two or three billion dollars into the economy without anyone's knowing about it. The reason he could do that was that he was head of something called the House Appropriations Subcommittee on Independent Agencies— and that's why they named the space center in Houston after Albert Thomas. That represented power to me.

Later on as I watched television and my role in it intrude more and more on the political process and the political process intrude more and more on television, I began to wonder what power really was. I began to think that television exposure meant power to a lot of politicians; being interviewed on television, going on *Face the Nation,* certainly going on *The Today Show* which then held primacy of place in the morning news shows. And gradually as the years passed, I began to think that politicians, and certainly the President of the United States, believed that going on television was not part of a process to influence legislation or change public opinion but became almost an end in itself. The very act of going on television somehow made them think that something had been changed like ice melting to water. In fact, I don't think that the physical property of the political process had been touched at all. I believe that every time that Richard Nixon went on television to explain away Watergate he buried himself deeper in a grave that he was digging for himself. Every time Lyndon Johnson went on television to explain away Vietnam he further, I think, complicated the process. And every time Jimmy Carter has gone on television, certainly in the last year, I think he has worn out his welcome, complicated the political process and confused a lot of people.

In the election we're about to watch unfold, we're going to witness a media blitz with much money put into it. You will also hear the cry go up for televised debates. I once wrote after the 1976 debates that I wish I could go into a court of law to seek an injunction forever forbidding two consenting candidates from performing unnatural acts in public, because as a participant in the 1960 debate, the first one, I tried to recall the main issues. One was that Kennedy looked better than Nixon in the first debate. One of

Kennedy's main supporters, Abraham Ribicoff who was driving that night from Sacramento to San Francisco, heard it on the radio and thought Nixon had won the debate. The other great issue of the moment was Quemoy and Matsu. The third was a nonexistent missile gap. If you tried to recall what the issues were in the 1976 debate, I think it was the remark that President Ford made about Eastern Europe which illustrated, not that he didn't know what he was talking about, but that he had no felicity for expressing that complicated thought. It revealed to some of us that Jimmy Carter was a man possessed with a great instinct for the jugular vein which I think we are going to see again in the forthcoming campaign.

But the thing that worries me which I want to explore with you—and my remarks will be very brief—is that those of us in television are said to be the prime source of information for the American people. As David Brinkley once said, "If that's the case then the American people are in deep trouble." Some people say that we're merely reflectors of the political process or of events. Dan Rather wrote a book called *The Camera Never Blinks,* the implication being that our reports were a very true and realistic view of the world, though I imagine anybody with any knowledge about the optical nerve system would tell you that an eye that never blinks is a distorted eye. But we go around saying that we're just a mirror on the world. I think that we're more than mere reflectors of the political process. I think in many ways, probably too many for our own good or for politics, we really threaten to become the political process itself because we decide by our very presence or by our very absence what's important and what's not.

Now unlike what Spiro Agnew said that we're in a state of collusion with each other—and I agree with what Gene McCarthy said back in 1969 when he was asked about Agnew and his charges on the press, Gene said, "I agree with everything he says; I just deny him his right to say it"—collusion and conspiracy is not what you can charge us with. I think the charge that can be made against us is not conspiracy, it's mindlessness. As Jean Genet has remarked, "innocence, which is a form of mindlessness, may be the highest form of immorality." And the thing that the politicians don't want to admit and we don't want to admit is that we're all in bed together. It's an incestuous relationship. On occasion we take in the pollsters and the media merchants; and the politicians may not want to be in bed with us but they're there; and I think they're there and we're there because the medium of television which employs, and in some ways produces both of us, is simply the most powerful form of communication that mankind has ever known. I don't think that after twenty-five or thirty years of television, about twenty years of what I call presidential television, we know very much at all about how our perceptions get across on television and what it does to the political process. We claim we do, but I don't think we do. I wonder how much we actually control it or how much it controls us. And with all the technological advances that are attendant upon this medium, I wonder whether we're ever going to control the medium again, if in fact we ever did. I think at an earlier time we did; I'm not sure. But I fear that we and the politicians, especially those who become presidential candidates, are somewhat like children playing with huge electronic toys, and we're delighted by the game despite our complaints about it. We're delighted by it. We don't think much about the consequences. In fact I don't think we think very much about whether there are any consequences at all.

The battle in the next presidential election is going to be fought on the evening news programs, those thirty second, one minute, five minute commercials plus the one minute-thirty spots if you've got that much time on the evening news programs, network and local. Everything is shaped around those because presidential campaigns, thanks to so-called political reform, places a limit on how much you can spend on a campaign. And to use that wonderful phrase that came to fruition during the Vietnam war, "cost effectiveness," the most cost effective way, according to politicians and their media managers, that you can get through to people is through television commercials but also on the evening news. So the schedules are arranged so they create media events. And what a candidate says and what a candidate does must be tailored to maximize that candidate's chances of making it on the evening news, national or local.

I remember in the 1972 campaign when I was in public broadcasting I wanted to see what a town was like after the candidates went through. We couldn't get any cooperation from the White House so we stationed ourselves in Billings, Montana, the week before to see how the town prepared for the visit of George McGovern. He came in on a Sunday night; there was snow falling, but he got in all right. The next day at a movie theater in Billings, he made a speech about land policy for the West, a terribly important issue then, a terribly important issue now. We then placed a camera in a hotel room showing me looking at the evening news shows. One network did nothing on McGovern; the other two had him throwing snowballs and then engaged in dissecting his views on abortion while saying nothing about his speech on national land policy. So I would think that the people who are running the campaigns—it is instructive that Howard Baker is to sign on John Deardourff and Doug Bailey who ran Gerald Ford's campaign in 1976—are people who both manage campaigns and also do the political commercials. The wit and wisdom of these candidates are very encapsulated in a fifteen to twenty second sound bite. If it's thirty seconds, for example, it's going to wind up, in that time honored American phrase, "on the cutting room floor."

As a matter of fact, a few years ago when I was at Duke University, Robert Squier—who worked for Muskie and ran a very successful campaign for John Y. Brown in Kentucky which will I think be a watershed in modern American political process because of how he did it—told a group of students that he had been coaching a Democratic candidate for the governorship of California, and he got that man to speak in twenty second fragments. Now of course the master of all this is Jerry Brown. He touches every chord. It is almost as if he parses the sentence as it goes on. And sometimes they're not even sentences because he understands us better than we understand ourselves. I'll give you a little story about Jerry Brown. I flew back with him in May after he came to Washington to get more gas for California. I didn't speak much to him on the plane; he was being interviewed by someone from the *New York Magazine*. When we got off the plane, this hoard of television people—we were in the media capital of America, in Los Angeles—were asking questions and Tom Quinn, one of Brown's aides, said, "Why don't you join us over at Lucy's El'Adobe restaurant later on?" That's where Brown hangs out. I got over there just a few minutes before ten, and there's a newscast that comes on at ten on Channel 5, and I noticed a television set being brought up to Jerry Brown. He watched himself and then the commercial came on. He put his jacket on, went outside, and a few minutes later I looked back and he was being interviewed by a mobile truck from the same station but now it was live. Then he came back, and we had a long argument about Hayden and Fonda. It was eleven o'clock and he was switching back and forth seeing how he did on the evening news and, so help me, at ten after eleven his state trooper brought him the *Los Angeles Times* and he looked at it. It's like sitting at Sardi's waiting for the reviews to come in. But Jerry Brown—and I urge you not to take the view generally spread by most of my colleagues that he's a flake—understands this process very well. He's made some mistakes this year, but I think in terms of understanding what this country responds to because of television, he knows more about it than anybody else.

Again by way of passing, Ted Kennedy is now looking around for somebody to do his commercials. One of the people being considered is Charlie Guggenheim and some other people too. Somebody told me as a measure of how fast the world is going by since the years his brothers ran in 1968 and 1960, that two of the people who came in to show their samples—after Guggenheim left—looked and there was a 16mm projector and they were not equipped to use it because they brought their commercials on video tape. I just throw that off because I think Kennedy's got a lot to learn about the political process; it's been one hundred years since 1968 in terms of what we have done to the political process.

I wish that I could see some ray of hope in what's been happening. I can't; because as we close out twenty years of presidential television I think the matter is getting out of hand. People will argue, maybe Fred Friendly would take this view quoting E. B. White's few lines about television back in 1947, about its bringing enlightenment and understanding to people. I only ask one thing and this is the only general proposition that I would like you to think about—all the rest is just window dressing. If the thesis is that we were supposed to spread enlightenment and that communication is supposed to be good is there any relationship—I don't know the answer—between the spread of television, it's involvement and predominance in the political process and the fact that the vote has gone down every year since 1960 from something like around sixty percent to thirty-four percent in the last election?

I don't know but I ask myself is there some correlation between the decline and—to corrupt Justice Holmes phrase about the law—television's role as a brooding omnipresence, sometimes I think a chuckling omnipresence, in our lives? Is there a possibility that Americans, having seen what they think is the political process spread before them on television, the idea that you're really there when in fact you're not, seeing something that is choreographed, unwittingly or very subjectively between the candidates' managers and television people, do viewers somehow think that they have participated in the political process itself; therefore there is no reason to vote? Add to that what they see on the screen in terms of the political commercials, the so called actual events, the pollsters activities, this seemingly never ending process going on before their eyes and is there a possibility that people then ask what is the sense of their getting involved in the process itself? I end on that. I don't have an answer. I'm not throwing it out to be coy, I don't know, but I think something has got to be done and I don't look for much improvement to come from those with whom I work.

NARRATOR: We've asked another communicator, Staige Blackford, present editor of the *Virginia Quarterly Review,* who has had a little experience in the political process himself and a common background with Mr. Vanocur in England as a Rhodes Scholar, to be our chairman in the discussion which follows. Staige is also perhaps the most active member of our Academic Advisory Committee at the Miller Center.

MR. BLACKFORD: Your remarks have certainly provoked me, Sandy. I come out of the print medium, so I would just like to make one observation on the modeling of this political process. About ten years ago, I was involved in a political campaign to elect Linwood Holton as Governor of Virginia, and a new word came into my vocabulary, "actuality." At that time I didn't really know what an actuality was, but this idea that we had to have somebody on the road—this was mainly for radio—getting a snippet of a Holton speech, phoning it back to headquarters and then having somebody else send it out to the radio network, seemed to me to be all false.

MR. VANOCUR: And the radios used it without saying where it came from.

MR. BLACKFORD: Sure. The other thing was that our campaign, although as I say I'm out of the print media, was aimed at television news, even on a state level. So I can see what you're talking about. I'd just like to open this up by asking one question which a friend of mine here, now teaching a very unusual journalism course uses as his first lecture entitled—and I'll ask you the question—are newspapers obsolete?

MR. VANOCUR: They are if they don't change. The first person— and this is in David Halberstam's book, but I take credit for telling him about it—to understand what television was doing to newspapers and how to change them, and then making the change, was a man named Nick Williams of the *Los Angeles Times,* which was then coming out of a very stodgy existence anyhow, to compete on fast breaking events. So he said that you had to extend the classic lead of the story which had been "who, what, when and where," by adding, "how". Therefore you saw on the off-lead stories that weren't news breaks as such, they got behind. The most successful practitioner of all this in the last twenty years, is of course the *Wall Street Journal,* and during its brief—and I thought its glorious— existence the *National Observer.* Yes, I think they have to.

I don't know how afternoon newspapers can work any longer. I think the problem facing the *Washington Star*—I don't think its facing the *Post Dispatch* or the *Milwaukee Journal* yet because they probably have inferior competitors in the morning—is that they will be obsolete unless they find a new existence on cable television. We keep hearing about the miracle explosion of cable TV, but a lot of people in newspapers are thinking about how they can get into cable TV. Every newspaper that is good, I know, in this country is thinking about that. But I think afternoon newspapers have a very tough time not only for the reason of television but also with the form of transportation in the afternoon, with rapid transit declining. I would think that if the subway ever got to be a full blown proposition in Washington for example, and you made the *Star* into a tabloid so it was easier to handle and the graphics were different, then it might stand a better chance than it's standing right now.

QUESTION: You made general criticism of the evening news on television on the grounds that the slots or exposure of the candidates was so short. The obvious initial response to that is to say let's make the slots longer. Now earlier in your talk you said that, in referring to Jimmy Carter's fireside chat on television, that in fact if you have longer slots, what you have is more tinsel. Do you think that's a fair statement; that in fact length would not solve the problem?

MR. VANOCUR: The half hour speech is requested by the White House, so that's under the President's control, not ours. No, I don't think a longer, like an hour, news program would change much, because I think what you would get, given the present state of many of the editors and the people they're bringing into television who have no print experience at all—and I confess to a bias because that's where I came from—would be what they're doing now, but at greater length. Double the number of spots. These spots on television, on politics, try to create some kind of narrative. It's the old question that's supposed to have been asked of Camus when he was told this old line, which Aristotle or Somerset Maugham used, saying that every story has a beginning, a middle and an end. Camus replied, "yes, the only question is which comes first?" The problem I have with a lot of television is that I can't tell where they start and where they end, and so you get the feeling that dramatic juxtaposition is everything.

I was reading today in *Fortune Magazine* Herb Schmertz of Mobil Oil who's responsible for the ads attacking the newspapers—but he's usually right—saying that in the Senate caucus hearing room where Senator Jackson's hearings were conducted on divestiture, that somebody had signed off: "from the Senate caucus room where the Watergate hearings were held." He said: "One could have said, 'from the Senate Caucus room, where John F. Kennedy announced his candidacy for President.'" The problem is that you're going for dramatic effect most of the time rather than for exposition.

Now I'm not for a moment suggesting that most newspapers are any better. As a matter of fact I think television is influencing newspapers in many ways because they have to compete with what people see on television; and the next day they're going to read it, so there is some kind of a subtle interaction. As a matter of fact, writing in *The Boys on the Bus* which is probably the best book written about the 1972 campaign, Curtis Wilke, who was working for the Wilmington, Delaware papers reported that Hubert Humphrey had been booed off a platform in Pennsylvania by students. His editors questioned this because they hadn't seen it on television. And it wasn't until a couple of days later that the corroboration was received in the form of having read in the *Baltimore Sun* the same story by Phil Potters, a venerable reporter, that they believed their own man.

QUESTION: I can see two solutions. One is longer exposure and the other is competing perspectives doing the exposition. The two programs that seem to do this most on television are *Agronsky & Company* and *Washington Week,* neither of which are on major networks. Why don't the major networks go for some competing programs?

MR. VANOCUR: They wouldn't get an audience. It's just out of the question because of the economics. That will have to come on cable. But my complaint is they ought to get better people to do this on television; and the spots on television ought to be a fraction longer and get behind the obvious. For example, right now the hard underbelly of American politics is media, the pollsters, the media merchants—David Garth, Charlie Guggenheim, Deardourff and Bailey, people who do the commercials—and the fund raisers. That's it.

Right now in the next week, for example, I'd like to see how much money Mr. Carter has raised. I think he's running into problems, and the only way I can find out is by looking at his quarterly report and knowing some things, such as that after he makes his announcement on the fourth of December he wants to go into California for a fund raiser. They don't know what to do with him out there because he's already tapped them once. They've got fund raisers for Senator Cranston the week before and so on. They don't know whether they're going to go for Kennedy or not. That's a good story. I can just see when I go in and say, look I want to do a story on finances. . . . In Ron Zeigler's phrase, it doesn't have photo opportunity. That's the problem we face. I tell you, if you did some of these things Americans would be interested. But right now the candidate getting off the plane, the music, the pom-pom girls, the walk along the fence, a sharp statement about an opponent and a man standing with a microphone, that's it. And I don't see any way to change that.

QUESTION: From your statements it seems that you say that the media is having a corrupting effect on the political campaign. And the question is, I guess, is there a rule that the media could apply that would not have such an effect? I was surprised at your beginning comments about presidential debates when you said that you would want to bar them completely. Here seems to be one opportunity where the candidates can address themselves to the people without the constraints that you seem to imply corrupted the promises. So what about something like presidential debates as a way of getting around the problem which you discussed and what about presidential debates with a format in which they are not directed by you, the television personality?

MR. VANOCUR: You answered your own question. I'm all for presidential debates, but the process has gone so far that we don't get out of it. I don't think these are debates. If we had the debates á la Lincoln and Douglas, I'd say fine; but it's a measure of our power in this whole process that we in effect set the ground rules. Now they would argue, CBS would argue: Well, they set the ground rules in collusion with the League of Women Voters because they didn't let us show reaction shots, so therefore it was a violation of our first amendment rights. I don't want us in there at all. But that's a measure of how deeply we are involved. I don't want to give you the impression, though I think you're absolutely right that I did, that I'm against debates. I'm not against debates as I understand debates, but not the way they have been done in 1960 and 1976. If you can get us and the printed press out of it that's fine. I think that's useful.

QUESTION: Well, to follow up; I've been looking at the questions of debates in 1960 and in the last presidential campaign, and a profound bias can be introduced by the question. And of course it makes the candidates speak about what they don't want to speak about but what you would have them speak about. The next question I have is that why is it, as just a matter of television history, that journalists have been able to get their position as questioners and why is it the candidates themselves have not picked the questions to be addressed by themselves directly?

MR. VANOCUR: This is subjective on my part. In 1960, a television debate had never flown before, and I think that Kennedy and Nixon were both anxious to get on television. The story is, (which is probably lore, I'm beginning to think I've been doing fiction for the last twenty years. I did have a discussion at Duke on the assertion that news is fiction, but that's another subject.) apparently when Nixon was watching Kennedy accept in Los Angeles he turned to William Rogers and said, I want to debate him and I can take him; or words to that effect. They just threw that thing together. If you want to pursue that sometime I think you might get Leonard Rensch from Cox Broadcasting to come up because he represented Kennedy. And a good deal of this is in Halberstam's book. But in 1976, my guess is, and it's very subjective, I think the candidates liked that association with celebrities. I think they liked to be on the air with Barbara Walters or Walter Cronkite.

When Carter held his first phone-in, with Cronkite, I wrote a column in the *Post* blasting the idea. But who's the bigger celebrity when Carter's being interviewed by Barbara Walter, Walter Cronkite or John Chancellor? I'm not sure that they want us out of the scene.

QUESTION: The Honorable Theodore Roosevelt McKeldin had a phobia against television and image makers, and other such flora and fauna that survey the land. I would like to have your comments on the issue of whether television has been near fatal to political nominating conventions?

MR. VANOCUR: Yes. I say that because I can change the imagery. I don't think that we're flora and fauna—and I include the print media—I think that we're not a too advanced form of carnivore who needs fresh meat to feed upon each day. And the biggest hunk of meat that can be thrown to us is a political convention. I've been asked whether I want to be a floor reporter in 1980. I have my doubts about doing it again. It isn't because the legs go first; they're in very good shape. It's because the political conventions now run us. Before, we ran them. The first real political convention, here, was 1960. Then it was full blown. CBS and NBC were competing vigorously. ABC was not in the picture. It did a truncated view. But then, you could get around the floor and act as a reporter with, I think, not undue interference in the process. 1964 was an interesting year. One thing that you ought to watch in campaigns is that each campaign builds on the one before. One of the things was that the Goldwater people were very, very shrewd. Remember, I don't think Goldwater won but one primary. He won California. But what he'd be doing was picking up all the delegates in caucuses and so forth. What Cliff White and Dick Kleindienst had set up was something that they knew that the Kennedy people had done in 1960, but now they bettered them. The Kennedys had a great telephone system. I went around the convention before, taking private numbers to see where they went and so forth and then matched them up on the floor. With Goldwater's campaign, knowing especially what a freak he was about electronics, they were in touch all the time with the floor, and it was at that convention that we sensed that we were somehow in competition with their communications system. Remember that was the convention where Eisenhower talked about self-styled commentators and got that tremendous round of applause. The applause was venom-filled applause. And we began to get a little worried about our role in all this.

But it wasn't until 1968 at the Chicago convention that I began to wonder what our role really was because we got pushed into the political process, maybe because of what was going on. We wanted to be in it. I haven't examined my own thoughts about that. You get awfully mad when you're being pushed around, Dan Rather was punched in the stomach, Mike Wallace was punched in the mouth. But I felt what happened there was that it got out of our hands. Lyndon Johnson, through a man who was also the treasurer of the Democratic party, had a console back there which controlled every microphone in the place. So on Tuesday night, the anti-Johnson people wanted recognition and they couldn't get the mike. The mike, that's power. That's information. I'll tell you exactly how the process got started. A man named Mark Shields, a political wit in Washington who once described Richmond as a hotbed of social rest, he came over to me and said, the chairman of the Wisconsin delegation is seeking to get Carl Albert's attention so he can ask for an adjournment before this gets out of hand. I knew I was being used. But, it was still a good story. I called up, got air time, stood with this guy—I can't remember his name but he was a McCarthy supporter—and he said, the reason why we're asking for it is because it's nationwide. Then minutes later Carl Albert recognized him and the convention was adjourned. Now I was no innocent. I knew that I had been involved in the political process.

Now 1972 came along. McGovern didn't run that convention. Nobody lets the presidential candidate wait until three o'clock in the morning to make his acceptance speech. Nixon's people by contrast had control of his convention from beginning to end. If they didn't want something on television, they lowered the lights.

Jimmy Carter in 1976, carried the thing through to a refined process I couldn't believe. He ran that convention, and we were all choreographed. So we were running around introducing Miss Lillian!

If I saw one more interview with Miss Lillian. . . . I'm sure she took out an equity card, she was bouncing around so much in the place. And now what I fear is that in 1980 it's all geared up for us. Except we think it's geared for us but they're really using us. They're in control.

QUESTION: I want to go back to 1968. I have always attributed Hubert Humphrey's defeat in November of 1968 to the Chicago Convention and the way that convention was presented to the public, primarily through television and to a certain extent through the newspapers, but primarily through television. You had riots staged by appointment. More attention was given to the rallies outside than to what was going on inside. I surmised, on the point of some, I'll call no names, that there was an earnest desire on the part of some of the journalists, both newspaper and television journalists, to start a draft of Teddy Kennedy. I'd like to hear you on this.

MR. VANOCUR: Sure because I've thought about it. And I think that just the Chicago Convention would make a good book because it was an important turning point in democratic government. Let me give you my opinion. You're right. It probably did cost Hubert Humphrey the election. But then too, it could have occurred because of Hubert's gutlessness in not accepting the peace proposals contained in a one or two sentence compromise that David Ginsberg, Richard Goodwin, Kenny O'Donnell and others were trying to arrange. Not breaking with President Johnson on the war until Salt Lake City at the end of September may have cost him the election. Or he might simply have said this is my convention, I want it, to control it. But he didn't do that. I just throw that out for sake of argument, but I do think your premise is right because of what was seen on the streets of Chicago. Humphrey had a hard time winning.

Then there is the question of reporters wanting Kennedy; I think that you can't prove these things. The only thing you can really fall back on is getting along in this business—because we're not a craft really but there is a sense of one's craft and a sense of professionalism. Teddy Kennedy was a very live possibility for the convention.

I remember I went down with Jimmy Breslin to the Standard Club, that's the Jewish Club in Chicago where a fellow named Hy

Raskin, who used to work for Jack Kennedy, had gotten rooms for Steve Smith. The only place Steve wouldn't be found is in a Jewish club in Chicago. And up there were all the cards with all the delegates from 1960 and also those from 1964. Well, you've got to assume that there's interest in Hyannisport where Ted Kennedy is sitting. Then on Saturday night I had dinner with Abe Ribicoff who said he had spent an hour with Mayor Daley in City Hall that day, and Daley had left the room twice to take phone calls, and he presumed they were phone calls to Hyannisport. Also on Sunday morning the Illinois delegation, historically, has caucused on Sunday morning, but Daley postponed the caucus. Well, that and some other atmospherics like Steve Smith talking to Gene McCarthy, Dick Goodwin saying something might be worked out, meant that we had to report an event in progress, which was the possibility of a Teddy Kennedy candidacy sponsored by Richard Daley.

Daley told me on Wednesday that what he really wanted was Teddy. But he said that Teddy didn't have the guts to do it. Somebody else told me that what Daley really wanted was a Humphrey-Kennedy ticket. We didn't know the truth, and I'm not sure we ever will know the truth. So it was a live possibility, but I don't think that anybody from television was pushing it; though if I had been sitting looking at our faces—and I remember one time when I went on the air and said I'm being followed by Hubert Humphrey's gum shoes; they're from the labor unions. They were following me and reporting everything on their walkie talkies that I was saying to my control room. I'm not paranoid, but why is that man following me? I'm sure we gave the impression as we fought the goons on the floor that we were pro-Kennedy, but the fact is we were caught up in a very tricky situation. I'm not sure we did very well, but we did the best we could.

Now as for the streets, I think about ninety-five per cent of the protesters did not come to seek a confrontation. Five per cent did. There was also an element of the Chicago police force that was seeking a confrontation. Mayor Daley didn't want that. Mayor Daley was very anti-war by the way. But there was a small element in the police department that wanted that confrontation and it's very easy to understand what would happen when one of these Chicago cops, probably Catholic, strict hierarchical education, familial upbringing, is faced with some young Cliffie or sweet young thing from Bryn Mawr calling out, up against the wall you

_____. It broke, it snapped, and you had a police riot. Now the other question, did we stage things? I don't think so. I suspect probably you go where the action is. There was in my judgment a provocation, but a good police force could have handled it a different way except something snapped, and they couldn't get control of it again. Now I'm on the convention floor. All I know about what's going on is what I see on television when I come in to have my battery pack recharged. The only time I got close to Grant Park was when I dropped John Chancellor off at Michigan Boulevard about two-thirty or three o'clock, after adjournment, and smelled the tear gas; that's all I saw.

Two weeks later, I was speaking to a group of Hughes Aircraft executives at the International Inn at Los Angeles airport trying to explain that what came across that box I know very little about because I, of course, didn't see what I was doing, I knew what I was doing but I certainly didn't see what was going on in the streets of Chicago. I came close to being booed off the platform because America's perception was that if you were in Chicago you were responsible for what happened. And I'm not sure how much America at that time wasn't very happy to see those kids getting their heads beat in and then feeling guilty about feeling happy about it. So it's the most complex period I've ever gone through in my life. I don't deny a thing you've said; I don't know if it's true, and I can't be quite sure about the accuracy of everything that was going on; but I could only say we didn't try to push a Kennedy candidacy. We didn't try to foment and stage riots, but the impression that came across must have been appalling.

QUESTION: I'm not sure of my suppositions either. I just wanted to hear your comments on it. But I do recall one scene from CBS where these rebellious young people were saying, "We've got to get closer, we've got to get closer to the television." That came over.

MR. VANOCUR: Well, I'm sure that happened, but you know who began that in this country? Martin Luther King. Martin Luther King was a master at using us.

QUESTION: Well, I agree with you. I think the manner in which campaigns are recorded, and the manner in which the media is used does present difficulties, and I don't know if there is any solution.

QUESTION: Politics have always been manipulative. The complexities of manipulating television are different and greater, but each side has those opportunities. Moreover, governing through television is important, as you pointed out. I wonder if there isn't a kind of alternative to being pessimistic as you are. I prefer optimism in that whoever can manipulate this medium best in the campaign might be likely to manipulate it best in governing. There is at least that kind of balancing, or possible invisible hand.

MR. VANOCUR: That's what, as they say in show business, is the flip side of it, and of course when you think about Roosevelt (who by the way did not like the idea of the fireside chat. There was no fire burning. It was Harry Butcher of CBS's idea), he didn't use it very much but he did use it well. I think you have to start with the premise that you can use it for your advantage certainly, to get elected. But then you will also use it and understand why you use it to gain certain political consequences. I think Roosevelt came up with a phrase about lend lease to your neighbor; it was a simple phrase about lending your neighbor a hose or a part of it to put out a fire. These public appeals all seem to have an objective or end. Bob Donovan's book on the Truman presidency has Truman using radio as an instrument to get things done.

I think some presidents use the media in a mindless way. They think it's very clever, but there's no connection between what they're saying and the actual political process itself. I don't know when this process began. I think it began with Lyndon Johnson. Kennedy was rather shrewd about what he could do. As a matter of fact he was rather amazed about it because he came into the White House thinking *Time* magazine was the most important influence on the minds of Americans. His father said it was television. So I think by the end of his term—or the end of his life—he had begun to realize what television can do. Yes, I agree with you, there is a flip side to it. And there are important consequences and good consequences, but what defies me is that why somebody hasn't grasped this.

QUESTION: I was interested in your remarks on Jerry Brown. I've been impressed by a number of commentators, writers and television people who have come back and said something rather like what you said, "don't dismiss him as a flake." And I wasn't clear from your own remarks whether you mean that he understands television or whether you believe he understands television and, more than that, is consciously using the symbolic power, which it obviously possesses, on behalf of a rather coherent set of goals. I've been very impressed with whatever I've seen written about him, the interview in the *Rolling Stone* most recently, as thinking in paragraphs not epigrams, and I wonder what your view is of his real capacity and secondly how you think that might work out in New Hampshire?

MR. VANOCUR: To answer the last part of your question; it's not going to work out in New Hampshire although he might beat Carter in New Hampshire, but I doubt it. If it had been a two-way race I think he'd have beaten Carter in New Hampshire. I spent an hour interviewing him—it's buried somewhere in ABC's vaults. I have this idea that he realizes that nothing works and all you can do in government is shuffle the pieces, and in a Rooseveltian way, stimulate people, throw balls in the air, and some fall to the ground, you catch a few, and one of the ways you do this is with a great deal of imagery through television. I brought up de Gaulle right after he said his hero was the Roosevelt of James McGregor Burns' *The Lion and the Fox*. But, I said, what about de Gaulle? I said didn't de Gaulle just really burn the incense of power, didn't try to fight the bureaucracy but burned the incense of power, and let the natural genius of the French people feel its way to some kind of fruition that they had not felt since the defeat by the Germans in World War II? He seized immediately upon the de Gaulle image. I think he's a juggler, and I'm not here to say that I'm not sure that isn't the best way to govern the United States today because I think that Roosevelt was a juggler too. I say it, and I don't think I say it in a pejorative sense. Now every once in a while all the balls have to come down though, and I'm not sure that Jerry Brown can catch any of them; that's the problem.

Do I make myself clear? Because I do think that the government is an unholy mess now, I'm not sure that any president who comes in now and tries to run it as Jimmy Carter is running it, is going to succeed. I'm not sure I like Richard Nixon saying to Halderman or Erlichman who tells him about the lira, "I don't give a 'expletive deleted' about the lira." Yet I'm not sure that that's too bad an expression for a president. And I have to say in reading parts of Kissinger's memoirs, Nixon is rather impressive in some foreign policy situations. And I'm not sure that that isn't the role of a president, to spend his time like a de Gaulle or Roosevelt—de Gaulle in a kind of mystical process, Roosevelt was rather like a faro dealer—in the political process; if that isn't the way of presidential leadership in this day and age? I suppose it's impressionistic leadership against literal leadership in the Presidency. And I think Brown is on the impressionistic side.

QUESTION: I agree. I just want to say that we know that if Jimmy Carter came in that he would run a clean government and organize it just as he did in Georgia. Brown is a governor, and I think many people who watch government closely think that's about the last place you ought to start, with the reorganization plan.

MR. VANOCUR: Carter never really had a good reorganization plan— not that good in Georgia. But this must be said about Brown, the two states in this country, thanks to Al Smith in New York and Hiram Johnson in California, that not even an idiot could botch up are New York and California. They have been set on such good courses by those two men and Brown hasn't even tried to botch it up. Anyhow what is the process of government? Isn't it a mystical process? Is the process, especially when your president merely sets out, as Mr. Truman said, the unfinished agenda of the American democracy, to hold out goals, and aspirations? Is it not a mystical function? I don't know enough about anthropology. As political scientists and reporters I don't think we know enough about myths in society. Is Carter running on his record or is he running against a myth; a myth by the way that never was? Is the whole Kennedy candidacy just based on this that we want to know how the saga or the soap opera ends?

QUESTION: What is your view on it, Sander?

MR. VANOCUR: I think that the American people have a fascination with this as a narrative, a saga. There's an ending to it and I say that in the best and the worst sense. I don't think he's going to have an easy time of it but that's an aspect of politics to which I don't think we pay enough attention. We're much too literal about it.

QUESTION: Well, on the other side, where do we go with the Republicans?

MR. VANOCUR: How do you go anywhere with the Republicans?

I'm beginning to wonder whether the Republican party has really had a leader since Theodore Roosevelt. Just look at it. You can't call Dwight D. Eisenhower a leader of the Republican party, though in fact he was much more of a politician than he wanted to admit. Who would say that being a general of the army is not being a politician? But look at the Republican history in this century; has there really been a leader that's come full-blown from the party? Even with Teddy Roosevelt he scared the wits out of most Republican leaders when he became President. They thought they were tucking him away for all time when they got him the Vice Presidency. I don't think the Republican party has thrown up any person who comes right out of the party and can then appeal broadly after he wins the nomination.

Reagan, on paper, has the best campaign I've ever seen (yet some critics are asking Sam Goldwyn's famous question whether the verbal contract is worth the paper it is written on.) His campaign may not be worth the paper it is written on, but right now it's air tight. I look for flaws and I can't find any; but the Reagan campaign wanted to buy television time, make an announcement on October 13th then follow with media events, storm into Orlando, Florida on the 17th, the straw vote convention, and really deal a blow to John Connally and the others. But the networks wouldn't sell him time. I thought at the time that Reagan wanted to make his announcement in this way. Maybe this is the flaw, that Ronald Reagan thinks that he can repeat the speech of the Goldwater campaign in 1964 and thereby win the nomination just by television. And he can't. You have to have the mix. You've got to be out there in the snow, you've got to be out there pumping hands through all those states. I began to think that maybe this reliance on television may be his undoing. I can't be sure.

QUESTION: You began by asking yourself about the culpability of television and its process. Two things that you've said in the course of your remarks seem to me that you suggest that we've got a chicken and an egg situation. You commented on the fact that if there were more detailed exploration of the issues on television, people wouldn't watch it and hence the shows cannot get financed and hence don't get on. The second issue is, when asked about Kennedy, you immediately responded as if the issue was not going to matter and that it was the image of Kennedy and the enduring image of the family that mattered.

I would wonder in my life if that had not always been so and that the people vote in elections by choosing mainly between different images presented them. Perhaps we in an academic environment may overrate the degree to which it seems to matter and that the fault then is not really television; it's just that television has now taken on the role that newspapers once had of producing the simplified images on which people are willing to make their choices. So it's not television's fault; television is reflecting something that's already there.

MR. VANOCUR: Despite what I've said about Kennedy, which is a special case; I think that in addition to the Camelot issue, the Camelot legacy, there are a lot of people who do respond to his issues. I don't think the country's as far right as everybody else thinks. Here we are in 1980. Since 1933, the country has only elected two Republican congresses, 1947–1949, and 1953–1955; has consistently elected these Democratic congresses that stand for big government and big spending; has elected a couple of Republican presidents, one of them in 1968 possibly by a fluke, given to them by the Democrats. So I'm not sure, for example, that issues are unimportant in Kennedy's campaign. He seems to stand for largeness of spirit for many people and for a complexity of reasons; the older because of comprehensive medical care, the younger because he seems to stand for what they think they remember of the 1960's, and his martyred brothers, and so forth.

However, we like to have it both ways in television. One of my brethren wrote in the last campaign, in the *New York Times:* it was a campaign devoid of issues. I'd like to suggest to you that if you are dumb enough to discuss an issue on television in a campaign you'll get your head handed to you on a platter. If you doubt that just ask George McGovern. Whatever the merits of his plan about the thousand dollar grant, he got skewered by it; his plan about cutting the defense budget. The trouble with us is we want to have it both ways. We say they ought to talk issues and when they do, as in the case of McGovern and the abortion and land policy questions in the West, it all comes out chopped liver.

I've got to confess after twenty years I don't know what moves people in a presidential election. My guess is it is character. The country decided somehow that they looked at Nixon like a probate lawyer who was brought in by the family to settle a messy will. He'd have to eat in the kitchen. You wouldn't let him have dinner with you. But as long as he settled the will he was OK. And McGovern, he was way out of the mainstream, and they made a choice and probably in terms of their perception and national interest, they made the right choice. In 1952, despite what they felt about Stevenson, they felt Eisenhower had the character for the job.

But having said that I don't think you can necessarily say that issues don't matter. Right now people say the single issue groups can matter. This is more on the congressional level than the presidential level. I don't think we know enough to be sure. But that is not my function.

What is news? I think Harold Ross of the *New Yorker* defined news as anything that makes you say, "gee whiz." I think that my duty as a reporter is not to educate the American people. I think my duty as a reporter, especially one who has been in the business for twenty-five years, is to try to give the news—if I'm on a newspaper in the space allotted me. There are ways to do it despite my feeling constrained about what I think is important and let them make their own judgment about it. And I'm not sure at all that an extension of the *Agronsky & Company* kind of shows— because that gets to be sort of choreographed after a while—is going to change the American peoples' perceptions one way or another. The funny thing is I think their perceptions are rather good, given the kind of information that we give them. Now you can argue back that we're giving them good information and that's why they have such a shrewd sense of their own self-interest.

QUESTION: Isn't it true that sometimes the journalists and the people on television have information—they all have it—which they feel is not proper to convey to the people at large? So you have the odd situation in which important information is held back from the public but distributed among the people who handle the material but the great bulk of the people don't get it. Often this is done with a sense of serving the good of the nation. It wouldn't be good for the people to know, but it would be for us to know. Are there any comments on that?

MR. VANOCUR: Yes, the stories are legion. We used to sit around and talk about all the Lyndon Johnson stories we could never put on the air. But let me give you two specific examples often addressed by students to us journalists. It's the question about why didn't we tell them about Wilbur Mills being drunk, or about Jack Kennedy's girl friend.

I talked about it one night with Tom Wicker at Duke University about Mrs. Exner's book. I never heard of Mrs. Exner when I was covering the White House, and Tom never heard of her. Did we know Kennedy was a womanizer? Yes, we knew about it. OK, supposing you knew it. What's your lead on your story? "President Kennedy today was seen with so and so walking to his bedroom at the White House. . . . " Who's going to print it? Even today who's going to print that kind of thing. Secondly, how germane is that to the running of the Presidency. Is it our role to be involved in gossip? The point is though, it's a question of taste. And in this post-Watergate retrospective morality that we're involved in which every public official is guilty until proven innocent I don't think that it's our job to be sermonizers about people's behavioral patterns unless it impinges upon their job.

I think had I known that Kennedy was fooling around with a woman who was also the mistress of a Chicago mobster and had been introduced to him by Frank Sinatra, I might have done something, even in those days. Now the question of Wilbur Mills. As a member of the Ways and Means once said: "I didn't know Wilbur Mills was a drunk until one day he showed up at a committee hearing sober." At Duke some students went after a group of journalists for keeping from them the fact that he was a drunk. Al Otten of the *Wall Street Journal* turned to me as the barrage kept going and said: "Did you know?" I said: "I didn't know;" he said: "neither did I." And he's a very good Washington correspondent. Now today if we knew about that and I don't think anybody did, we'd print it. We knew Hale Boggs was a drunk, we knew Russell Long was a drunk, we knew Harrison Williams was one. I think we'd write about that now. I'm talking about the personal side, but each one gets to be a different kind of judgment. You can't make any generalizations.

Where I think we get into trouble is this idea about national security. I think that is one you have to decide on the merits each time. I am prone now to think that my judgment or my editor's judgment about national security is as good as the people in government because they always use the phrase, "if you only knew what we know but we can't tell you" or "if you could see the traffic." That's the great line in national security; "if you could see the traffic then you wouldn't do this."

I had the experience when I broke the Kennedy/Khrushchev Summit meetings story in 1961; and Pierre Salinger knew I was on to something and said, "Before you do it, all I ask is come to me." I called him after I checked with my superiors in New York, and said: "We're going to run with this story if you can't give me any overriding reason of national security." He said: "I can't;" so I did it.

But right now I'm prone to feel that if I have something, I'm going to go with it. I don't approve of the CIA going to the papers about the Glomar Explorer; or the *New York Times* sitting on the Bay of Pigs story, and then Kennedy saying, "If only they had printed it, I wouldn't have done it;" and so forth. I think we're showing a heightened sensitivity to all this but on the national security issue, I'm very prickly on that score.

QUESTION: But if twenty journalists have a piece of information and certainly the people whom we least desire to have it, then the only people left are . . .

MR. VANOCUR: I told you I agreed with you but I think that's becoming less and less a practice in Washington. Anyhow if twenty journalists know, then somebody is going to print it.

QUESTION: With respect to the drunks, you don't have to print it because sooner or later they will come out and admit it and become reformed alcoholics, and . . .

MR. VANOCUR: And get reelected.

QUESTION: In the last of his presidential campaign books Theodore White did point out that the American people cannot vote their preferences on any important issue no matter for whom they vote. I think that is the answer in a sense to the last of the queries that you posed in your formal remarks. And I think you expressed it well yourself in describing the destruction of issues by television and the media. Now the question I would raise is this: if government has some purpose, if the political process has some purpose other than that of simply electing people to office, then under what circumstances do we really recover again a responsible government, given the tendencies that you have described so well?

MR. VANOCUR: For a liberal Democrat to make an Agnew attack

on the press, I don't desire it; I think it's coming. The President could speak out not to run against the press, but to get out from under, if he wishes to, and I don't know if he wishes to; this debasement of the political dialogue in which I think both sides participate could be changed. That might do it. And I don't want to leave the impression that there aren't a great many of my colleagues who don't feel the way I do. We do get caught up in systems and they are difficult to change.

Let me go off on a tangent. I'm trying to make a point. I wasn't being coy when I expressed a wish I'd had more historical background about politics in this country. I don't know the role of advertising in this century. I think you could make an argument that Albert Lasker, the father of modern advertising, is at least as responsible for the genius of the American economy as are Eli Whitney, Henry Ford, and whoever invented the computer. Advertising is such a pervasive force in our society and—digression within a digression—as I read about the interest rates apparently cooling off the economy, I think to myself, well what effect is television advertising having on people's consumption? I don't know. I don't think an economist has thought about that yet. What I'm getting at is that advertising is so much a part of our lives.

John Cheever said in a story in the *New York Times* that he watches television commercials with fascination. Why don't we report on television commercials? I think so much of us is wrapped up in that, plus so much the people who live within spitting distance of each other in New York and their perceptions of us that unless you get a handle on that, and then see how that impinges on the political process, I don't think we know much, really. Nobody is writing about these things. So I can't give you an answer because the political process is so much involved now in packaging and imagery. And I can't say advertising hasn't been good for the economy. It has been good. I'm not sure it's good for politics. There is so much overlapping, and I am groping now as somebody who has been in the jungle all these years to try to find some daylight and to get some answers. And I think you have to address those questions before you can address the . . .

QUESTION: Question of responsibility.

MR. VANOCUR: Well this is the real issue. How do you get a handle on responsibility? Who is responsible in this world of media? You

go on the *Today Show,* you go on *Meet the Press,* "I'm responsible."
But where does the buck stop? You can diffuse it all through the
use of television and the press.

QUESTION: Years ago when the phrase, "the free and responsible
press," was heard a great deal young James Reston appeared on
what was then the hot medium of radio and spoke on the question
of, "When will we get better newspapers?" And his answer was,
"When the public demands them." It seemed to me that that was a
problem of responsibility, and I'd like to bring it home and see if I
can make you wear the shoe for a minute. Is there any difference
made by good guys or bad guys? Has any television executive done
anything to make the process more responsible; or are they all
caught up in the photo opportunity premise, the ratings competition.

And conversely, as you describe all the occasions when choices
had to be made by reporters like yourself and the choice was made
honorably when there was a great opportunity for venality or
prejudice; are all the others honorable men? Or have villains been
in there? It sounds to me as though we're caught up in a system
where, on the one hand, you describe a lot of people behaving
responsibly in a small area but on the other, everyone is paralyzed
when it comes to the large question.

MR. VANOCUR: I suppose I should begin by saying that compared
to most of the press in this country, television is rather pristine.
Newspapers are terrible in most parts of the country. Having said
that, I think you'd be surprised how many smart, decent and
ethical people there are in the running of television news or have
been in the years that I've been there, and still are. What I fear now
is a certain debasement of those standards by the people who are
coming along who haven't had much to do, not with print so much
(I'm not wedded to the idea you have to come up through print,
though I like it), but with the canons of taste, professionalism and
literacy.

I've worked at all the networks. I get mad or I think somebody's
offended my sense of professional pride and I quit. I don't do it
thinking that people are going to come following me in a mass
movement. It doesn't make any difference. Remember that scene
in *Network* where Bill Holden is in a room? He's the network chief,
he kicks the table down and he says, "So I can go write another
book exposing television news which nobody is going to read." The

reason that I fret about improving television is because it's a juggernaut. It is powerful. It rolls along and it seems that in television news the most important thing for you to do is to make sure you keep on being famous. As David Brinkley said when Chet Huntley died: "He was famous for being famous." That is very important in our business. The pressures of this enormous juggernaut, this lucrative juggernaut are so great that it has a tendency to run roughshod over questions of taste and professionalism.

QUESTION: I've heard that Congressman John Anderson from Illinois is a fine man, a man of character and intelligence, but that he doesn't have a TV image; that the TV people aren't interested in him and that he hasn't a ghost of a chance. Is there some way that if a good man—and I'm just picking on him for an example—comes along he can overcome being ignored? Can anything be done about the man who doesn't have resources, but only has intelligence and character?

MR. VANOCUR: In the first place, John Anderson is sensational on TV. He's just sensational. Remember how Paul Douglas, that quiet economist, was really a tub thumper on the political circuit? Another person from Illinois, John Anderson, is terrific. That isn't a problem. The problem is the polls. He's low in the polls. So how, if you're a candidate, do you get around that? I have got some ideas if I were John Anderson's campaign manager on how I could do it. I'd tell him to look at what McGovern did and what Jimmy Carter did. Take Jimmy Carter, he was low in the polls too, but he knew studying McGovern's campaign—and this goes back to what I said about all campaigners studying the one before if they're any good—that if he won the Iowa caucus he'd capture the press's attention. So he was in Iowa a lot. Then Jerry Rafshoon came up with the idea that he'll put those five minute segments that are usually done by local news from 7:25 or 8:25, 7:30 or 8:30 on the *Today Show,* and show these little biographies of Jimmy Carter: farmer, naval officer, and so forth; he took out ads in the papers pointing to the commercials, in effect. For an expenditure of $7,600 Carter won—plus his campaigning of course—he won not only Iowa but he won the imagination of the press. We then had a front runner. We had a new face.

Now remember what happens after a while with the press; we get tired of a new face. Along comes Jerry Brown in 1976. We'd become a collective set of roundheels for Jerry Brown. You should have seen what was written in the Washington papers when he came to Maryland, aligned with the most corrupt elements in Maryland politics, but as a new man. George McGovern was ignored by the press in 1972, but he came in third in Iowa behind uncommitted and Muskie. He came in better than people expected in New Hampshire because we said that Muskie had to win by sixty-odd per cent of the vote. How did we know that? Because there was a Becker poll in the *Boston Globe* and we said if he didn't win by sixty-odd per cent, he wouldn't win. Muskie won New Hampshire but we awarded it, in a sense, to McGovern, who hadn't even won. None of this is done consciously. We don't sit in a room and say let's plan this tomorrow. Fresh meat. Then McGovern got on *Time* magazine's cover around the time he won Wisconsin. Then about May—and McGovern contributed to this—having decided that McGovern never should have had a chance—and now seeing him running away with it; and since it wasn't supposed to happen, newsmen start to beat up on McGovern. This scenario can go on for hours. The press right now is going to decide, since we are supposed to be in Kennedy's pocket, that we're going to chew up Kennedy. We haven't decided it, we haven't had a meeting, but I know what's going on. So a man like John Anderson has to figure out a way and say, where does a man like John Anderson get a place in the American presidential race? Why are the networks ignoring me? I said a liberal Democrat before, it could be a liberal Republican. All he has to do is attack the press. He'll get attention. We're very deep into sado-masochism.

MR. BLACKFORD: Thank you for your presentation, and if you get fed up with ABC and jump somewhere else just remember Lyndon Johnson's famous words "power is where power goes."

III

The Media
And The Presidency

The Presidency and the Press
PAUL DUKE

NARRATOR: Throughout a rich and very creative career Paul Duke has demonstrated that he is capable of doing a great many things. He began his career as a student at the University of Richmond; he went into the Associated Press after college, thanks, he says, to a professor who encouraged him to think this was a respectable occupation and one in which he could work with distinction. A rather remarkable group of writers came together and fanned out in various directions at that time: Roger Mudd, Charlie McDowell, Guy Friddell, they all were part of this little complex. So the idea of a Virginia gentry in one of the professions at least is not dead.

He went on from Richmond AP to Washington AP, then reported for five years for the *Wall Street Journal* on international and national affairs; he then joined NBC and went from NBC to *Washington Week in Review* which celebrated its fifteenth anniversary this past Friday. *Washington Week* needs no introduction to anyone around this table. Some of you may know less of another program that Mr. Duke has founded, *The Lawmakers,* which throws the spotlight on a neglected area of American government, the American Congress.

Paul Duke is one of the very few American communicators who has distinguished himself in two ways: (1) he has worked in print, radio, and television communication; (2) in contrast to some who have established noteworthy programs, he definitely undertakes not to intrude his own opinion into the conduct of *Washington Week.* For all of these reasons and also because we consider him a native son who has shown warm and sympathetic interest in the Miller Center, we are pleased to have him with us to talk perhaps for a moment about some recent developments. And then in response to your questions and also to some thoughts of his own, we shall have an opportunity to explore with him a little bit some of the underlying principles that he sees in the working of executive/legislative relations, in the working of the presidency and its relation with the press, and in whatever other issues he may want to discuss in this more general way. It's a great privilege to have you with us, Paul.

MR. DUKE: Thanks very much, Ken. You've confirmed one of my basic suspicions again and that is that there are three kinds of lies: lies, damn lies, and speechmaking introductions. But I must tell you that your introduction does beat one which I received a couple of months ago when I was in Columbus, Ohio. There was a party beforehand for this speech which I had to make at night and the man who had to do the introductions enjoyed himself just a bit too much and when he got around to introducing me he said, "You all know this man because you see him every Friday night on *Washington Week* and you know that his reports are just incomprehensible." So I'm delighted that you invited me to speak in the morning. I am truly delighted to be here and feel flattered that you would invite me to join such a distinguished company in being one of the participants in the Miller Center program. So, thanks very much for having me.

My roots in Virginia do go back aways. As a matter of fact they go all the way back to the fourth grade at Dumbarton Junior High School right outside Richmond where Paul Saunier's father taught me to be in the rhythm band. There were a few Dukes before that though, I must confess, as well. I also appreciate the kind words that many of you have had for *Washington Week* and one of the pleasant discoveries I've had being down this weekend is to find that there are so many people in Charlottesville who spend their Friday nights before the television set. There must be other things that go on in Charlottesville on Friday night but in any event I am very flattered.

The interesting thing I think about *Washington Week* is that it is a television program which has been successful by using newspaper and magazine reporters who happen to have the facility, the ability to articulate and tell their stories. There are many people who regard us as "nattering nabobs of negativism," to use a somewhat discredited phrase. But I think that's because there are so many negative things to talk about and because the nature of our society and the nature of our world. But actually we just have one fundamental purpose and that is to try to shed a little bit of light on a lot of darkness. It's not an easy job and we do miss the mark on occasions but this program has been remarkably successful. We have an audience of about seven million people and the loyalty to the program is just what really does amaze me. Our reporters, for example, have been recognized on the streets of London, Rome, Paris, Jerusalem, at the Great Wall of China. And not long ago a child in Canada had everlastingly inflicted upon him the name of Cordray. As yet no one has had the name Duke inflicted upon him.

I think one of the reasons for the success of *Washington Week* may be found in a story about the late great Supreme Court Justice Oliver Wendell Holmes. A young reporter went to call on the old judge when he was about eighty-four years old, finding him in his study, improving his mind as always. He asked him the reason for his success and Justice Holmes replied, "Young man I discovered at an early age that I am not God." We discovered at an early age that we're not gods either. But I'm sure whenever I go around the country and whenever I speak, I think that there is a notion that a lot of people have that as members of the press corps in Washington we lead glamorous lives. And let me just take a few moments perhaps to disabuse you of your fantasies.

For one thing there is a difficulty we have in pursuing the truth in Washington. Mark Twain once said that "Washington is a city that regards the truth as a precious commodity and therefore it should be rationed." There is a great deal of rationing which goes on in Washington at all times. Somebody also suggested that what we really need is a truth-in-politics law, but I'm not certain that would work either. When Fiorello LaGuardia was the mayor of New York City, he was a member of Congress before that, when somebody once asked him what he thought about Prohibition he replied that he was quite certain the good Lord never intended grapes to be made into jelly. So we have our problems in terms of getting the politicians always to enunciate the truth.

Then there are all the letters which we get from our viewers, and I must tell you we do get a great deal of mail. The grammarians are an especially active lot. All you have to do is to make a simple mistake of grammar and you will be deluged the following week. Not long ago I referred in the program to "an old cliche," and I had this woman in New Hampshire write me this long letter in which she said, "Please, Mr. Duke, give us some new cliches." When I was at NBC I once did a commentary on gun control and I got a twelve page letter from one of the gun freaks from Florida who wrote me, just excoriating me, ripping me apart, winding up by saying, "It's people like you who are ruining the country and should be put before the firing squad."

Then there's all the bureaucratic bafflegab that we have to put up with as reporters in Washington. I must tell you I've always had a special fondness for the English language as I was an English major when I was in college, but sometimes I feel that the English language is a foreign language in Washington. For example, Congress approved a tax increase last year, only they didn't approve a tax increase, it was revenue enhancement. Interior Secretary Watt keeps talking about "deprioritizing" past programs. Prioritizing is bad enough but he keeps talking about "deprioritizing" our programs. But my favorite of favorites was a phrase which came out of the dear old CIA which once referred to one of its assassination units as a health alteration committee.

And then I must tell you that as reporters in Washington and as television reporters we have a special hazard which we have to endure and that is that if you make a mistake when you are on the air you are exposed for everybody to see—the emperor is always exposed—and we do make our share of mistakes. When I was at NBC I was doing a radio newscast one day and I had a line in my copy in which I referred to Senator Everett Dirksen who at the time was in a hospital recovering from a lung operation, and the line said, "Senator Dirksen is recovering satisfactorily after an operation for removal of his right lung," only when I got to that what I said was, "He's recovering satisfactorily after an operation for removal of his right wing." So you have to think fast on your feet sometimes. I readily admit I'm not as fast thinking on my feet as an announcer we had at NBC who was on duty one Saturday when a bulletin came in about an attempt to kill a certain prime minister of South Africa, and the editor who was on duty gave this announcer the bulletin and told him to go into the booth and so he rushed in and they gave him the green light and he looked down and this man happened to have a very difficult name to pronounce. The announcer realized he was in trouble, but thinking quickly if not brilliantly, what he said was, "There's been an assassination attempt against the prime minister of South Africa. His name is being withheld pending notification of the next of kin."

Anyway, I am truly delighted to be here today and delighted to get back to the real world in a sense. I guess I'm all too aware of something which Disraeli once said, and I think when you are in Washington you have this feeling that somehow this is not always the real world but Disraeli said that "The older you get, the more ignorant you realize you are," and I guess that is something which strikes me as all the more true when I do get away from Washington. Somebody asked me for my political affiliation last night and I said that after being in Washington for twenty-five years I now regard myself as a genuine nonpartisan cynic. I must tell you that I don't see anything wrong with a political joke so long as he doesn't get elected to office. I've covered a lot of political campaigns and I remember once being in Louisiana when one of the Longs was running for public office. This Long happened to win—Earl Long happened to be elected governor after he plastered the state with a series of billboards that said, "I am the best of a sorry lot of candidates."

Amidst all the disarray and the guff and the chaos of the political process, somebody occasionally voices one of those eternal truths. And I remember something which Dwight Eisenhower said when he was President—I've always remembered this because I thought it was profound in its simplicity—he said, "We progress in this country by bits and pieces." The great irony of course is that when Mr. Eisenhower was in the White House there were a lot of people who felt that this was a somnambulant period and we didn't have much progress and that things were basically at a standstill. And now, considering what's happened during the past twenty years, we find a lot of people look back in joyful nostalgia to the Eisenhower period and would like to see something more or less like that, when we had an inflation rate of around one percent, for example.

There are a lot of other things which I remember about those years, too, because they were my rookie years coming to Washington. Basically during that period I was covering Congress. I remember, for example, that it was the Congress of Carl Hayden, the first representative of the state of Arizona, a man who served into his nineties; it was also a Congress of Theodore Green, a peppery senator from Rhode Island, a man who gave up tennis at the age of eight-seven because he couldn't work it into his schedule. It was a Congress of H. R. Gross, the Scrooge of Iowa, one of few members of Congress to vote against honorary citizenship for Winston Churchill because Britain had not repaid its World War II debts. And it was a Congress of people like Sam Rayburn, Adam Clayton Powell, Everett Dirksen, the famous wizard of oozl, and for a new boy in town just in from the backwoods of Virginia as it were, it was like having a front row seat to the greatest show on earth.

I remember a group of us were sitting around once talking to Hugh Scott who later became the Republican leader in the Senate, and he told us that the Senate was the only institution of its kind where one man, one man could get up on the floor and say nothing, absolutely nothing and immediately a dozen senators would leap in to disagree.

But then political fashions do change as we know and a lot of changes have occurred since then. I was just thinking the other day—remember the New Left? We all remember the New Left, we called it the Goofy Left, and now we have the New Right and the New Left has vanished. And if you want to buy some stocks you can call up Jerry Rubin on Wall Street, for example.

The point I'd just like to make here is that the political process is characterized by change, just like other areas of life. And it's also characterized by inconsistency, though. For example, among the Presidents I have known and observed, John Kennedy made a lot of fancy speeches and talked rather boldly, but I remember him as a rather timid President who didn't always act very boldly. Lyndon Johnson was a President who launched the great war on poverty and yet we know that his presidency was practically destroyed by the Vietnam War and he was the President who really did expand the Vietnam War. Richard Nixon was one of the most experienced and well-trained Presidents of this century and yet he was driven from office and corrupted by Watergate. Jerry Ford was a formidable congressional leader and outstanding member of Congress, somebody you would expect to be able to work with Congress, and yet as President his relations with Congress, for the most part, were in shambles. Jimmy Carter was one of the most intelligent men we've had to occupy the White House this century and yet he couldn't make up his mind on almost anything, and sometimes in the same speech would take different positions. Ronald Reagan yet the great warrior who has taken an unusually tough line toward the

Russians one of the first things he did when he reached the White House was to lift the grain embargo which probably was the single most effective weapon that we've used in our foreign policy against the Soviets. So the point I want to make here is that there is an inconsistency among Presidents, just as there is an inconsistency among most political figures.

Now, when we of the press corps point all of these things out, when we point out the imperfections and the peccadilloes of the Presidents and lesser political mortals, people really do get mad. I know that because we get a lot of mail from people who get mad at *Washington Week,* people who never heard of the art of flattery and have no hesitancy about letting you know they never heard of the art of flattery. And in election years especially we get a lot of mail from people who think that we are biased to the Left or we are biased to the Right. And now that Ronald Reagan is running into trouble we're getting mail from people who suggest that we're doing the country a disservice by pointing out that Mr. Reagan is having trouble with Congress, that he's having trouble with the right wing of his own party, that the White House is having trouble with the press as well. For example, a man in Indiana wrote not long ago to say he found one of our programs filled with a lot of bad ideas, subversive ideas that could cause great damage to the country, suggesting we had a liberal bias. I wrote back saying I was sorry he felt that way, that I didn't recall hearing from him during the Carter years when we were accused of having a conservative bias. Another man in Illinois wrote to say he found it disgraceful that we used reporters from the *New York Times* the *Los Angeles Times,* and the *Washington Post.* To him I replied, "Do you feel it disgraceful that we use reporters from the *Baltimore Sun,* the *Wall Street Journal,* and the *Richmond Times-Dispatch?*" But my favorite of favorite of letters was the one which we received a few years ago from a Milwaukee woman objecting to something that was said on the program about Jimmy Carter. "You were wrong in saying Mr. Carter is dumb, he isn't, he's stupid, you're dumb."

Now these letters illustrate something which I have long observed about people who watch television news and that is they get upset about things which they don't like or things which they see on the tube which they don't want to see. When somebody accuses us of bias I could only think that what they want is for us to reflect *their* biases, that's what they are really interested in. Of course, just let me digress for a moment to say I should tell you that all of these letters about bias are balanced by the many letters we get from our straight thinking fans. A woman from South Dakota wrote to say she felt we should be running the country: "You always seem so wise and knowledgeable, incorruptible and sincere." I of course wrote back and said she seemed like a very wise woman.

But actually, to get down to brass tacks, all of this is really old hat. It's an old American tradition, as we all know, to attack the politicians, to attack the President, to attack the Congress, and to attack the press. Thomas Jefferson, to mention a name that's well known around here, felt so vilified that he felt the newspapers should run a special section called Lies. Alexander Hamilton called the press "a wild animal in our midst." John Kennedy got so disgusted with the press coverage of the old New York *Herald Tribune* that he ordered all copies stricken from the White House. Lyndon Johnson broke with Walter Lippmann. And I remember there was a great cartoon which Herblock did in which he suggested that Lyndon Johnson had launched a new war on a second front against Walter Lippmann. Katherine Graham says Lyndon Johnson didn't talk to her for five years because he so resented the *Post's* coverage of the war. So the conflict between the press and the politicians obviously is not new, it's been going on for a long time.

I think what is new now is that we do have an administration in Washington which is employing new tactics in an effort to manage the news, to try to manipulate the news and to try to control the flow of information out of Washington. I think it is really a pretty clever crew, too, and one example is something that happened just a month ago. To my knowledge it was the first time that we've had a White House news conference that was turned into a birthday party for the President. There it was in living color one morning. What happened was that the President called one of his impromptu news conferences. The commercial networks are inclined just to leap in and cancel whatever program is on the air at the time and to switch immediately to the White House on the theory that the President may really make some news. Usually he doesn't but you never can tell when he might have a major announcement. And they did and the President obviously didn't have much to say but right in the midst of this news conference Mrs. Reagan comes marching into the room to the snickers of the press and she's carrying this birthday cake and put it down, and there the networks are, they're covering the birthday party. The networks weren't very happy about that because they obviously felt they were being used.

But this is really only the flashy part of this administration's new offensive. More flagrant is what they are really trying to do in getting the press to run more upbeat news, to be more positive in the coverage of the White House and developments concerning this administration. The White House press secretary, in a rather audacious mood not long ago, suggested that the nightly news programs should run a good news segment every night. This in their eyes would counter what they see as the negative flow of the news, and obviously they were thinking that some of the good news segments would involve this administration. And in certain cases the White House is now trying to be the messenger which takes the good news to the country. Hence we had the recent appearance of the President himself at a Boston bar and at an automobile assembly line in Missouri, the idea being that Mr. Reagan himself would take the glad tidings to the country that Reaganomics is working, that it would be the salvation of us all and that happy days would soon be coming back again. But messengers, even presidential messengers, can make mistakes, and when Mr. Reagan was at the Boston bar quaffing his ale with his new blue collar friends, all of a sudden he blurted out the opinion that the corporate income tax wasn't really a very good thing. The White House aides obviously were appalled by that because they immediately could see the next day's headlines and they could see what the nightly news segments of the presidential visit would be and they were obviously right because the goodwill which they had hoped to engender by showing the President mixing it up at a Boston bar, being a hail fellow well met, was lost in the ensuing coverage of the fact that the President was suggesting during this time of austerity and hard times for many people, that maybe the corporations of America were paying too much in the way of taxes.

All of this underscores, I think, the hazard of trying to manage the news and specifically of staging events to make a President look good. But every administration tries to do it and this administration is clearly no exception. The Reagan White House has now brought in a man who is supposed to be a communications wizard, a naval officer, and he is moving to the White House with a clear purpose of trying to polish up the presidential image. As my old friend Peter Lisagor used to say, "They all want to make us cheer-leaders." So here again we have a new chapter in an old, old story. The press again is under siege and is being attacked by the adminis-tration in power, their contention being that we are somehow undermining the country because the great good things which this administration is doing are not being accurately and fairly reported to the country. There is, as a headline in the *Wall Street Journal* said not long ago, "a great deal of new lashing out at the unpatriotic press."

I don't think any of this is surprising to those of us who've watched Presidents come and go. Political paranoia seems to go with the White House turf. I think what is different in this case is that this administration is bolder and more heavy-handed in its attempts to manage the news and to manipulate how the White House press corps covers the news. And it even instituted just during the past few months some additional steps, such as requir-ing the keeping of logs of White House officials who have contacts with reporters and even if a reporter calls somebody on the tele-phone they are supposed to take note of this as well. So all of this is designed basically not just to put pressure on the press but also to intimidate staffers of the White House, some of whom have been very outspoken in the past six or eight months in talking about disarray at the White House and the fact that there had been innumerable clashes and divisions of opinion about some of the ways that the President has been conducting his business, and in the way decisions are being made at the White House.

Now sometimes these tactics backfire. The White House rather bravely decided to go after Bill Moyers when he did his documentary a little over a year ago about the plight of the poor and how this administration's budget cuts were affecting the less fortunate people in this country. There were some people at the White House who didn't think that was a very good thing to do. One of those who spoke out was Richard Darman, one of the wiser presidential aides, who compared the White House attack against the press at that time to the action of former Virginia Senator William Scott, who, when he was cited in a magazine poll as having been voted the dumbest member of the Senate, promptly called a news conference to say it wasn't so. Anyway, the complaints of the politicians and government officials always remind me of something which Gertrude Stein once said of writers, "They want three things: praise, praise, and more praise."

To go beyond this for just a moment, there is a more disturbing side about this, though, and that is some of the criticism which we of the press corps are now getting from our own ranks, from those who contend that the press is out of step, is out of control, and that the press somehow should be using its power more wisely or more responsibly. Michael O'Neill who is the editor of the New York *Daily News* not long ago in a speech accused the press of making a considerable contribution to the disarray in government, suggesting that the emphasis on investigative reporting is crowding out what he called "other more significant kinds of reporting and is making it more difficult for our leaders to govern. We should," he said, "make peace with the government"—his precise words.

Then there was Kurt Ludke, a former editor of the Detroit *Free Press,* who said in a speech last year, "The press makes public opinion. There are good men and women who will not stand for office because of their concern the press will find their flaws or invent them. Furthermore," he argued, "there is no such thing as the public's right to know." Again, the precise words.

Now this is really pretty heavy stuff, and my response to all of it is—hogwash. To begin with, if the politicians and the bureaucrats make such a mess of things, as they frequently do, think how much worse off we'd be if all the news coming out of Washington, everything you heard was good news, telling you how rosy things were, that inflation really wasn't bad, unemployment really wasn't bad, that the economy really was coming back. Suppose you got nothing but good news. I think the time to be concerned is when the politicians and the press are really backslapping and sweet-talking one another. And the notion that we should make peace with the government has the same ring to it as those people who write and say we should get behind the President no matter who the President is. My response to that is that we should get behind the free press because the free press is the only free press we have and the First Amendment is the only First Amendment we have. The constitutional guarantee of a free press means that we have an institution outside the normal organs of government which is supposed to be standing on the sidelines and it is absurd to me to think that you can preserve a free government by giving up one of the basic freedoms, or in any way temporizing one of the basic freedoms of that government. James Madison, the father of the Constitution, gives us, I think the real answer when he says, "Knowledge will forever govern ignorance and the people who mean to be their own governors must arm themselves with the power that knowledge gives." More recently in the Pentagon Papers case, U.S. Judge Murray Gurfein put it well when he said, "A cantankerous press, an obstinate press, and an iniquitous press, must be suffered by those in authority in order to preserve the even greater values of freedom of expression and the right of people to know."

Thus, the First Amendment applies not just to the virtuous press, to the good press, to the responsible press, but to the irresponsible press, to that part of the press which does engage in perhaps malicious gossip, which is wrong, which can't always be trusted. I must say parenthetically that as a journalist I share many of the frustrations which some of the people who write us, which probably some of you here today have. I think there is too much irresponsible reporting, too much poking into private lives, and I think too much reliance on unnamed sources, and I think that there is too much reporting at the national level which is superficial. I think there is too much instant analysis which turns out to be instant bologna. I still remember waking up, turning on my television set after the Iowa caucuses in 1980 and hearing my old colleague Tom Pettit of NBC saying after those caucuses that Ronald Reagan was politically dead. All too often we undermine our own credibility. Nor should the press be as thin-skinned as it sometimes is. William Fulbright once said that the press should not regard every criticism as a fascist attack against the First Amendment, and I think he's right. All the same, it is far better to have the press and not the government making the mistakes.

Perhaps some words of retired Supreme Court Justice Potter Stewart are worth citing. "Newspapers, television networks, and magazines have sometimes been outrageously abusive, untruthful, arrogant, and hypocritical. But it hardly follows that elimination of a strong and independent press is the way to eliminate abusiveness, untruth, arrogance, or hypocrisy from government itself." Few politicians have the notable view of Harry Truman who used to say that if the press stopped criticizing him he'd know he was in the wrong pew.

For the most part the press and the politicians in Washington coexist in a state of tension and you might describe it as friendly and unfriendly tension, but we know that in the case of the Nixon administration it became open warfare. What happened during that administration is worth remembering because here we had, not just a clash between the press and the presidency and presidential aides, but a systematic campaign to discredit the press, to try to get the American people to feel that what they were reading actually was not the truth. It was just ten years ago that Charles Colson was given the assignment of organizing a systematic campaign to try to persuade the American people that what they were hearing on television and reading in newspapers was just not so, a campaign in which they not only harrassed editors with phone calls but they also made up letters and sent letters to the editor and did all kinds of infamous things to try to discredit the press. The press won that battle but I think all we have to do is to think, what if the *Washington Post* had been intimidated, suppose that newspaper which bore the brunt of the attack, suppose it had been somewhat timid, suppose it had decided to pull back. As it was the press corps was late getting on to Watergate and the *Washington Post* had to carry the ball on that story for a long, long time. The big lie technique did not work in that instance but it certainly means that we must always be vigilant.

So the fundamental point here, as far as I'm concerned, is that the greatest danger comes not from an aggressive press but from a timid press. Senator Sam Ervin of North Carolina, who was the sage of Watergate and long one of my heroes, said something which I've always remembered and that is, "The First Amendment is designed not to protect the press but the people." It's really a very tough amendment, because as Senator Ervin added: "The First Amendment extends its freedoms to all human beings regardless of whether they are wise or foolish, profound or shallow, learned or ignorant, devout or ungodly, and regardless of whether they love their country and its institutions."

Well anyway, to wind all this up, I think we will survive the latest occupants of the White House, just as we have survived other assaults in the past. I think we do have a rather rich tradition to preserve and I think it will be preserved. I think the press corps has over the years become a lot tougher and has in a sense become immune to a lot of this. I also remember something which my old colleague, David Brinkley of NBC once said, "There have been many instances where the politicians have seized power to muzzle the press but there's never been an instance where the press has seized power and muzzled the politicians." Thank you very much.

NARRATOR: Before we ask for your questions I'd like to make one announcement that if the Miller Center had a good news column, the item at the top of the good news column would be that Dumas Malone is back after having been away for a few months with a little upset, and nothing could be more important for Miller Center Forums and all our activities to have Dumas with us. The other item affecting Dumas that I think some of you but not all of you know was that Wednesday he was awarded the Medal of Freedom. And whereas the press of the United States chose to put the picture of Billy Graham on the front page, they somehow neglected to put the picture of Dumas on the front page, and that's why I'm making the announcement.

MR. DUKE: See, you can't trust the press.

MR. MALONE: Here it is, see. I don't know how long I'll have the courage to wear this but I thought I'd wear it for a few days.

NARRATOR: Well, it's a great honor for the University, to scholarship and to all that Dumas Malone has stood for throughout his career. Usually we ask him to ask the last question. If he should want to ask the first question, why, having stored up a certain number of questions, he can do it or not as he sees fit.

MR. MALONE: Well, I certainly am in full agreement with Paul about the freedom of the press. It is of the utmost importance. It's too bad that there can't be a better distinction between the public and the private, which Jefferson always made so much of. Public things have got to be examined with the utmost scrutiny, but this private stuff, I must say this sort of gets me. We are in a way faced with a dilemma. We've got to expose the administration but how can anybody withstand the amount of scrutiny that any President now gets? I mean it's just so—Washington and Jefferson, those people they wouldn't have stood it at all. So I don't know any answer to it except good manners and restraint and good judgment that has got to come from the press itself. Or maybe Paul has thought of a better way to meet this difficulty, yes I'm sure you've thought of that. The President now is subjected to such intense scrutiny that people frequently say that we may be in an era of one-term Presidents. Nobody can stand more than four years of it, and I sometimes think that we have more reporting than we need. I think that some of these things are reported and interpreted to an absurdity, really. I'm sure you will agree with that. But at any rate, we never would have gotten rid of Nixon but of course we are not rid of him yet.

MR. DUKE: He's coming back. He's now going to star in a movie.

MR. MALONE: We are eternally indebted to the press. I don't suppose the Vietnam War would have been done but for the press, that the degree of the public opposition would have been as great. So I'm all for the press. But they need to practice restraint, good judgment, and good manners, as I'm sure you'll agree.

QUESTION: There is something more than good manners involved here, Paul, and it seems to me that those who are responsible for the press, particularly in television, have an enormous question to address. It seems fair to say that because of the advent of television, not because of you on television or other individuals, that the role of political parties in this country has badly disintegrated. Political parties played an important part in the integrative function of our government, and I would suggest that perhaps one of the reasons for the additional tension between people and the White House and the media stems from the fact that this problem of government has become so extraordinarily difficult. It's harder to get together to integrate policies and what Dumas is saying about the one-term President is very much appropos, in part because of the sharp focus on Presidents. In effect we expect much more than a President can ever possibly deliver, and in the period of office he is stripped to his underwear virtually so that any President who could maintain that kind of support needed to govern is almost difficult to see.

My question is: Does the press, particularly the TV press, acknowledge or accept that it may have some responsibilities for contributing to the integrative function that it has destroyed by its effect on political parties? This is certainly related to the capacity of governments to govern and the tendency of TV reporting to focus so heavily on the immediate. It seems to me they generate an enormous burden on any kind of policymaker who is trying to make some kind of policy that makes the attempt to look at longer range considerations more seriously.

Lastly, the one thing, having been in the bureaucracy side of it, one of the things that bothers bureaucrats of course is that the difference between being in the White House and being in the press is the White House does have to pick up the chips for what it does and the enormous power of TV is there without the responsibility. Is there any way that as an institution TV needs to develop something that expresses in an operative sense its responsibility?

MR. DUKE: Well it's difficult to deal with your points in that sense because I think basically what you are saying is that you feel that there is too much irresponsible reporting on television or that at least there is too much superficial reporting.

QUESTION: Too little perspective reporting.

MR. DUKE: Too little perspective reporting. I would agree perhaps fundamentally with that because I think there is a tendency at the commercial networks to look at Washington news through a rather glamorous lens. One of my contentions is that television over-covers the White House and tends to trivialize every little incident at the White House or what the President does and that it under-covers Congress, which is more important in the scheme of things than you would gather from watching the nightly news programs. And I agree that there is a lack of coherence to television's cover-age of the news. I mean, something may be dramatized this week but next week it's completely forgotten. But by the same token the newspapers are much the same way. If you look at today's newspaper and you see the headline, they may be dramatizing something which next week is just completely forgotten. And so we depend on other institutions, we depend upon the historians or some of the better magazines to give things the longer range focus.

In addressing myself to your point about the troubles of the political parties I find myself more in a defensive role of television. I think if we take the example of the Democratic party, I think the Democratic party brought on a lot of its own troubles, for example, with some of the reforms which it instituted, and it was those reforms, the attempt to democratize the Democratic party and to give a greater voice to a greater number of people which led to the nominations for example of George McGovern in 1972 and Jimmy Carter in 1980 which had a lot to do with really hurting the Democratic party. And I think here again like in the nineteenth century, the latter part of the nineteenth century, I think we're going through a period of, for lack of a better expression, some kind of political turmoil perhaps, but I don't regard it as permanent. I don't buy the notion that we are headed for nothing but one-term Presidents hereafter. For example, if the people didn't want Jimmy Carter to be their President, and I don't think it was television which did in Jimmy Carter, I think it was a perception which the people had that he was an ineffective President that did him in. And television reported that story just as the written press reported that story. But what troubles me is the suggestion that maybe Presidents should be given eight years. I mean if you disagreed with Ronald Reagan, his conduct of the presidency, why shouldn't you vote him out if you are the American electorate and you think he should be voted out in 1984? On the other hand, we might elect a President in 1984 or 1988 that the people really do care for and whose policies really do endear him to the American people who would be given an eight-year term. So I find that there is maybe a suggestion in your comments of looking upon television as something of a scapegoat, of the press as something of a whipping boy for these troubles which have developed.

Now I would certainly hasten to add that I think there should be a more responsible and more serious kind of reporting in the television press because I am troubled by a lot of the pop journalism which we have. Nonetheless, I think that there is, like the White House is contending today, their contention that there should be more good news reported, I think implicit in all this is somehow a misunderstanding of the role of the press. And the press has a day-by-day function to perform at the same time that it has the function of trying to tidy up all the developments and give some perspective and focus to them, too.

NARRATOR: Sander Vanocur is part of another Forum. Would you react to this? He recited the history of his television career and then he said, "Gradually as the years passed I began to think that politicians and certainly the President of the United States believed that going on television was not part of a process to influence legislation or change public opinion, but became almost an end in itself, that the television coverage became a political process," and then he talked about campaigns.

MR. DUKE: Well, I think that's true. And a more pertinent point here, I think, is that politicians really try to use television, too. They want television to report in a fashion which they think reflects well on them but at the same time they try to use television to their advantage. When Mrs. Reagan walked into that room with a big birthday cake she was there because she knew that it was going to be on live television and the whole notion was that this would be image-building. We're going to give the country back the image of Ronald Reagan as a good guy, and so it was all light-hearted and festive and very, very meaningless. So it's really a two-way street here.

QUESTION: Mr. Duke, I've watched over thirty years the process of government. The unelected congressional delegations of committees and staffs have grown tenfold. I also watched a reform called Political Action Committees, the combination of which is making the presidency almost forced to fight through another medium, i.e., the press. They can't manage the Congress the way they used to or as well. Apparently there is no leadership capacity there. Have you observed any of that in your time there?

MR. DUKE: No leadership capacity from the White House?

QUESTION: No, in the Congress. I had Senator Byrd of West Virginia admit one night that he had such a fractured Senate due to the individual concentrations that he almost could not get them into the line.

MR. DUKE: You mean the individual senators?

QUESTION: Yes, well, the Senate as a whole. He was the leader.

MR. DUKE: That's a common complaint which you hear. Tip O'Neill has said the same thing. We have a rather new breed of congressman who sees himself now as a computerized manager. There are some people who are really quite worried about the future when you can punch a button—for example, if an important vote is coming up and people will have these computer terminals in their home and the congressman or somebody in his office can punch a button and you can ask people back home in your district, "How shall I vote?" and they'll get the response and then the congressman will trot over to the floor and he'll cast his vote. But we have a new breed of congressman now who is very tuned in to public opinion in his district and they perform all kinds of constituent services. They are less devoted to the national interests, they're not really national congressmen as we used to know, and hence that has created the problem for the congressional leaders who have to build support, who have to build a consensus for national policies because there are these more managerial kinds of members who resist the leadership enticements to go along on certain issues.

The question again, though, is where public opinion is because we had the spectacle in 1981 of Congress following public opinion right down the road voting for Ronald Reagan's program, of the Democrats in fact, going overboard in trying to appear to out-Reagan the Republicans to a certain extent in terms of giving tax cuts. And I well remember talking to some members of Congress who were fearful of the Reagan program and felt the Reagan program wouldn't work but they felt the country was really behind the new President and wanted to give him a chance and wanted his program voted in place. On the other hand they felt that it just made absolutely no logic whatsoever, this program, a program of tax cuts, of budget cuts, vastly increasing military spending, that it would only exacerbate our economic problems, which of course it did. But the program was approved because the politicians felt that politically they had to go along with it, and that is even a more frightening thing to me.

QUESTION: Some years ago H. J. Liebling wrote a series of articles on the press and he was much concerned with the failure of many newspapers and the concentration of power of the publishers for the newspapers that remained. He thought this might be a most unwholesome experience for the press and the opportunity for emphasis to be exerted by the owners of the newspapers and of course television and elsewhere. It does seem that our best investigative and, in the best sense, objective reporting comes from the noncommercial sector. I wonder if what Liebling had to say was still something to worry about or whether it has not turned out that way or whether you have any opinion on this or whether it is of concern to people practicing journalism today when they look into their own house and think maybe that might be a problem.

MR. DUKE: Well, I think it is certainly of concern but I also remember Liebling writing about the 1936 election when Franklin Roosevelt carried every state but two and ninety percent of the editors of this country endorsed Alf Landon for President. So it's a worthy example to cite when people say that the press becomes too powerful, for example.

QUESTION: Well, I was thinking of what the publishers say about what emphasis his paper should take and you'd have reporters who would not necessarily agree with that. I think that was the emphasis that Liebling was worried about, the owners of the papers.

MR. DUKE: Setting the policy and the press feeling that it had?

QUESTION: Yes, and on television, and so forth.

MR. DUKE: Well, when I was on the *Wall Street Journal* we never felt any compulsion whatsoever to follow an editorial line and the *Journal* was conservative in those days; today I would regard it as ultraconservative. They were two separate entities, I mean, the news department and the editorial department, and the twain never came together whatsoever. As a matter of fact some of the best political pieces I think being written today are in the *Wall Street Journal* despite its far right views on the editorial page. And even more than that the *Wall Street Journal* has a bureau chief named Mike Miller who wrote a piece I well remember a year ago, the best piece I read anywhere about the effect of the Reagan budget cuts on the poor in this country in which he said they really did savage the poor. So here you had the bureau chief writing a column on the editorial page and next to that were the editorials saying, "Right on." There are instances of that obviously in this country but I think not very many.

QUESTION: Mr. Duke, isn't it nevertheless true, that there is a major problem with power about the press in this country in that the line in your remarks that rang true to me was the thin-skinness of the press today? I ran a thing where people from the press, a lot of your colleagues, came through and said that the kinds of things that you said about the First Amendment. And an invariably quick response to criticisms of the press was repeated again and again and again. I saw Richard Valeriani's cord standing out on his neck when I quizzed him about Pat Epstein's book about television nightly news and lots of other examples. There is a reason out there for the concern out there and for the concern in the broad public, not very well formulated, and not only in the White House but everywhere. And it's not only politically conservatives, it's sort of across the board. And back in those roots in our Virginians, in Jefferson and Madison, what they were worried about was an open society and the problem of great centers of power, concentrations of power, and they were talking in an age of a press that's like the lemonade stand that General Motors runs when it runs an ad talking about free enterprise. But the actual press, with which we now deal, is what an economist would call an oligopoly, and you've got a monopoly in most places. Mr. Liebling was working on it, he had a twist on it, but you do have a giant center of power. It doesn't muzzle governments, it does have an enormous effect on the culture, with television now, and the numbers, God look at the numbers of the commercial networks—the hours people listen and watch, that's power. It's power not of the same sort as things like tyrannical government, but it's power, and it was very hard to get members of the press to respond otherwise than by saying "the First Amendment." For freedom everywhere can at some point turn into power.

Technology and economics have made the press very different from the age in which the theories of the press were formulated which we are still using as a frame. But I think today's press wouldn't respond the way the newspapers did to the Hutchins Commission in 1948 but it is still there, they wouldn't hear it, it would be like an outsider saying something, something you ought to listen to about the press. But there is still not only thin-skinness but a difficulty getting a real problem examined. I think the University ought to grapple with the press in thinking about how this different kind of an entity fits with democratic theory. The First Amendment is insufficient anyway.

MR. DUKE: Well, I certainly don't think that the press should put itself on a pedestal and feel that it is inviolate to criticism or to responsibility, for example. I differ with some of my colleagues who, for example, take the absolute view that reporters never should testify in court cases, that if you cover the story and you have some information pertaining to a criminal case that you can't go before a grand jury or offer pertinent testimony. I think, as members of the press, we also have a duty to be citizens as well, too, so I sympathize with that. But there are two problems I have with your basic contention and one of them is: what is the press? The press is not a monolithic force. We're not all in the same boat.

Are you talking about *People* magazine, are you talking about *Time* magazine, are you talking about the *Richmond Times-Dispatch,* are you talking about the *New York Times,* are you talking about the *San Francisco Chronicle,* are you talking about PBS, are you talking about CBS? You see, the press is very, very diverse in this country which I think really is the fundamental strength of the press in our society, the fact that we don't have a monolith or we don't have a press that's going entirely in the same direction even though editorially it is still a one-sided press, it is still a press in this country which editorially endorses and supports Republican candidates for President and most Republican candidates at the local level as well.

QUESTION: It's hard to get into it, though. Another Liebling line is "Freedom for the publishers." It's hard to get into that conversation. It was a lot easier in Jefferson's day, harder to get your voice into the conversation of society through the press, which is what the press ought to be, the conversation of society. It's hard to get into that with the present economics and technology.

MR. DUKE: And the second point I would raise with you is if there is a suggestion of reform here, who makes the reform? How do you conduct reform? I mean the press has to be self-vigilant and self-governing, really, in a free society. I just don't think it can be any other way, basically. You can offer an amendment on that if you wish.

QUESTION: My only comment on that, Paul, is that anyone who read *Time* magazine last week ought to feel better about the American press after reading about the British press and the Queen.

I would like to ask one question. You referred to the Reagan tax bill of 1981, I've been puzzled over this for some weeks because I haven't gone back and looked. I wondered, did the press get carried away by the tide of public opinion? Because I can't remember that the press was really pointing out across the board, even a great deal, that you can't have the greatest defense increase in history at the same time you have the greatest tax cut. And I can think of a couple Democratic congressmen who may have cynically voted for that tax cut. But refresh my memory.

MR. DUKE: I think the press did. I know on *Washington Week* we did. I know we discussed that a great deal and I know it was always in the context that some people felt, that some economists in particular felt that this was a program that just couldn't work. And the great revelation which the politicians had—the members of Congress approved that program in July 1981 and then they went home and they thought they would be greeted by brass bands in the street because they really performed this miracle. They'd come out with a new economic program that was going to be our salvation. The only thing was when they got home instead of brass bands they were greeted by lynching mobs. And the reason was that inflation was continuing to skyrocket and interest rates were way up, and businesses were beginning to enter a period of enormous bankruptcies and closing of doors during that period. And the Republicans, I well remember, came back from the August recess in September of 1981, and they were frightened to death, they were in a state of panic because they realized that this program which they approved was not really that strongly supported by the people at home because they didn't understand it and it didn't work the magic which they thought would be worked almost immediately. And if you remember, the stock market nose dived at that period. But it was a classic case, I think, of the politicians not really doing what they should have done because they just willy-nilly supported the program. But I think the press by and large did point this out, maybe not as sufficiently as it should have but it pointed it out.

NARRATOR: Who would like to ask the last question?

QUESTION: I would not like to ask the last one since I'm finding this so delightful. Paul, I'd like to ask you about what kind of spectrum, if you could give us a kind of rough spectrum of, say, programs similar to your own, are doing a different thing, or what you think are the most important contributions of different kinds of journalism that are made today that really do contribute to the public good, aside from your own, of course.

MR. DUKE: *Washington Week* and *The Lawmakers!* Well, let me start with the written press. I think the *New York Times* in particular does a good job today of covering Washington. I think the *Times* is far superior to the *Times* of, say, ten years ago or even seven or eight years ago. I think they have beefed up their Washington staff, and there was a period when the *Post* was in the ascendency and the *Times* was in decline. I think the *Times* has had a notable comeback because I think they really do a good job of covering Washington now. I think the *Post* does a good job but I think the *Post* may have dipped just a little bit. But there are other publications that I think are reliable and trustworthy: the *Baltimore Sun* has a very good Washington staff, I think they do an excellent job—good, solid, experienced people; the *Los Angeles Times,* I would say the same thing; I think the *Chicago Tribune* has a very good Washington staff now. At the magazine level, *Time, Newsweek,* and *U.S. News,* fine, basically good reporting.

My basic complaint is with the superficial nature of much of television reporting. Interestingly, the viewing habits of Americans seem to be changing. The audience for the commercial networks is going down. It has been going down now for the past three years. The audience for PBS, I'm proud to say here today, has been going up, rather it was going up at a rather modest curve and now it has turned into a rather sharp curve. And one of the reasons, I think, is that a lot of people have discovered that there are good things on PBS, responsible things, for the most part, even though we do our share of things that I'm not always proud of, in the documentary area in particular. Also cable television is coming along as well and that's cutting into the commercial networks. McNeil-Lehrer is now going to go to an hour and there's an interesting question, they're going to go to a new format which is going to be a newsier format and the interesting question is whether that will really cut into the nightly news programs because the nightly news programs are still a kind of slam-bang kind of journalism.

I felt enormous frustration when I was at NBC doing nightly news segments. There were many, many instances when I would have what I thought was really a good story and I would be told to hold it to a minute and thirty seconds which meant that I couldn't get in some very, very important facts, so I felt this frustration, and so one of the great satisfactions which I have as a journalist and doing a program like *Washington Week* is that I feel that I can take the news and give it a certain comprehensibility and focus which I never could before, to give it some context for people to more clearly understand what's going on. I don't know if the commercial networks will ever come to that. Being a product of that school myself I know their thinking is not along that line, they are more in terms of "Move it along and dress it up a bit." Anyway, we can all hope for a new day.

NARRATOR: We also can be thankful that *Washington Week* has the largest viewing audience apparently of any public affairs program in the country, so that's a good sign. We hope that Paul Duke will continue with not only his two programs but maybe someday a program a little bit like this where he tackles some of the things in greater detail that he has around the table with friendly critics and strong supporters who are bound to be with him Friday evening whenever his program airs. It is a great pleasure to have you with us.

The Presidential Press Conference
RAY SCHERER

NARRATOR: We are very pleased that Ray Scherer could be with us. He and I were graduate students at the University of Chicago in the "Golden Age." That was a time when postwar "refugees" from the Army, the Navy and the Air Force of the United States took haven at Chicago, which was then Mr. Robert Hutchins' university. In this period, few professors were able to finish more than two or three sentences in a lecture without being interrupted, challenged or questioned by a G.I. If the professor said something about Italy, Iran or Indonesia, some student had been there; it was indeed an exciting period.

The other source of excitement was the presence at Chicago of two towering figures in international relations, Quincy Wright and Hans Morgenthau. The first day I went to breakfast at the University of Chicago, I found my way to the Windermere East which someone had told me was the place for Sunday morning brunch. I saw fifteen students seated at a big table shouting at one another, pounding the table and arguing. I thought to myself the subject of controversy had to be religion, politics or intercollegiate athletics which Chicago had banned. Instead it turned out that half of the students were followers of Morgenthau and half were disciples of Wright. This kind of debate continued throughout the period we were there.

MR. SCHERER: I wrote my thesis for Wright and Morgenthau. One was power and one was law. I don't know how I managed to please them both.

NARRATOR: From that point the story becomes a more public one and Ray Scherer went on to major responsibilities at NBC. He became White House correspondent for NBC and his reports were a household word for many of us.

The last element in the story involves a recent article in the *Wall Street Journal* by Vernon Royster who discussed the changing character and the evolution of presidential press conferences. It stimulated our interest in today's subject. This more or less reviews the history and background of our invitation to Ray Scherer. I thought it would be interesting to have Mr. Scherer reflect on the changing patterns of presidential press conferences and then, at the end of our discussion, we might consider whether the Miller Center might have a role to play in further study or suggestions for improvements. We found when we came to the Miller Center that a great deal of good work had been done but most of it had been kept on ice and it was not getting out to other people. So we thought one way to begin to rectify this would be to get something down on paper and make it available to scholars and interpreters for their use. This is the history of our efforts to publish Miller Center Forums.

In any case, the relevance of our subject was brought home in a recent visit with the foremost Woodrow Wilson scholar, the historian, Arthur Link of Princeton University. Professor Link asserted that presidential press conferences began with Woodrow Wilson. Wilson tried holding press conference from 1913 to 1915 and then stopped them because he found the strain was too great. He turned to other methods of communication with the public. So I suppose a first question one might ask is who initiated presidential press conferences.

INTERJECTION: Louis Brownlow said Theodore Roosevelt started the presidential press conference.

A BIOGRAPHER OF THEODORE ROOSEVELT AND JOHN W. DAVIS: No, I think he talked to the press informally.

INTERJECTION: He called them in.

QUESTION: Oh, yes he called them in but . . .

INTERJECTION: So that was the beginning of it.

QUESTION: Well in a sense, yes. But it was not formal.

MR. SCHERER: It depends on what you call a press conference.

What sort of a meeting with reporters was a press conference and what was just an informal gathering?

NARRATOR: Well, you've not come to hear us; we've come to hear you.

MR. SCHERER: You want me to reminisce? Well, I came to Washington in the Truman days; and Mr. Truman was still doing news conferences in the same format Mr. Roosevelt had introduced. They were all put in the third person, and you were only allowed direct quotes occasionally when he said something that was particularly incisive or newsy, in which case you had to ask, "May we have that in direct quotes?" And he would say yes or no. Roosevelt held them twice a week and Truman held them generally once a week. He was pretty irregular about them. One week they would be in the morning and the next week they would be in the afternoon. I think he held them on Monday; Eisenhower changed to a Wednesday format. Truman's conferences were, as I remember them, very peppery and informal. Some of them lasted only ten minutes and there was a lot of give and take and a lot of banter. He had certain people that he knew very well, particularly the Missouri correspondents with whom he fenced; he was very free and uninhibited. More often than not after the news conference, Charlie Ross, his press secretary, would call us in and say, "He didn't really mean to say what he said; he meant to say this. . . . " But none of them, of course, ever appeared on radio or television.

Toward the end of the Truman era, somewhere in 1951 or 1952, we were occasionally allowed a little bit of it to use on radio—little excerpts. I remember Morgan Beatty being very excited one night about bringing people in who participated in the Truman news conference, and they had an excerpt of something or other. I think they were always recorded though. A stenographic report was kept. I think there is probably a recorded version of the Roosevelt conferences too, but they were always reported in the third person which took out a good deal of the juice. Truman's news conferences were direct and to the point. He wasn't given much to philosophy. There were fairly sharp questions and fairly sharp answers.

When President Eisenhower came along, James Hagerty immediately sensed that the news conference was a good political vehicle for a president in communicating with the people. And I think from the beginning we were allowed to have it on tape for radio purposes. We were never allowed to broadcast them live, but we were allowed to tape them. Then Hagerty would clear the quotations just in case the President misspoke himself. Clearance was generally pro forma. At the beginning, Hagerty would take out a sentence here and there—that is from the radio tape which we were allowed to use—but it soon got to be more and more pro forma. I remember hanging around the White House—the news conference would be from, say about ten-thirty to eleven o'clock on Wednesday mornings—for clearance and once the clearance was given we were allowed to use it on the radio.

After several years, when television became more and more a factor in American life, Hagerty sensed that we ought to have television coverage. I can remember him calling us in and asking whether we could do it without a lot of fuss and commotion, without, as he put it, a lot of bright lights shining in the President's eyes. At that point, sometime in 1954, or maybe 1955, we had available a new film which was called Tri-X. It was 400 speed which was fairly fast so you didn't have to use a lot of bright lights. We put a row of cameras in the back row of the Indian Treaty Room where the news conferences were held in the Executive Office Building. Truman was the first, by the way, to move the news conference from the Oval Office across the street to the Indian Treaty Room. He wanted to give them a little more formality and a little more room because more and more reporters were coming. It's an extraordinary old room in the old State, War and Navy Building, now the Executive Office Building, but with very bad acoustics. It had marble walls and we used to sit in little funeral parlor chairs. The President would come in and hold this news conference. When it was over and he left, we'd all bolt for the door.

With Eisenhower's press conferences, they took out the two back rows of chairs and installed a wooden platform. There were perhaps six film cameras: one for NBC, one for ABC, and one for CBS, one for Tele-news, one for another network, etc. The old-timers among the press corps resented it because they thought it would make a show of things. They didn't like the cameras coming in and intruding on their preserve. But it went pretty well and, from then on, you saw excerpts of Eisenhower at his news conference on the nightly news. It was in black and white and the news conference ran thirty minutes. It so happened that a 1,200 foot roll of film ran about 33 minutes so it was a very congenial marriage of technology and subject matter.

After this, the news conference took on still another dimension. Instead of being only on radio it was also on television. There were some people who carried the whole thing at night on TV, some of the local stations. So you could watch all of Eisenhower's news conferences on the eleven o'clock news or whenever it was broadcast. I think networks may have carried the whole thing at the beginning because it was a novelty, but later on they used only excerpts on their news shows.

We used to go to Hagerty and ask why doesn't the President take the next step which is to hold live news conferences. We urged him to persuade the President to go on live television. Hagerty could never get Ike to agree to that because the feeling was that he might misspeak himself. We used to say that he rarely did and this was not a great chance to take, but Eisenhower always wanted that final control of never going live in case he should say something which would be upsetting. Truman had said a number of things, notably about the atomic bomb on one occasion, which sent Prime Minister Clement Attlee of Great Britain coming over on the next plane to straighten things out. So news conferences did have worldwide ramifications.

The next chapter involved President Kennedy. Kennedy was very sure of himself and so was Pierre Salinger. They decided news conferences would go on live television—which gave us still another dimension—and they became a good vehicle for projecting Kennedy's image as a young, self-assured and well-spoken leader and president. They moved the news conferences from the old Indian Treaty Room to the State Department auditorium. It was an immense place which put Kennedy on a larger and impressive stage. He generally held his press conferences either in later afternoon or early evening. Sometimes the early evening ones were at seven o'clock which put him on prime time, or pretty close to it. Here was a chance for the whole world, so to speak, to look in and watch Kennedy as reporters saw him, answering questions off the top of his head. This diminished the role somewhat of the press corps because people were getting it live. AP and UPI would simply take it off the tube and file it as he ran it instead of the reporters coming out and interpreting it and filing one bulletin after another. Kennedy held his press conferences fairly regularly and, I think, did a pretty good job of communicating.

Then suddenly he was gone and President Johnson came in. Johnson never quite figured out a format that pleased him. One week he would have a news conference which was in the old format in the Oval Office where you took it all down and reported it afterwards. Another week he might have one in the East Room which would be open to live television; and on another occasion he might try one from the theater in the White House which you could record and use afterwards. He never found an ideal format and I think the press conference retrogressed in his administration a bit. He never felt comfortable. Sometimes he did better than other times but I had a feeling that the camera inhibited him and only rarely did we see the real Johnson with the bark off.

At that point I went to Europe and no longer covered the Presidency again, but that, in capsule, is the way it developed from a news conference that was for the writing press only to one that was carried on live television.

And now we have Jimmy Carter who holds them at various times, not quite as regularly as others. Again they're back on live TV, and he holds them from a refurbished room in the Executive Office Building. At this point I think I'll take a breath and see what questions there might be. I've dwelt rather heavily on the logistics of it because they provide the background for the institutionalization of the presidential press conference.

QUESTION: Did Kennedy have the greatest rapport with the press? Of all the presidents that you have mentioned, he seemed to get along best with the press.

MR. SCHERER: Yes, he had a lot of contemporaries in the press corps—people who had grown up with him and covered him while he was a member of the House and the Senate. He was very graceful about it; he had a turn of phrase. He never seemed to be afraid of the press corps, never seemed to feel that he was on trial or trapped as other presidents did, particularly Johnson. So I would say he had a lot of rapport.

QUESTION: What are the disadvantages and perils of press conferences in terms of the last format, that of live coverage? We are all aware of the benefits and the importance of the democratic process but what, in your view, are the disadvantages?

MR. SCHERER: Well, if you have a president who was cocksure of himself and wasn't always terribly thoughtful, as occasionally with Truman, he might misspeak himself and his words would go out to the whole world by satellite, but I think that's a fairly rare phenomenon. I don't think that happened terribly often. The other peril, I suppose, was being drawn out on something you weren't ready to speak about in which case you'd have to parry it and become sort of bland. I think Carter's news conferences are bland. I think he's pretty well in control of the facts but you rarely hear anything startling new. You get a pretty good feel for Carter the man but less of a feel for the substance of his views.

QUESTION: Obviously in diplomacy there are certain matters which should not be raised, especially at sensitive times in international relations. It is quite conceivable that the President can more or less be coerced by the environment of the press conference and by his desire to establish rapport with the people who are interrogating him to go further than he should. I'm just raising this in a hypothetical sense. I come down clearly on the side of open press conferences, but I do think there are problems. As I remember Franklin Roosevelt's conferences, he was extraordinarily facile at parrying, at not saying what he didn't want to say. President Coolidge was remarkably revealing, but it was all off the record.

MR. SCHERER: I've often wondered what Roosevelt, with his grip on the public imagination, might have done if he had had television.

QUESTION: Yet he had many of the columnists and most of the publishers against him. But apparently a very good working relationship . . .

MR. SCHERER: . . . with the working press. Truman carried on that same thing. He always said he liked reporters but he disliked publishers.

NARRATOR: May we stick with the disadvantages for a minute? Some diplomatic correspondents say that President Carter said things at the very beginning of his administration that made negotiations difficult. For instance, he made claims before Secretary Cyrus Vance's first visit to Moscow, holding out prospects of almost total nuclear disarmament in certain new projections that went far beyond anything Secretary Kissinger had proposed. When the

Russians abruptly rejected the new proposals, you got a sharp reaction in American public opinion against talking with the Russians.

MR. SCHERER: The perils, as I see them, are almost exclusively in the foreign policy field. Domestically it doesn't seem to happen. Maybe domestic questions are easier to answer; maybe presidents are more at home with them. But with foreign policy there's certainly a definite peril. Once you blow one, it tends to make a president inhibited and takes some of the gloss off future news conferences. The pattern generally is that presidents come in all charged up, tend to hold press conferences regularly, and then, as the months and years go by, the process tends to wither and decline. Presidents tend to feel that they are a nuisance. I think that's almost a universal pattern, although I don't think it was true of Roosevelt.

QUESTION: Is there another pattern, that of presidents increasingly using the press conference as a platform for making statements? Can the advantages and disadvantages of this be measured? That is to say, I have the impression that presidential statements are getting longer and longer and the actual interrogation shorter and shorter. Or is that wrong?

MR. SCHERER: Well, sometimes the President comes in with something he wants to say and reads two or three statements.

QUESTION: But you don't see a pattern?

MR. SCHERER: Well, Carter hasn't done too much of that with opening statements.

QUESTION: I'd like to ask a question about the degree to which what happens in the press conference is programmed in advance from what the President learns through his press secretary and his staff in his preconference briefing. Is it fairly predictable what's going to happen?

MR. SCHERER: I think it's fairly predictable. I remember having to see Pierre Salinger after one of President Kennedy's news conferences to clear up something, and there was Jack Kennedy sitting there. I asked him, "Was there anything that surprised you today?" He said, "No, but I thought surely I was going to get one question I wasn't asked and I was surprised by that." I think more often than not presidents anticipate questions. Of course, there is always the wild one that comes out of nowhere. In Carter's case, he tends to recognize known people sitting up front who are fairly predictable. You often wonder why something didn't get asked but it just happened that way.

QUESTION: Let me state a proposition if I may. You respond to it as you wish. I have the impression that there is no true follow-up on most questions.

MR. SCHERER: Because of format . . .

QUESTION: I've been disappointed repeatedly by the tendency of the President to make an unsatisfactory, sometimes evasive response, and the failure of reporters to pursue the question, and get to the root of the matter. Now that's one dimension of it and the second is this: I'm distressed by the quality of a great many of the questions. A conference will start with a question on an important matter. The President will make an answer which is sometimes unsatisfactory. Then another reporter pops up, not only changing the subject, but introducing the most trivial kind of gossipy, personal question which makes good news but doesn't add to our knowledge.

QUESTION: Could I add one more question. One of the things I have wondered about is the effect on news conferences as the old hands such as yourself have tended, one by one, to move out of the picture. At the very moment reporters have achieved mastery of certain key subjects, newcomers come in. I can't help thinking of Edward R. Murrow's last years of reporting when, after a lifetime of reflection and after covering the Battle of Britain, he came back and tackled the threat of Senator McCarthy and McCarthyism. Could he have conducted his last days of radio and television journalism with such courage and skill if he hadn't grown wise in understanding American democracy and the political process, if he were a rank newcomer? Does the country lose something when, for one reason or another, those of you who know the most go on to new responsibilities? Do you get people who come in with knives sharpened, in an adversary role, with very little knowledge and not much experience who take on the responsibility of asking questions for me as an American citizen? I'd be delighted to have you and other experienced reporters that I have known over the past thirty years asking questions for me, but I'm not so sure that I'm always happy with those who speak for me today.

MR. SCHERER: Going back to the first question, it's a format problem. Everybody comes there with his own question. There's a psychic quality that you want to be recognized, I suppose, and there is an element of show business about it. One question is asked and then the President recognizes somebody else, and reporters come there determined to ask their own questions. They have a device now where before you have asked a question you say, "Mr. President, I'd like to follow that up," and he says, "O.K.," so he's warned in advance. Then you stand on your feet to follow up his first answer. I think for the most part, the questioning zig zags all over the lot. It's an unsatisfactory device. Everybody knows it and there have been various proposals to change it. But none of them have been tried and few of them probably would have worked. One of the proposals is to have two or three senior people represent the whole press corps.

QUESTION: This comes down to a matter of size. Are the press conferences too large?

MR. SCHERER: Yes, they probably are too large, but how are you going to make them smaller?

QUESTION: How many attend now?

MR. SCHERER: I suppose several hundred attend now. Because press conferences are on television, a lot of people don't attend. And because they're not as rewarding as they used to be in bringing out the President's personality, I think a lot of people tend to stay in the office and watch in on TV.

QUESTION: How many attended the Truman conferences when you began?

MR. SCHERER: I always thought the news conferences were more authentic, so to speak, when reporters crowded into the President's office and stood around his desk in the Rooseveltian format. The door would open and everybody would flock in, and there he would be. Of course, there is always a little bit of electricity in the air at presidential press conferences, but it seems to me there was more then.

QUESTION: Wouldn't it be fair to say that the press conference has ceased to be the exclusive vehicle for the President's communication and for his using the media, or speaking through the media to the public? There are a great many more contacts and avenues of communication with the press . . .

MR. SCHERER: Perhaps, but Roosevelt in his day would go out and make a speech anytime he wanted to be covered.

QUESTION: What about the role of staff? Over the period you were covering the President, the number of staff involved in the general area of press relations grew larger and larger. What effect does this have, not just on the press conference, but on relations with the press in general? What do you see as their role and how does it affect the working reporter's access?

MR. SCHERER: Press conferences have grown larger and larger. When I first went down there in the Truman days, I was the number two man for NBC. There were only about a dozen people who followed him around regularly for the *New York Times,* the *Herald Tribune,* the *New York Daily News, The Baltimore Sun, The Washington Post, The Washington Star,* CBS, ABC, NBC, *Time* and *Newsweek* — that was about it. If it was a trip, you would call the *St. Louis Post Dispatch.* You might have the *Wall Street Journal* and of course the wire services were always there; AP, UPI and Reuters covered Truman wherever he went, even if it was on a boat for the weekend. If he went down the Potomac, we'd have to charter another boat and go along. But the coverage got more and more extensive. The advent of radio brought more people into it and the advent of TV brought even more who covered him for special networks, etc.

It seemed that coverage took a quantum jump everytime we got a new president. It got much larger with Kennedy than it was with Eisenhower. So now, whenever you go any place you have several hundred people and you have to hire two jet planes.

But to return to the question of no follow up, I think such issues are large questions that have always been there. It didn't matter so much in the old days when the public wasn't looking in. A reporter would organize the story and report it in such a way that it read very well. Now that the press conference is a public institution, the flaws are a little bit more evident.

QUESTION: I wonder if it is true or not that the flaws are more evident today? Since you have been in Washington for a long time, you recall that when you started out it was pretty well-known who was the heavy drinker in the Senate and who chased after women and all this sort of thing. You reporters knew about it but you never put it on the wire. In the last fifteen years all of this has come out, all this knowledge of drinking and other things.

MR. SCHERER: There are no secrets anymore.

QUESTION: Do you think that the public is better served by the kind of knowledge that we have today of what senator does this and what president does that?

MR. SCHERER: It's an arguable matter. My standard always was that if it didn't hurt his performance why report it.

QUESTION: Take Wilbur Mills. Was Wilbur Mills a good congressman?

MR. SCHERER: For most of the time he was. Toward the end he wasn't. And maybe somebody should have blown the whistle on that. I don't know how many people knew it, but toward the end he was out of control and did some very irrational things. However, until he fell into the Tidal Basin, it didn't come out.

QUESTION: Did you know about Mrs. Rutherford or Kay Sommersby?

MR. SCHERER: No, I didn't at the time. I didn't cover Roosevelt but there were people who knew about Mrs. Rutherford because when they travelled on a train with Roosevelt to Hyde Park suddenly the train would stop and he would have his rendezvous. I think they knew something was going on but I don't think that they knew everything at the time. There are always some people who know and there are always some people who suspect things. But the guideline was unless you know something exactly and precisely, why report it. It's true; that's changed.

QUESTION: Well, certainly reporters knew what was going on with Jack Kennedy; it's incredible to think how the relationship with the President has changed because today you would report everything. Then it was quite evident what he was doing but nobody said a thing.

MR. SCHERER: I used to hear from Secret Service men that there was a lot going on but I always tended to disbelieve it. I couldn't quite believe that he could be president and carry on all this extracurricular business.

QUESTION: All of us who knew him, knew what he was doing. It seems to me amazing that you were muzzled.

MR. SCHERER: Yes, we would go to New York for something or other with Kennedy and he would disappear and we wouldn't see him until he left. You could speculate. No, I think the standard again would be that, unless it affected his performance as an elected president or elected member of the Senate, you didn't report it.

QUESTION: Is there something more basic in the fact that such things are being reported? Lippmann used to argue that the greatest danger to democracy was that private lives would become politicized and the public interest would be trivialized and formulated in wholly private terms. If this has in fact happened, is there anything one can do about it? For instance, everytime I read about the personal affairs of Kennedy or Roosevelt, I think of all the gaps in our knowledge about the diplomacy of wartime conferences, about what went on in Vienna between Kennedy and Khrushchev. We have James Reston's reports of what Kennedy told him after the first meeting with Khrushchev at Vienna and we have scraps here and there, but in terms of the public philosophy, is what we would most like to know being crowded out by the scandal?

MR. SCHERER: Well, the scandals all seem to come out later, those about Kennedy and Roosevelt. There's even a Wilson story this week that I had never heard before in reference to a woman with whom he was enamored.

QUESTION: Is the press divided on all this? For example, on *Agronsky Speaks* the only person who defended the press on the coverage of the last hours of Rockefeller's life was Jack Kilpatrick. All the others said this was bad, that the press had kept dredging it up, going over it again and again.

MR. SCHERER: Well, in Rockefeller's case it was bungled at the beginning. I think it might have been different if Hugh Murrow had said: "Gentlemen, as you may know, there are some odd circumstances here. I'll tell you what they are and then leave it to you whether or not you want to write it." I think if they had told the whole story from the beginning nobody would have written it, but when they started to dissemble and people knew they were dissembling, they set the hounds trailing the pack.

QUESTION: What determines whether a president is reputed to have good press and media relations as against poisonous ones?

MR. SCHERER: I think it's determined by his honesty. If he's honest and gives it to you straight, he probably has good press relations. But once he starts to hide and dissemble, and maybe tells a few lies or gets a little nasty, then relations go sour. I think they go somewhat sour in any case toward the end of his regime because relationships become corrosive. Some, of course, grow worse than others. In Nixon's case they went almost totally sour.

QUESTION: Was Johnson better as a senator than as a president? He switched and became defensive as president but he was more candid as a senator, wasn't he?

MR. SCHERER: Well, even as a senator, Johnson was always a great backroom operator, though, of course he didn't have the spotlight shining on him every day. He could get things done and you admired his finesse in those days, balancing one force or group against another and taking political tradeoffs. He was admired as a wheeler-dealer in the Senate because he would get things done by giving everybody something. But doing the same thing on a presidential level is a little different somehow. It takes a different coloration. You can do it in a semi-hidden way in the Senate, but you can't do it that way in the White House. The same traits that might be admired in a Senate leader would not be so much admired in a president. And, of course, the war is the thing that really soured the press. I think Johnson's manipulative qualities, had he not gotten into the war, might have enabled him to get a lot of legislation through and probably would have been seen as the mark of an effective leader. But once he applied it to the war and once he set out on a big military buildup without ever admitting it, I think then the press became suspicious and it turned people against him.

QUESTION: Is the discussion of improving press conferences really an academic question given the authority of the press and the first amendment, all of these rights? Is this something which won't change anyway, no matter what anybody says? Should a center like this therefore disregard the subject inasmuch as anything that comes out won't have any influence?

MR. SCHERER: I don't know. I think it's worth looking into. I think the White House regulars have had informal meetings about it. They have had sessions among themselves and I think they have agreed on ways that would improve it. But it means giving up some prerogatives and delegating people to carry on the questioning. It's just hard to do. Some presidents, perhaps Kennedy was the first, would sit down with one man from each network for an hour and hold presidential conversations. Johnson carried that on. I was involved in one or two of these conversations. Nixon did it too. That's another way of doing it. Or you can sit down exclusively with one man from one network representing all the rest.

QUESTION: Truman did that with Arthur Krock, didn't he?

MR. SCHERER: Truman did it with Arthur Krock. They were great exclusives. It made the rest of the press corps very angry, especially when Krock got a Pulitzer Prize.

QUESTION: But following up on the question of good press relations, accessibility to the President beyond the press conferences, which turns out to be a sham for many of the press people anyway, is the primary factor isn't it? Hasn't this varied from president to president?

MR. SCHERER: Access is a considerable factor. Another factor is the quality of the press secretary. The press secretary keeps the confidence of the press corps and that of course is a great help. Jim Hagerty was very good at that. He was excellent on all the mechanical details of the coverage. He would hold long briefings for the press before the President went on an overseas trip. He would tell them every last detail; when the bus was going to stop, who would wear what badge, where the luggage was going to be and where the phones were located. Those things are peripheral but they helped a lot. Accessibility with some presidents involves the press secretary who can either get an answer for you or not. I think that's still done to a great extent. There are always people quoted as "aides."

On the nightly television show, that "aide" of President Carter, more often than not, is probably Jody Powell or somebody around him. You can funnel things through such people. In Johnson's days a lot of stuff would come through Walt Rostow. Bill Moyers, when he was press secretary, was very good at telling you exactly what the President was thinking. He might soften it up a bit and refine it, but a good press secretary can be a channel. And as I say, if you had something that you really needed to know or were working on a special program, such people would get you an interview with the President.

QUESTION: In your opinion who were the better press secretaries?

MR. SCHERER: Opinions differ. I can go through them briefly. Charlie Ross was the first one I knew. He was, of course, a contemporary and mentor of Truman in many ways because he was the correspondent for the *St. Louis Post Dispatch* when Truman came to Washington and he knew Truman as a Senator. He was very good and widely respected; he died in office. Then Truman had Roger Tubby, a younger man who was pretty good.

James Hagerty came along and always enjoyed Eisenhower's confidence and in many ways was a policymaker. He was in on things at the White House. He was particularly good during Eisenhower's heart attack, which I happened to cover in Denver. They told us everything, almost more than you wanted to know. They produced Dr. Paul Dudley White to tell about such things as bowel movements, and they did get enormous credibility. I think they told us pretty much the straight stuff.

Then came Pierre Salinger who in many ways was the court jester and liked to play the buffoon, but he had the confidence of Jack Kennedy, although he was never quite the imposing figure that James Hagerty was.

Then we had George Reedy who was a good man, and in retrospect turned out to be very wise about the presidency but who somehow wasn't a good press secretary largely because he'd been with Johnson too long. He was somewhat inhibited and probably afraid of him and was often beaten down. Johnson had a terrible way of doing that to people. Then Johnson had Moyers who was awfully good at the beginning because there was a father and son relationship with Johnson; that eventually went sour, and Moyers bailed out. Then Johnson brought in George Christian who was a

Southerner and a gentleman; I always thought he was quite good. He had a very difficult principal, but he never told you any lies that I can think of. He would say "I can't get into that," and back off.

Then you had the Nixon era which I didn't cover but which I watched very closely. Ron Zeigler was something of a salesman and later became almost totally distrusted and disliked by the press corps.

Then you had President Ford and he picked Jerry Terhorst, and old friend who went out on a matter of principle. He didn't approve of the Nixon pardon, but I've always wondered if that was the main reason. He only lasted a month. Then Ford picked an old friend and colleague of mine, Ron Nessen, who seemed to start out very well but later lost credibility with the press corps because he had a combative nature and apparently fenced with them too much. I don't really know what happened firsthand because I wasn't there, but that got to be a bad relationship.

And now you have Jody Powell who started out very well. I guess the jury is still out on the recent Carter Middle East trip for meetings with Begin and Sadat. Powell angered a lot of people by seeming to mislead them. He put a very pessimistic tone on things, and, of course, at the last minute it turned out well. I don't know whether Powell was doing this, as the Israelis say he was, to make the eventual triumph of Carter look all the better, or whether that's what he really thought. But a lot of people who covered it thought they were being handled rather badly.

Hagerty is generally looked upon in retrospect as being, I would have to say, probably the best all-around press secretary. He wasn't a terribly articulate man but he was very good at going off the record and good on background and was a thorough professional. He came up through Thomas Dewey's campaigns and served Eisenhower very, very well.

QUESTION: I have a question on the relationship between the presidential press secretary and all the other spokespersons in the government. Hodding Carter has recently become somewhat of a celebrity. In the old days, you would have only one person speaking for the President. But now the spokesman is identified as Hodding Carter instead of an anonymous spokesman. What's the relationship among the several press people? What's their relationship to the White House press office?

MR. SCHERER: In Hagerty's day, he pretty well dominated all the departmental press spokesmen. They would come in and confer with him once a week and would talk about their problems. If there was good news to be announced, he would put it out at the White House, and if it wasn't so good he would see that it came out from the Departments. That's been done with varying degrees of success ever since. I don't know how press staff are coordinated today. In the Kennedy days, they would all meet the night before a news conference. You knew there was going to be a news conference because you would see all these people coming in. They would sit down around Salinger and would tell him the questions that had been asked at their various news conferences—whether at State, Defense, or wherever—during the week. They would put all these questions down in a list along with suggested answers. Then an hour or so before Kennedy was to appear, Salinger and others would sit down with the President and review the questions and answers and he would soak them up. I think there is still a great deal of preparation; they get a black notebook together for every presidential news conference. How much Carter leans on this I don't know, but that could certainly be determined.

QUESTION: Hagerty had the reputation of having the most centralized news flow from the Executive Branch of any of the press secretaries. And that made him a much more authoritative person to deal with.

MR. SCHERER: And he had a president who didn't particularly care and was glad to deputize his press secretary to handle reports. Eisenhower as a general had always been used to speaking through a press spokesman.

QUESTION: Could you generalize about that and say that a strong president doesn't want a spokesman in the press room whereas a weak president does?

MR. SCHERER: I don't know.

QUESTION: Maybe you don't think Eisenhower was weak.

MR. SCHERER: Well, I read a piece in the *Washington Post* the other day by somebody who said that there was a consensus about every president except Eisenhower. And this was in answer to a professor who wrote a rather critical piece about Eisenhower as a "do nothing president." He was saying that Roosevelt was seen as a great war leader and Truman's hallmark was decision making and not mulling over things. He left a blank on Eisenhower and said that Kennedy was skillful and graceful and then Nixon came along. But he said that the jury was still out on Eisenhower. I suppose maybe that's true of Eisenhower, not only as a press conference performer, but as a president.

NARRATOR: Fred Greenstein, the Henry Luce Professor at Princeton, is coming here to re-examine the Eisenhower presidency.

MR. SCHERER: I don't think anybody's ever done it.

QUESTION: It's been sort of a neglected modern presidency. Nothing in depth has been done and Greenstein is trying to fill that gap and is discovering some rather interesting things. He's done a lot of work at the Eisenhower library. A lot more of the material is now open than had been open in the past. He's also found that Eisenhower kept a private diary. He gained access to it through Ann Whitman and found it is very revealing in what it tells you about his feelings about people and his methods. It's been discovered that there was much more method to his conduct, including press conferences, than he's generally been given credit for having.

MR. SCHERER: He liked institutions, he liked the National Security Council, which had regular meetings. He liked the Cabinet. And all these things went into decline under Kennedy.

QUESTION: He apparently was a person who had a very set and clearly defined style of leadership, and in the shadow of the Roosevelts and scholars who preferred the activist flare, he comes out rather poorly as somebody who didn't know very much about politics. That's being re-examined.

MR. SCHERER: Well, my own hunch is that Eisenhower, as the revisionists look at him, is going to come out better.

QUESTION: They are already doing it and Truman is being downgraded.

MR. SCHERER: The whole Truman presidency is a phenomenon.

QUESTION: It's a personality matter I think, don't you?

MR. SCHERER: He had a peppery quality that people seem to admire in retrospect. It's of course heightened by people like James Whitmore who goes on the stage and you see an hour of Truman. Truman as a person is collapsed into an hour. Truman really wasn't like that and the best authority I know on that is Robert Donovan who has written a fine biography. He's probably the greatest living authority on Truman with the definitive book. He has found a lot of new stuff in his interviews from people that nobody had ever interviewed before, ex-Secret Service men and others that you'd think wouldn't know anything. He really has pulled together a lot of new information. The real Harry Truman isn't the Truman in the Merle Miller book who was a senile Truman, who was bored sitting around while they were doing a television show and was giving off these rather peppery opinions. Those are things said by a man in his senility and didn't really represent him. A lot of people have formed their ideas about Truman from the Merle Miller book which is not a fair picture.

QUESTION: He remembered things that never happened. A phenomenal memory.

MR. SCHERER: Many things, such as his relations with McCarthy, a lot of things like that.

QUESTION: Is there any way through a study of press conferences that one can place presidents in their historical context and period; for example, Eisenhower healing the country after McCarthyism? Or Roosevelt saving the capitalist system despite his so-called radical ideas, preserving capitalism despite the opposition of the business community, or at least some parts of it. Or Gerry Ford after Nixon? Can you do that kind of thing?

MR. SCHERER: I think you could but it would take a very skilled person. The press conferences must be a reflection of the man unless he's hiding himself behind his words as Johnson sometimes did. It must be there, but . . .

QUESTION: There is President Johnson in some of those informal and impromptu conferences he held in the rose garden as he walked with reporters and then to some extent bared his soul. They were rather appealing.

MR. SCHERER: I used to spend hours with Johnson when he talked at great length, but afterward, it seemed to me that while the conversation was interesting at the time, it appeared inconsequential in retrospect. He somehow held himself back. He would tell you things about people he didn't like, particularly reporters, but it was the stuff you didn't print anyway. He distrusted anybody that was close to Kennedy, the eastern people, because Johnson never got over his sense of inferiority with Ivy League intellectuals. And that's why he liked to have so many around him because he thought it gave him cachet, people like Walt Rostow.

QUESTION: One of the things that appears to have crept into and is now an accepted part of reporting about the President are the ratings by the press, articles and comments on his performance, his standing and his popularity. This was not a part of press reporting back in the Roosevelt years, maybe because there was nothing to write and interpret. The facts were so obvious. But the whole question of how the President is doing, how he's managing his job, where does that come from?

MR. SCHERER: A lot of that stems from the polls where everybody has his own poll. The *Times* has one, the Associated Press has one, and CBS has one. I think that can be overdone. It used to appear on page one. I notice now it's generally in the back of the papers, because even newspapers sense that they're overdoing it, although polls about Carter seem to be reported about every other week judging and evaluating his performance.

QUESTION: Also the assessment of his relations with Congress, how he handles issues, and what his work habits are. Where do these insights come from? Who's feeding out the data to the press on which these articles are based?

MR. SCHERER: Well, if you cover the Hill, you talk to people up there who talk off the record and who see a lot of any president, people like Tip O'Neil and Senator Robert Byrd, and maybe Howard Baker and John Rhoades on the other side. More often than not they come from people who are critical.

QUESTION: That's apparent. And one wonders why that is? Why does the press want to find primarily negative evidence about a president nowadays?

QUESTION: To supplement the question, I've been told that at a meeting of the Ford Foundation Trustees recently, the main subject discussed was "the ritual destruction" of the President. Their thesis was that the adversary relationship that has grown up between the press and the President means that sooner or later, whoever the President is, he will go under. Eric Sevareid said in his annual New Year's broadcast that he thought we were entering a period of one-term presidents. One reason was that we faced problems that no president could solve, and another reason was that with leaks, disclosures and adversary relations, no president could survive.

MR. SCHERER: I think you said it very well. I think that is something we should all be concerned about, this adversary relationship which came out of Vietnam and Watergate, and it's going to take a long time before we get that out of our system, out of our national psyche. One wonders whether we ever will. But I think it is very true.

QUESTION: Is part of it due to the development of investigative reporting?

MR. SCHERER: It is. All the younger reporters want to investigate, and you can't investigate everything because it just isn't there. The old-timers decry this, possibly because they didn't do it, but, largely on moral grounds, they're afraid of it. If everybody is out investigating, you're automatically going to tear everything down.

QUESTION: Also, there is just so much available in the way of information due to the various new laws. The young torpedoes who are products of the Watergate period go for the jugular vein; and this is pretty obvious, not just at the presidential level, but down to the small town.

MR. SCHERER: It pervades everything, it is a new thing in journalism.

QUESTION: Isn't it the main source of scandal material. It doesn't matter who the figure is, does it?

QUESTION: Well it's not just scandal; it's picking up as the major sources of information people who have knives, sharpened knives, out for public officials in this large Washington establishment.

MR. SCHERER: For decades people like Drew Pearson did it. Now the celebrity status that Woodward and Bernstein have attained accounts for a lot of it. What do we do about it? People who run journalism schools are very concerned about it and about the all-pervasive tendency of younger people to cross over immediately into advocacy. And that isn't just peculiar to the television world; people throughout the media want to make an early and instant reputation.

QUESTION: I've often wondered if Woodward and Bernstein had been two sixty-eight year old men, would they have had the same effect on the young people?

MR. SCHERER: There aren't many graybeards on the networks. Television being the somewhat cosmetic media it is, they mostly run to the younger people. Sevareid was retired at the height of his power because of the mandatory rule that applies to everybody but Bill Paley at CBS. At sixty-five David Brinkley is still around but there really aren't that many old-timers on TV. CBS has more than others.

QUESTION: Walter Cronkite?

MR. SCHERER: Cronkite has always been very careful and I don't think many people know what Walter thinks. They love and trust him and he's their uncle. He's been every place and still has the highest rating, but I don't think people associate him with particular opinions. They just think about him as a very nice man that they trust. He's that kind of guy. I don't think he has pretensions to any particular intellectualism. He's a guy who reports what happens.

QUESTION: Do you regard it as the kind of trust that we all had for Edward R. Murrow during the war?

MR. SCHERER: Yes, but it's different. I think you associate Murrow with terribly exciting times when something was happening across the Atlantic that we all felt strongly about but couldn't see. He stood out on the burning roofs and had an enormous integrity, not that Walter doesn't, but with Walter it's a different kind of trust.

QUESTION: Murrow had a deep, authoritative and mature voice, even when he was young. And people did not see him.

QUESTION: You'd think we'd need every ounce of wisdom on the problems to which no one has any clear-cut solutions, and yet the way we are going, we act as though we didn't need it in our public commentary.

MR. SCHERER: In radio, you had Raymond Swing, Elmer Davis, and other marvelous people. Television isn't given to that. People have an impatience with it. You do longer commentaries once a year; Sevareid will sit down with Cronkite for the year-end show. Murrow used to gather all the NBC and CBS correspondents at the end of the year and talk for an hour about everything that was happening in Europe and around the world. Now, those things are passé, but they were wonderful. Why have we given those up? Because they don't get a rating? Or because the young people don't perform as well?

QUESTION: Getting back to the press conference. In the handling of the foreign press in the press conference situation, how do they relate? Do they wait for the domestic press corps to sort things out for them? What part do they play in presidential press conferences?

MR. SCHERER: Well in the old days it seems they used to participate and ask questions—everyone joined in—the old-timers, the foreign reporters, and the writers. Now they don't seem to. There seems to be an unwritten rule that they don't intervene and, as I say, it's so competitive that only the people in the front seem to get recognized. You seldom get anybody who is not a regular. Occasionally Carter will pick somebody out of the back of the room.

QUESTION: Are the seats assigned?

MR. SCHERER: The seats are apparently assigned now.

QUESTION: On what basis?

MR. SCHERER: The regulars sit in front and the others sit in the back.

QUESTION: How do you get to be a regular?

MR. SCHERER: You get to be a regular by going there every day.

QUESTION: When you trace the demise of the role of participation by the foreign press how far back do you go?

MR. SCHERER: I would guess it was somewhere between Eisenhower and Kennedy. Just as there aren't as many American foreign correspondents spread around the world, there are not as many international correspondents in Washington as there used to be. There aren't the old-timers who were well-known. A few are still around but the others are gone or they pursue a quieter role. I think a lot of them turned their back on the press conference as such as a useful institution. They can watch it on television but they don't feel constrained to go there and sit up front.

QUESTION: Did Lippmann ever go?

MR. SCHERER: Lippmann used to show up occasionally and sit in the back of the room.

QUESTION: All this has come about apparently as the press conference becomes much more a forum for the President. As the press conference has become a public relations forum for the President, its true news value has probably declined, hasn't it?

MR. SCHERER: I think that's so. I think that's probably where you come out.

QUESTION: What about the hostility that would well up in the Nixon press conferences, say, with Clark Molenhoff sitting to Nixon's right, all six foot twelve of him jumping up and never being called on?

MR. SCHERER: I think what's happened is that the news conference has become a public event for the public to watch. In Roosevelt's day it was a kind of club. You went there and fenced with Roosevelt and only the privileged few could go. You didn't want to miss it because you gained great insight. The only time the public saw the President was on newsreels, and they were largely staged. Then the news conferences became more of an institution and more public; their intrinsic value to a thoughtful reporter has probably declined.

QUESTION: Are you suggesting, then, that perhaps they would be more effective if they were controlled in a smaller group.

MR. SCHERER: I think the President should vary them. He should have some in which he's not so conscious of cameras going out to the whole world, where he could speak out loud more. Toward the end of the Eisenhower days there were several occasions in which Hagerty would tinker around with the machinery and Eisenhower would give a dinner and we'd all be there. I remember one of them in which he touted Robert Anderson to us as a man we ought to think about as his successor. Anderson has faded since as a public figure, but he was the only outsider at the dinner. It didn't occur to us until afterwards that that's what this vehicle was. Ike had great reverence for Anderson who was Secretary of Treasury at the time. He had various names that he floated from time to time. They weren't always very eminent people, but he brought them forward, because he was never fully comfortable with Nixon. In 1956, he advised Nixon to seek some other post and get some experience. I've often wondered if that was Eisenhower's way of getting him out of the way. It didn't work and Nixon inherited the mantle.

QUESTION: We've talked about the disadvantages of press conferences and indirectly we've talked about reforms and improvements. If one had to tick off three or four viable, realistic, practical reforms, what would you suggest?

MR. SCHERER: Part of the reason for the present format is that the President is trapped by technology. Because of television, he almost has to perform for the people. If not, there's a great hue and cry that he's not reaching the public. But he could have a news conference in which three or four old-timers were delegated to ask the questions, were allowed to ask two or three questions in succession and follow up.

QUESTION: Giscard d'Estaing in France does this. I've see several press conferences in Europe.

MR. SCHERER: There would be a terrible hue and cry from the rest of the press who were left out unless they voluntarily agreed to this. He could have some news conferences in which he sat in his Oval Office and reporters filed in; this is what Johnson tried in the old Truman way. He would philosophize and the releases and reports would be in the third person. The reporters would indicate broadly what the President said, not precisely what he said. Carter has done a lot of news conferences with regional groups. Some were carried on public television and have been pretty good. However, they haven't been terribly newsworthy, largely because the regional news conferences seem to dwell on regional issues, which are not of national interest.

QUESTION: What about a conference devoted only to a single subject?

SCHERER: That's a good idea but I doubt if you could carry it off unless you could devote a news conference to the pluses and minuses of nuclear power or some other urgent subject. Or you could devote one exclusively to foreign policy. But any time you try to structure things, reporters grow suspicious and worried. You'd have to get them somehow to go along with it. Or have them propose it.

QUESTION: One thing that has always intrigued me is the care and feeding of the press and providing all the amenities.

MR. SCHERER: Yes, they charter the plane for you, they rent the hotel rooms, etc.

QUESTION: All of that and I have wondered, in the case of the presidency, would it not be more effective to have the kind of thing that Roosevelt and others did in a more intimate situation? What if part of the press does raise sand? Are they going to ignore the story? How important is it, really, to cater to such a great extent to the press corps?

MR. SCHERER: It's done by custom and they expect it.

QUESTION: You would make a lot of enemies if you ignored them.

MR. SCHERER: Nixon tried to do that. He said you've got to charter your own plane and that sort of thing and it didn't work. It made relations worse. The care and feeding of the press is just something that's built in. When Jimmy Carter suddenly goes to Cairo, there's no way for the press corps to go unless the White House makes the arrangements, largely because the Secret Service has a hand in things and its very cumbersome. Some of them get over there and they find they're three or four to a room, but they have to go along with it. I must say, if you are a reporter and all you have to do is put your name on a list and report to the airplane it makes it very easy for you.

QUESTION: When did presidents begin to court women in the press?

MR. SCHERER: That's a good question. Some like Sarah McClennan have always been around. She was around in Eisenhower's day. And she always asked some oddball question and he used to like to recognize her just to see what she had on her mind that day. She worked for a number of papers, and every time she got up she'd cite another accreditation. In many ways she was everybody's maiden aunt and you knew she was going to raise cane. She was lovable in a way, although she was a little bit of a gadfly. Doris Fleeson was another pioneer woman reporter.

QUESTION: And now we have the pretty blonds.

MR. SCHERER: That's because of television and some of them are quite able. They have an easier time being hired. I guess there are simply more women reporters than before; it's just part of the business. I don't know if media executives set out to court them. It's just that they have become so prominent that they're now present in the nature of things.

NARRATOR: Well we mustn't hold any of you, most of all Mr. Scherer, too long. We're grateful. I do hope we can follow up. You've give us a lot to think about now and for the future and we thank you.

The President and the Press
JODY POWELL

EDITOR'S NOTE: The discussion with Jody Powell on the president and the press proceeded on the basis of questions and answers with members of the National Commission on Presidential Press Conferences.

QUESTION: Have you thought of releasing the transcripts of the daily press conference? I think it's a scandal, the badgering, etc. The press believes in everything being public, why not let that be public?

MR. POWELL: I don't think there will be any quarrel from the reporters if I did that. The reason I didn't do it was because I felt that those briefings were, in a way, too important, anyway, and I didn't want relatively informal sort of things primarily being circulated all over the government and becoming some sort of daily bible that people were analyzing and interpreting and trying to decide what they ought to be doing inside the government when in a lot of cases it was just the best feel you could give folks at the time for what the president was dealing with and where he's heading. That would raise the language and the words to a level of importance that they ought not to enjoy. I also agree that it would help the tone of the briefing period. I thought about inviting a group of boy scouts who would come in and sit along the wall.

QUESTION: Well, it is true that reporters behave with more decorum at, say, Hodding Carter's conferences than they did at your background briefings.

MR. POWELL: That is true, I think. Then again, you have a little bit of that in both places.

The physical set up is different. The crazies that go to the State Department briefings are about as crazy there as those at the White House briefings.

COMMENT: They're the same people, the same crazies. But, I must say that there is a little more decorum. Nothing approaches the yelling and shouting that takes place in the televised presidential conference, neither in Jody's sessions or the State Department sessions.

COMMENT: That's television.

COMMENT: Among other things, yeah.

COMMENT: In recommendations for random drawing of those who have indicated in advance that they have a question there's one alternative we proposed. The president has the right to announce that he will not recognize anyone who shouts; you have to hold up your hand if you want to be recognized. The alternative would be to put your name in a hat if you had a question and then you draw from a hat. But the danger there would be, by accident, to draw a bunch of crazies.

MR. POWELL: The odds are that if you let everybody who's eligible to come to those things and submit questions, you would have more people who don't come to the White House regularly and don't really follow what's going on, who are likely to have either silly questions or very narrowly defined, special interest type questions and that you're going to have more of those people in your pot that you have now.

The question is, have you improved the quality of information that the public gets? Presumably that is what you try to do with live, televised press conferences. You are attempting to inform the public directly of what the president is thinking, let them see and hear him. You are using a question and answer format as a medium to do that.

People may have problems with that definition, but that happens to be mine. I think you have a problem too, that what we found when we were doing these things twice a month—and I don't know if once a month helps—it was not in our interest. It may or may not have been in the interest of people who were looking in. I assumed that it was, but it was not primarily, at least in my judgment, in the interest of those who are asking the questions. Their interest was more to refine knowledge that they already had which the general public does not have and to take this or that particular aspect of it a step or two further. Frankly, our conclusion was that the things were irrelevant to what we were trying to do there and the indication was certainly that those who were watching or used to watch them were finding it to be largely irrelevant too because the interest was going down considerably.

I frankly think the town hall meetings probably would have been more informative to the public had they been televised live than the press conferences were because people are going to ask what they're interested in. You certainly get no more narrowly defined, parochial sort of questions at a town hall meeting than you get at a press conference. Occasionally, more but not a great many more.

QUESTION: If you were to advise Mr. Reagan on how to handle the televised press conference, what would you tell him?

MR. POWELL: I don't know. I would certainly advise him not to lock himself into having a couple a month as we did. I would advise him, maybe, not to lock himself into having any given number, to hold that decision to himself and hold them when he felt like it was appropriate. If it turned out to be twice a month or once every three months, then to try to deal with the pressure which is going to arise and which should arise for access and contact within the press through some other device: small groups or smaller groups or something like what you're talking about here. Live, televised press conferences I think in retrospect, are something that ought to be used sparingly and when there is a good damn reason to use them.

QUESTION: You mean on the part of the president?

MR. POWELL: Yes; which doesn't necessarily mean every interest that the president has is, surprising enough, contrary to national interest.

QUESTION: But it's his decision?

MR. POWELL: Yes, rather than saying I'm going to have one every month or I'm going to have one every couple months or couple weeks or so.

QUESTION: But how would he manage it? Or would he? Or would you just go ahead with the same . . .

MR. POWELL: If I could come up with a way to make them work better I would certainly suggest it. I can't . . .

COMMENT: It's the shouting aspect that we're . . .

MR. POWELL: That bothers me less maybe than it does you.

COMMENT: It bothers the viewers a great deal.

MR. POWELL: You can try.

QUESTION: Can I go back to the weekly informal conference? Roosevelt did this twice a week and it was pretty good. You could ask as many questions as you wanted. It was on background. If you wanted a quote you had to ask for it from the press secretary, and it seemed to me to be a pretty good way of doing it. Many times the press conference would take place and he would say, "I don't have anything to say," and the press would ask two questions and it would be over in five minutes. It was just print journalists then, but I always thought they got a lot more out of it. Would you buy that? I don't mean excluding television; there's no way to do it.

QUESTION: You're talking about keeping the television crew out?

COMMENT: Yes, the reporter could come in and then he could walk out and say: this is what the president said.

MR. POWELL: I think something like that is probably a good idea. Something like that makes a lot of sense. If I were Governor Reagan or any other president I would not commit myself to doing anything once a week or once a month or on any other schedule during my whole administration. It's perfectly fine to urge that sort of thing on the president. However, I would not recommend it.

COMMENT: Both Truman and Eisenhower, we thought, benefited in credibility by not holding news conferences only when it suited their particular propaganda purpose. But, unless there were good and overriding reasons, they held them on a weekly basis. Where this group is somewhat divided—I think—is on bringing the TV camera, as opposed to the television reporter, into the room. Television has so vastly changed what the conference used to be that it does have to be thought of in a different context.

MR. POWELL: It's a cop-out to lay all the problem on television. The real problem is that the relationship between the two institutions, press and the White House, has changed significantly since the 1950s. It will never be the same again. Maybe it ought never be the same as it was even in the early 1960s. Television is neither good nor bad but it's here.

QUESTION: What's the change?

COMMENT: The adversary relation.

MR. POWELL: Yes . . .

QUESTION: But wait; I went to every one of Eisenhower's press conferences and although it was done with perhaps more geniality, there was a definite adversary relationship. He was given very sharp questions.

MR. POWELL: Can you go back—you were there and I wasn't—and look at the way—forget the format—the president is handled or treated or covered in columns, stories and so forth? I don't believe you can even come close to claiming that the coverage was the same for the president I worked for as opposed to Ford or Nixon or Johnson and, I suspect, as opposed to Reagan when he gets in there. I think it ended basically with Vietnam and Watergate, and John Kennedy was the last president that got the sort of treatment which read: we're all part of the same deal here; gee whiz, Mr. President, we'll have a few talks with you tonight and work this thing out. You know, that sort of coverage. It "ain't never going to happen again," I don't believe. It may come around somewhat.

I'm a great believer in the public's right to know and the president's obligation in keeping them informed. But I think the problem right now is how all that fits into the much larger question which is the ability to govern. And the ability to govern, I think cannot be taken for granted. I think, obviously, public communications between the president and the people is a tremendously important part of that. So when I say I wouldn't commit myself to a thing if I had to do it over again, that's what I'm concerned about. There may be some way to design a system that takes into account that new and different relationship which would not be the same a year from now as it was last year; but clearly it is different.

COMMENT: In the days when I first started covering presidents, which was Eisenhower, there was a certain aura about the president and the presidency. I was in awe of the President of the United States, I don't feel that way anymore at all. And I think that what Jody is saying is absolutely correct. The whole atmosphere has changed. Now there are good aspects to this and bad aspects to it but it is a fact that no longer do the White House correspondents who cover a President of the United States think that he is some God-given figure that we should look up to. I can remember early on reporters who covered the White House saying, "We respect the office and we have to stand when he comes into the room and we have to treat him with respect." There are a lot of reporters who don't now.

COMMENT: I suggest that you reincorporate that . . .

COMMENT: I don't think that's possible. I think that what Jody says about the Vietnam War and the Watergate period which lead us to distrust a president is going to be a pervasive attitude for a long time to come.

COMMENT: I thought the whole purpose was to examine the decline of the presidential news conference as an institution and try to find some ways to encourage both the president and press to restore it to some of its former meaning.

COMMENT: With the questions I hear on a television press conference, not just a few but many of them, there ought to be a fellow going around after the question tapping, "All right, out!"

COMMENT: How are you going to do that in a free society? Are you going to arrest them?

COMMENT: I would throw two or three out and the rest would get the idea.

MR. POWELL: If you can create that position I would be glad to apply for it. I'm bigger than most of them.

COMMENT: We can't even get rid of the certifiable nuts.

QUESTION: I want to ask Mr. Powell one question. You started in 1977, and with what you now know, what kinds of rules, even if you didn't promulgate them, would you put into effect?

MR. POWELL: Pretty much the same thing I said before about what I would say to Governor Reagan. I would not commit us to two a month. I would do them when I felt they were—the president felt they were—needed, mainly when there was something important to be said; or when an accumulation of things added up to some undefined critical mass of things that are worth doing. I would not just stand up there and see if you can find something that makes news. I would try to handle the access of the president in informal, not available for broadcast, smaller groups. I don't know how I would do that. That's the guts of the problem. I would certainly take a harder run at it and spend time thinking about it and come back again if this didn't work or that didn't work with something else.

We did try a little bit of that, but we had all sorts of problems on ground rules. Lots of TV people didn't like it, but the big problems we ran into were the print people. They did or didn't like this ground rule, they would or wouldn't participate. At one point the *New York Times* informed me that they would not participate in a "not for attribution" session with other reporters but they would be glad to participate if the session was exclusive which I found to be one of the more hypocritical postures.

QUESTION: To repeat something we've already argued about this morning, would you give wire services first crack at the live conferences?

MR. POWELL: You might as well. It doesn't make much difference to me.

COMMENT: If you don't, you might start off the first question with a crazy.

MR. POWELL: Yes, I don't see that there's any problem in continuing to do it.

COMMENT: It gives it a certain decorum.

COMMENT: The first two questions, theoretically, are going to be sensible.

MR. POWELL: I started off by staying away from advising the president on whom to call on and whom not to call on but I dropped that.

QUESTION: Doesn't that confuse him—trying to find out who to recognize?

MR. POWELL: Well, I suppose all I ever did was say, "You might want to stay away from these three or four."

QUESTION: But how does he know where they are; and in the shouting matches, what catches your attention?

MR. POWELL: Well, part of the problem is sometimes you'll call on somebody and if the other person who is of this type is generally in the line of fire and the person he calls on can be intimidated and give way, then you've got the floor . . .

QUESTION: These last two news conferences, the informal ones, is there notably less hostility? Would you say the communication flows perceptibly more freely?

MR. POWELL: Yes, but this is a very unusual situation. I don't think it says very much about the overall situation. I mean, the guy had just lost an election. What they're interested in is not so much hard political stuff. For the first time in almost four years his answers are not immediately subject to the interpretation, whether he chooses a, b, c, d or none of the above, that whatever the choice is he is motivated entirely by political considerations. That's the norm.

QUESTION: But if you had been re-elected, I take it you would have had more of those?

MR. POWELL: More of something like that.

QUESTION: You do find some virtue in that, then?

MR. POWELL: But I don't think you ought to commit yourself . . .

QUESTION: For four years we've had a standing request into you for an interview with the *London Observer*. We haven't had one. We finally got one with Reagan. What was your mentality about not doing carefully spotted interviews that would have some broader effect?

MR. POWELL: It's something I wish I had done more of. I think we paid much too little attention to the press overseas, in general.

QUESTION: Jody, it has been said that presidents like to keep the news conference the way it is, people shouting, because it makes them look like they're dealing with a pack of jackals. In other words it plays better with the public, the image of the beleagured president, a leader put upon. Is there any truth in that?

MR. POWELL: No, I don't think so. I don't know what you could do if you come up with something to get even a modicum of consensus amongst the people actually doing the jumping up and down and shouting. Everytime I've tried to go through this thing I reached some point where you say—not that you couldn't work it out but as I said earlier you're going to get one chance in seven— there are two thousand people with White House press credentials. There are probably twenty that are serious—more than that I suppose—serious reporters cover the White House every day. Now you get five hundred requests for questions or a hundred or one hundred and fifty, you're going to have one chance in seven of any given question being from one of the regulars. Is CBS going to get three chances because they have three White House correspondents and the *New York Times* get one or two and the *Post* gets a half because they have a White House correspondent that doesn't go over there? When you start to make these things mechanical you've got a problem too. If the primary concern is people jumping up and hollering, I suppose you could see if moral suasion could keep them from doing that.

QUESTION: Why can't the president say: this is the way we're going to do it; you put up your hand and . . .

COMMENT: The way the secretary of state does.

MR. POWELL: I think that's a different setup over there.

COMMENT: They sit down . . .

MR. POWELL: They're seated. You only have microphones for the regulars up there.

QUESTION: Do you think part of the hostility is that the press secretary, I guess starting with Zeigler, has taken on a much more expanded role? It seems to me that Salinger, Hagerty, were much less into policy than you have been. Something that has occurred to me is there is hostility among reporters because they think you are trying to be the president: who the hell elected you? And they can't get often enough to the president.

COMMENT: Well Hagerty was into the policy a great deal.

QUESTION: But don't you think that's expanded a lot? You don't think that's part of the current hostility?

MR. POWELL: I don't know. You might be better off asking somebody on the press side. But, it hadn't occurred to me as being a factor.

COMMENT: I think that would only be the case during a time such as the Watergate period when you went for two or three months without a chance to ask the president any questions. Then that hostility was partly due to the frustration you were feeling. You've got this guy up there who doesn't know anything and is stonewalling.

COMMENT: But the fact is that Dwight Eisenhower was almost as regular as clockwork. He was asked, particularly during that period when he was trying to play footsy with McCarthy, some very tough questions but they were asked with more civility than is asked now. And the question we are addressing is how do you put this relationship back on a fairly regular basis; with nothing absolute. The president has the right to cancel any time he wants to and that's still an adversarial relation—in the better sense of the word—but not an antagonistic, a bear-baiting contest.

MR. POWELL: I see the televised press conference as primarily an opportunity to provide information directly to the people, with a question and answer format being a device by which information is conveyed. I think I would agree that the televised press conference is not the best way to provide information to the press so they can analyze it and then convey it in in-depth analysis and understanding to the public. I don't think televised press conferences work well for that. I do think I would try to substitute something for that as a way to . . .

COMMENT: That's about where we are.

QUESTION: How much would you say that communication in the age of mass communication that electronics brought is the number one dilemma of the president?

MR. POWELL: From my perspective there is a dilemma, but I feel I can't speak for the president. But it seems to me that its not only what's happened in communications but what has happened elsewhere, they've all contributed: the difficulty of reaching consensus, the fragmentation of power in the country and on the Hill, the decline in the seniority system, the dying of the parties as a mechanism for conflict resolution on the way up, all of those things; increased responsibilities of the federal government, the change in the relative power between the executive and the legislative branches. All of those seem to me to have put more pressure on the communication aspect of it and made it a much more difficult problem.

QUESTION: If you had to do it over again, do you think the president would have fared better if there had been about five televised debates, including Anderson, but stretched over a five or six week period?

MR. POWELL: I don't know. It's hard to see how we could have fared worse! It's interesting, while Anderson did get seven percent, he probably would have gotten more than that.

COMMENT: I think the president could have worn them down with ongoing superior knowledge, but he couldn't do that in one.

MR. POWELL: We would have been better off with more than one.

QUESTION: Going back to the news conference and your campaign. In earlier years other presidents, as they got close to a campaign, they would hold press conferences like clockwork because it was a half hour of free television time. I would have thought during September and October you would have had one every week. Why didn't you?

MR. POWELL: I think you have a good example there of how things have changed. I don't think the networks would have covered them, do you?

COMMENT: No, that's right. We would have covered maybe the first one or two and then we would have said: wait a minute, we're being used.

COMMENT: This is ancient history but when Adlai Stevenson and Eisenhower were running they said they just weren't going to have them. Adlai had one that was sort of a disaster and Eisenhower had another one. They don't want to make mistakes during a campaign.

MR. POWELL: I don't think that is the usual history, is it? Ford only had one.

COMMENT: I was thinking back to Eisenhower when he came up in 1956 and of the time when Nixon was running . . .

COMMENT: But those weren't live, televised, either.

QUESTION: Did Nixon do it in 1972 (once a week conferences during the campaign)?

COMMENT: No, I don't think Nixon did.

COMMENT: Ford had one in the very last week which was a disaster for him.

QUESTION: But only a president can command a national audience, whether or not he's a candidate. The president can have them as often as he wants to and the networks don't have to cover them, but I would have thought you would have taken advantage of it?

COMMENT: It's very dangerous in a campaign when a president is tired, going at top speed.

COMMENT: That apparently is one of the considerations.

MR. POWELL: If the networks would have been willing to cover them, we probably would have had them, but I don't think they would. I may be wrong, but—if you had an event, fine.

COMMENT: But, we're saying you should have them when you're having an event or not. You should have them as a matter of regularity and frequency.

MR. POWELL: Except during a campaign.

QUESTION: Jody, on another issue, but related, do you favor getting, somehow, the White House Correspondents Association or some other institution to take over the accreditation problem? Is that what you referred to earlier?

MR. POWELL: That wasn't exactly what I was referring to but I think if you had some sort of congressional system—I don't know enough about what the thing on the Hill does; it seems to me it doesn't do very much now. But, if you had a peer group operation with some guts and some clout that would do that, I think it might work. It's clear that a White House press office can't do it. We're nothing but a paper shuffling operation. We just about have to accommodate anybody. Now, whether you can do that and exercise any real discretion without being subject to the same sort of legal problems that we have, I don't know.

QUESTION: How about a psychological test?

COMMENT: The crazies are a real problem. For one thing they forced you into holding a lot of your briefings on an informal, ad hoc basis which worked for us regulars. But instead of having them every day at 11:30 when you knew the crazies of this world were going to be there you started holding them in your office on short notice. Wasn't that primarily because of the crazies? And I don't see anyway of eliminating those people. They are a large part of those people standing up and shouting.

QUESTION: Other people in the press corps—peer pressure?

COMMENT: They love it. They love it if you go after them. Then their stories are about how reporter so and so attacked me today and . . .

MR. POWELL: That's exactly right. I don't hold it against the White House regulars that they're not able somehow to control it . . .

COMMENT: There's nothing in the Constitution about: "you put your hand up and keep your mouth shut."

COMMENT: It's harder to see them if they're sitting down. Maybe you could tell the crazies to wear a distinctive sweater or something.

COMMENT: Well, one of the crazies held up a sign with "Mr. President" printed in it on a live press conference.

COMMENT: If the American people could listen in on this and discover that there is no way to apply the rule of reason in the office of the President of the United States in relating to the press, they would be overwhelmed.

COMMENT: It isn't that there's no way; it's that it's difficult. And it really comes down to whether the president and his press secretary are going to enforce some kind of control. I mean you almost have to become a policeman.

QUESTION: Well what about your White House Press Corps Association?

COMMENT: I have no power. Constitutionally there is no way to do it. You're the lawyer, you should be telling me that I can't do it. I can't say who should be accredited because the First Amendment says the government can make no laws of that kind and Jody can't even do it. The White House got taken to court on an issue like that and lost.

MR. POWELL: We lost the case on the guy that had been convicted of carrying a concealed weapon. I don't know what the exact decision was. It was something like: it hadn't happened recently and there's no reason to believe that even if he carried a concealed weapon he was going to shoot the president.

QUESTION: What do you think of the talk that's coming out of the Reagan camp of not having a luminary or a prominent figure, but having four subsidiary press secretaries who would cover various fields. Apparently that's one of the views.

MR. POWELL: I really don't know so I hesitate to comment on it. I'm sure at some point I'll sit down and chat with those folks and whatever I've gotten that they might be interested in . . .

QUESTION: If you get a briefer who is not in on the policy he can't do a very good job, it seems to me.

MR. POWELL: It cuts both ways. But they've got a right to sort of work things out for themselves and listen to people privately if they want to and give what consideration they want to to these ideas. I really don't know what they have in mind.

COMMENT: Well, we don't either.

COMMENT: Johnson once said he was going to have three or four press secretaries. He said he was going to alternate.

QUESTION: "Experts in subjects," is what they're suggesting?

MR. POWELL: Yes, I don't think it's necessarily a bad idea to try to set up an operation like that. We did that to some extent, for example, at The National Security Council.

QUESTION: These fellows worked for you, didn't they?

MR. POWELL: Well, they work—traditionally—to try to serve two masters, both the advisor for national security and the press secretary. That was never a problem.

COMMENT: But it was more developed than it was even under Kissinger though. Your man served as kind of a personal press secretary for the special assistant for national security. That never happened, certainly under Bundy and Rostow, and I don't think it happened under Kissinger.

COMMENT: No. Kissinger had one.

MR. POWELL: That obviously is proof that whether you have a person with that role or not has nothing to do with whether the national security advisor does or does not adopt a high public profile.

QUESTION: Mr. Powell, the Miller Center got into this thing for a double reason. We thought the whole role of the relation of the president and the people and the role of the president as educator and communicator was important. The other thing which we haven't mentioned today but which kept coming into our earlier meetings with reporters and press secretaries was what Ford Foundation Trustees described some months ago as the ritual destruction of the president. The Trustees at a meeting went around the room and asked what everybody thought the single most urgent problem was. Everybody thought they'd say inflation or something like that, but seventy-five percent of them agreed that the ritual destruction of the president was the most vital issue leading to the one term president.

With the people we've met with before, they've described what they called the turning point. There came a point somewhere—for you it was supposed to be the Lance affair—where relations soured and where, even though you had good will in the beginning, nothing you could do on either side helped in the relationship with the president and the press. Is there any truth in this view in terms of your experience?

MR. POWELL: Well, that's sort of what I was trying to get at when I talked about the ability to govern. That's not all of the problem, probably, but that is certainly a part of it. And I'm not sure you're not chasing a red herring when you look for turning points. They do happen, but the question is whether they're going to happen anyway, whether that is a natural process which is triggered early or late by something. You can always find a reason for it, looking back on it, but whether it is . . .

QUESTION: But is it built in, in the relationship? Is it inevitable?

MR. POWELL: That's the question I would raise. Frankly, I doubt I'll ever be in a position to be objective about it. I might be more objective later on than I am now, but that does worry me. I'm torn between wanting Reagan to get the same sort of treatment we got and not wanting him to fail.

QUESTION: Do you think the fact that you were, from outset, considered an outsider in Washington had any effect on your relationship with the press?

MR. POWELL: More indirect, I think; it had an effect on the coverage. I don't think it had a major impact upon my relationship with people at the White House. I had a lot to learn and I maybe would not have had quite so much to learn if I had been around town.

I haven't really thought this through so this is a distorted answer, but there are so many sources of "information" in the town, and in our case so few of them had any loyalty to, or inclination to support, the goals of the president or the administration. Capitol Hill is just a . . .

COMMENT: A sieve.

MR. POWELL: It's not a sieve, it's a fire hydrant, you know, just gushing. The executive branch's adjectives are a little better in terms of their . . .

QUESTION: Loyalty?

MR. POWELL: Well, it's not so much loyalty or disorder. It's almost indifference. The one thing nobody wants to say is that they don't know. In fact it's just the opposite. They want to create relationships, they want to cultivate them for a variety of reasons, policy, ideology, careers, you name it. So there were maybe four or five of us at a time on a given issue that were competing with, literally, hundreds of people all over town who were spreading, in many cases, stuff that had little or no relationship to the president. You sort of felt good if you were able to catch up with a few of them and get them knocked down before they went on the air or before they got in print. Usually you weren't. That's something I suspect any president will have to deal with, to some extent.

If we had come to the White House with a network and also developed a mechanism to keep that network informed and operating and moving in support of the administration, which is easier said than done, that might be helpful. But it is a tremendous problem. There is very little currency for an individual in the agencies or on the Hill to be consistently helpful to the president. If you're trading with a reporter, a little bit of information that is in support of the president's foreign aid bill or windfall profits tax is a lot less valuable.

COMMENT: It isn't news.

MR. POWELL: Yes. It isn't worth two cents. If on the other hand, you've got a study that shows that the thing's screwed-up, or the figures are wrong and so-and-so's got a particular interest in the matter that might appear to be illegitimate, or that several members of Congress have decided they're not going to vote for it because they didn't like the engraving on their last invitation to the White House, now that's, by God, big news. And you can sell that.

QUESTION: Is there a definable problem granted they're here, but do you ever find a definable problem of the lobbyist using the press?

MR. POWELL: Oh, yes sir. And they're good at it too.

QUESTION: You could tell it when you saw it?

MR. POWELL: Yes.

QUESTION: Not always?

MR. POWELL: Not always because quite often you had people on the Hill, and in some cases people in the executive branch, who were carrying water for them. A lobbyist, I understand, if he is any good doesn't need to do that directly. He can always get somebody so that a reporter can attribute his actions to an administration source or a source on the Hill. Anybody worth a damn can get that; you don't have to do it yourself.

QUESTION: No cure for that either?

MR. POWELL: I think there are probably some things that could be done, but there's no guaranteed cure for it. If there's a little more coverage of that part of the process of it, it would help a lot. And if people who consistently spread false information live with the thought that they might end up getting exposed publicly every now and then, that would have a very salutary effect. If reporters felt no obligation to continue to protect the identity of a source. . . . I had one do it to me, frankly, even though in my case it was certainly a much more commendable thing I was trying to do! But if a few people got blown for—again, one of the things we had to deal with in this campaign was an organized operation on the Hill that was using highly classified information in a very vicious sort of way. And one of those guys did get blown; it ought to happen more often.

QUESTION: Did that stop the others?

MR. POWELL: I don't know. I suspect it made some people think, but it doesn't happen frequently enough that you . . .

QUESTION: Did you know that some of the Reagan people were using the Iran thing to leak false stories?

MR. POWELL: Oh, yeah.

COMMENT: I was appalled when one of the television networks went on the air with two stories by the Reagan people. The stories had been checked out and were found absolutely false.

QUESTION: Was one of them out of the UN?

COMMENT: No, it didn't come out of the UN. One of them was a retired military general who was circulating the stories. As to the other, I don't know the exact source.

COMMENT: With a serious thing like the hostage issue which everybody knew could swing the election one way or the other, the reporters, it seems to me, had the responsibility to check out the stuff, rather than go on the air with it.

MR. POWELL: I have never tried to get a reporter to print a story that I knew to be false, except once and that was on the hostage situation and the rescue plan. I did try to get people to write stories that indicated that that was the last thing on our minds.

COMMENT: And you should have!

MR. POWELL: I think so, but other people may think differently. Yet the business of people in this town feeling absolutely no compulsion to tell the truth is a serious problem. There is no real penalty for being a bald-faced liar ninety percent of the time; continuing to be a source of information is a problem particularly if you're trying to go into the thing halfway honestly. If you assume everyone in government is a liar, then you say, "Okay. What the hell, everybody lies so don't worry about it." But if you assume that, pretty soon that's what you're going to get from government. Because nobody that's honest can survive.

QUESTION: Well, what are the cures?

MR. POWELL: Other than the sort of thing I suggested, I don't know.

QUESTION: Blow their cover?

MR. POWELL: That's one. Failing that—which is another thing that will never happen—I dream of the day—which will never come—when CBS thinks it's legitimate to deal with the fact that such and such a reporter for NBC is whoring for a particular biased source on Capitol Hill or in the executive branch or the White House; you name it. He'll have on his particular story, broadcast to the public, a clear and consistent pattern of misleading and inaccurate information, all from the same source. The other network would say this is the relationship between that reporter and his source, it goes back this many years, and this is this source's relationship with these different people that have a particular point of view of the thing. That would put a stop to it, maybe.

COMMENT: The trouble is these fellows all belong to the same union.

MR. POWELL: Well, as I said, I don't expect it to happen. Maybe when the *Times* has got what it takes to do that to the *Post* or vice versa, or the *Star* and the *Post* or vice versa, that will be the year of jubilee! But, I'm not holding my breath on that.

QUESTION: Can we go back a little closer to our subject. How did Jimmy Carter look on televised news conferences? As a chore, as a kind of occasional responsibility, or did he have a certain relish to get into the cockpit so to speak?

MR. POWELL: He enjoyed them. In fact, we had to talk him out of them.

COMMENT: I always thought he was pretty good at them.

COMMENT: He handled them well.

MR. POWELL: I also thought he handled them well. But, they weren't doing anything.

QUESTION: I think they were. How do you mean they weren't doing anything?

MR. POWELL: They weren't informing people.

QUESTION: But the one where he had the hour press conference on Billy helped him, didn't it?

MR. POWELL: Yes, sir, but that's exactly what I'm talking about. That is the time for a televised press conference. That is one of *the* best illustrations. There are other times too. But by God, that's exactly what you want to do. It serves a purpose not only for the president but for the public and for the press. But you do it when you want to do it and when you're ready to do it.

What if you were committed during that period to having—I don't remember how long that thing lasted, long enough—and you were committed to one of these regularly scheduled press conferences sort of half-way through? What if the president had been in the position I was in of having to deal with the thing sort of mid-stride when he didn't know what you knew. What if the president stood up there and said, himself, on camera, "I never talked with the attorney general on this thing," which he believed honestly to be the truth at the time, and didn't find out it was not the case until several days later? What if he had done that? It wasn't much fun for me to say it. But it would have been even worse, particularly given today's atmosphere, if the president had said it.

QUESTION: Is there any way for a president to get away in a press conference with saying, "By golly, I want an answer to that as much as you do. Let me say why we haven't got it now and what we're going to do, and I promise the moment I get it I'll come back on another conference and let you question me about it?"

MR. POWELL: I don't think that's the problem. It's not the sort of off the wall question that the president just doesn't know about. It's the things that you think you know. That case was one that we thought we knew. We could have waited three more days—to take that for an example—until we had a chance to go through all the logs to make exactly sure that we knew all the facts.

You also had the other pressure—both pressures going to the credibility of the White House—which was to provide answers on a timely basis. You're trying to balance those two things just as the press does when they publish. How sure is sure? Do you go with it today or do you wait until tomorrow to check one more place? How many things do you do that with?

I don't think I'm being overly protective of the president, but if he's going to be dealing with the press, say on a weekly basis or something like that, he's got to have some protection against the inadvertant error of commission or omission. And that's very hard to design. Without something like that, given the attitudes today, I think you end up eroding the power of an institution, namely the presidency, which is in enough trouble as it is.

COMMENT: But the only way to do that is to keep television out.

MR. POWELL: It's not just television.

COMMENT: I think, frankly, that the people are looking for what they believe is an earnestness and honesty. They're not looking for the specifics. The reporters are looking for the nitpicks.

MR. POWELL: And I would submit that as a rule, with certain exceptions but as a good working premise, that's what people are looking for. Before any president's four years are up, the press is looking to see if they can't find a way to show that this guy's exactly the opposite. They do this not with malicious intent but to make sure, putting the best light on it, that if he is just the opposite they'll find it out.

QUESTION: But you're saying that the town meeting is a better way of reaching the people without the intervention of correspondents, press people, because there they see their president in action—a small town with pressing problems that are meaningful to them? Do you think that during the four years of the presidency, the president should make this meeting more effective and have more town meetings?

MR. POWELL: Let me clarify one thing. I said that I thought that the town meeting was more effective in communicating directly with the public in a question and answer format because the type of questions that were asked there are more likely to the sort of questions that people in general want answered.

COMMENT: But they're awfully general.

MR. POWELL: But that is exactly what people are interested in.

COMMENT: What we're talking about is informing the public.

MR. POWELL: That's right and I did not suggest—it was really more of an example—that I thought it ought to replace either televised press conferences with the press or other exchanges with the press. There is another function which is that the press has an obligation to gather information from the president and other sources and then explain things to people and help them understand. That's a very legitimate thing. But I don't see how you can have very many more town meetings than we did. The problem was that they were not covered—except for the first one. Perhaps because we had so many, they tended not to be covered. Because we were having press conferences, the town meetings tended not to be nationally televised, although you usually could get some sort of coverage either in the city or nationally—they weren't all small towns, by the way.

QUESTION: Are you saying that the president himself got more out of them than those meetings with the press?

MR. POWELL: Both. I'm saying that amongst the many things that make up communication between the president and the public, one is direct. And I think that those town meetings served that purpose better than some other things for that part of it; not that the president ought to do nothing but town meetings by any means.

DR. GALLUP: Could the format of the press conference be changed so that you could accomplish these two purposes that we're talking about? I think I would put it this way, that the press is obviously news oriented; the people are problem oriented. They want the president to talk about the problems that they feel are most important. And that's why at the town meetings, he gets the kind of question he gets. Now this thought occurs to me. It may not have any particular value, but supposing that the first two or three questions answered by the president were questions put to him in written form, maybe a day in advance, or two or three. The questions that would be answered would be the questions that related to the major problems of the country such as inflation, and so on, questions of this type. These are the questions I think that the people want to hear. They want to know what's being done on the inflation problem, what's being done on the crime problem, what's being done on the unemployment problem. These are the gut issues for the people and this is where they want enlightenment. Maybe the press conference could start with two or three questions of this type in which the president could take the time and really do an educational job. Then let the press come in and question, or do anything they wish with those answers and add others of course.

MR. POWELL: Sometimes you get your head handed to you when you say something that the press knows but the people don't. That's the difference. The press know—or the ones who care, know—very well what the president is trying to do about inflation for example. The public generally doesn't know, or they've sort of heard it one time. Either they've forgotten or they haven't thought of it for awhile. They don't know whether things have changed. I suspect that written questions submitted in advance have an aura to them that would cause you some problems if you ask these folks to do that.

COMMENT: I don't think that would go over.

QUESTION: One thing the president hasn't got enough of is time. I know we're talking lightly about one press conference a month, one each week. How much does this take out of his life to prepare?

MR. POWELL: We probably spent, in terms of the president's time, a total of three and a half hours, counting the thirty minutes of the press conference. We probably took less time than most presidents have taken.

COMMENT: Yes. I'm shocked.

MR. POWELL: It's not just the president's time. His time is the most valuable. It takes a fair amount of time to prepare the briefing books. I'm not sure that's not a good exercise for the government, to make them go through thinking about what the questions are and whether they've got answers for them. If I could have I would have abolished the press conference and made them keep doing the briefing books!

COMMENT: The president's time is the more important time.

MR. POWELL: It's the most important. But even that's a fair amount of time, if you figure what percentage that is of the number of hours that a president has, even with very long days. A couple of hours a week is a lot of time on one thing.

COMMENT: But communications is a big part of the president's job.

MR. POWELL: Yes it is. But, my belief is that was not the purpose.

QUESTION: Can I get off the subject again? Why has every presidential debater wanted to have the press there in the middle?

MR. POWELL: I guess a combination of reasons. In part, to assume the role of the heavy, which is, frankly, part of what the press is supposed to do, to ask those questions and followups and really drive the points home.

QUESTION: But if you did that it would make you look too mean?

MR. POWELL: That was certainly our experience.

QUESTION: We're about to make some recommendations. They are nothing startling. In fact, the more we looked at it the more we thought they should be simplified. We don't want to sound presumptuous, but do you think this is a useful exercise we're involved in?

MR. POWELL: Yes, I think it is.

QUESTION: If we had given them to you four years ago do you think it would have . . .

MR. POWELL: It would have been helpful.

COMMENT: Listening to you, some of these problems seem more intractable then we might have guessed.

COMMENT: The one about the crazies still seems to be the one we haven't faced yet, head-on.

DR. GALLUP: Is there another problem? Not only the crazies but the reporters, themselves, who keep asking the same question. As a viewer, you sit there and say, "My God, hasn't he been listening? Does the president have to answer that same question the third time, the fourth time?"

QUESTION: Would an IQ test be unconstitutional?

COMMENT: But the crazies are always visible in every medium, in every public arena.

MR. POWELL: I think they're a bigger problem at the White House press briefings than at the press conferences. The president can not call on them if he doesn't want to.

QUESTION: The crazies haven't really come out of Vietnam and Watergate. Haven't they really come out of the expansion of the definition of what is press, which has come out of court decisions?

MR. POWELL: I don't know where they come from. You all are probably better equipped to answer that question.

COMMENT: I don't think we're talking about crazies as much as we are about the point Jody made where out of the couple hundred or more that go in there, you've got maybe twenty-five who really follow the presidency and the issues. If you don't get their question you don't get good communication. And yet by this lottery system we're relegating them to about one out of eight shots.

COMMENT: It might make it worse.

MR. POWELL: If you're anybody in this town that's got a credential, you're going to make sure that you get a question in because, you may be in town seven years and never get a question at the presidential press conference. And here you got the same chance as a senior columnist or anybody else of getting a question to the president. I don't think you ought to have the same chance. I think the people that come down and sit through those awful briefings every day because they have to and grub around down there and try to get people on the phone and try to do at least a workmanlike job of covering the White House deserve a better shot at a question at a presidential press conference than somebody that never comes in that gate except for presidential press conferences. I would say most people, where a couple of hundred is all you can get in, probably a good half of those people are not people who make any semblance of an effort to cover the White House and the president on a day-to-day basis. It sort of surprises me how few people do that. It's a very small number.

COMMENT: The lottery system actually was tried and practiced—and I was one of those that advocated trying it—was in the Ford administration. We did it, and we did it when we were out of town, when the president would go out of town and hold press conferences. The first time he ever did it he held one in San Diego and we signed up before we left for San Diego. But, you eliminate a lot of this when you go out of town because those people who aren't really serious White House regulars don't make the trips. So you really have an advantage then.

QUESTION: Does the president consciously try to call on people he knows?

MR. POWELL: I think even subconsciously, he tends to turn to a familiar face.

COMMENT: But also a few in the back, to make it look democratic.

MR. POWELL: I don't know, I've never really told him about that.

COMMENT: He does.

MR. POWELL: Yes, he may, on occasion do that. And you get—I've had delegations from the black press who come in to complain that the president isn't calling on enough people representing the black media. I finally broke down, against my principles, and I said: okay, I'll suggest to him that he take that into consideration, and he did. I personally thought that was one of those things where your principles get in the way of your procedures—I felt that their concern was legitimate and that segment of society deserved, perhaps, a better chance. On the other hand, I thought it was not generally a good idea for the president to be trying to keep track of the percentage of questions as defined by how many women he calls on and that sort of thing.

COMMENT: But it worked all right.

MR. POWELL: Usually things work out all right the first step. It's where that path leads you that concerns me—not what was going to happen to me but what's going to happen to some president three terms down the road.

COMMENT: You ended your May 3rd speech by quoting Thoreau's precept—one to speak and another to hear—as a solution. There is a deep feeling in the country, I think, that for some reporters it isn't so much to ask a question or seek information but to create an image and to get an increase in salary. It's to become a public figure. Is there anything at all anyone could say that would communicate the idea that if reporters speak for the country and ask questions for the country, they don't thereby also have the credibility in themselves to warrant answering, by implication, the question? We've struggled for six months now, and always come back to the First Amendment and always come back to the limited power of the White House Correspondents Association. Is there anything one could say about greater responsibility on the part of the press itself?

MR. POWELL: I suppose there's a lot of things you could say about that! I don't know if I see that particular part of it as that much of a problem. Sure, there's some of that. Correspondents are human beings and they want to look good. But, I think it's asking too much of anybody that covers the White House regularly to do anything other than ask that sort of question that attempts to get at the still undefined nuance, moving the story ahead in this or that specific, and sometimes narrowly defined area. If you ask these people to try to ask the sort of town hall meeting questions, in essence, you're asking them to serve as sort of props in a presentation to the public because you're asking them to ask the president a question, an answer to which they already know.

They know what the president is—they should know; if they've forgotten they certainly would be the last person to want to admit it—trying to do about inflation, the budget, deregulation or cost containment. And it may be too much to ask them to say, "Mr. President, a lot of people in this country are concerned about inflation. Just what are you doing about this thing?" You don't ask people to do something they're not going to do anyway.

Report of the Commission
On Presidential Press Conferences

EDITOR'S NOTE: The history of the Miller Center project on the Presidential Press Conference had its origins in discussions in the autumn of 1979 between Mr. Lloyd N. Morrisett, president of the John and Mary R. Markle Foundation, and Professor Kenneth W. Thompson, director of the Miller Center. The Foundation and the Center share a common interest in communication among the president, the press and the public, and in the improvement of public understanding. The Center had launched its review of the subject in a Forum conducted by Mr. Ray Scherer, Vice President of RCA and formerly White House correspondent of the National Broadcasting Corporation, which was subsequently published in *The Virginia Papers on the Presidency*. Officers of the Markle Foundation expressed interest in the Forum and generously provided funding for a further investigation of the topic.

The staff of the Center first organized interviews and round-tables with a broad cross-section of White House correspondents and press secretaries organized into two groups. In stage one of the project, the staff interviewed participants in press conferences conducted by Presidents Franklin D. Roosevelt, Harry S. Truman and Dwight D. Eisenhower, with more limited attention to those of Herbert Hoover and Calvin Coolidge, drawing on the first-hand knowledge of living correspondents. In stage two, the staff turned its attention to the live televised press conferences of Presidents John F. Kennedy, Lyndon B. Johnson, Richard M. Nixon, Gerald R. Ford and Jimmy Carter. The review called attention to the growth of the White House press corps, greater specialization by reporters (including full-time coverage of the White House) and the impact of television on the press conference.

In the next phase of the project, a National Commission, cochaired by Mr. Scherer and Governor Linwood Holton, was created to examine and study the information collected in the first stages of the project and to make recommendations on the future of the presidential press conference. The cochairmen selected members of the Commission, who proceeded to consider whether the presidential press conference, having undergone important changes, continued to serve useful purposes, and sought to define these purposes. The Commission set out to prepare a report based on the preceding discussions, setting forth the origins, evolution and present functioning of the press conference. It undertook to weigh changes and modifications which might lead to improvements, as well as alternatives to the present format. The Miller Center looks forward to other activities based on the project, including publication of a separate monograph by a Miller Center scholar, followup discussions and colloquia, and the maintenance of archival materials on presidential press conferences. Other projects relating to the president and the press are contemplated.

INTRODUCTION

This report deals with the problems and suggested reforms of the presidential press conference. (In this report, the Commission is employing the term "press" to include all forms of mass communication, broadcasting as well as print.) While we are not calling for sweeping changes, we have felt it worthwhile to formulate and publish these proposals for the following reasons: First, the age of electronic communications has radically transformed the press conference, making it a much more public event. Second, despite these changes, the importance of frequency and regularity in holding press conferences has remained. Press conferences derive their credibility from the regularity with which they are scheduled, yet recent presidents have held them only irregularly, to the detriment of all. Third, the press, although it has as great a stake in the operation of the press conference as anyone, has been unable to arrive at recommendations to deal with these problems. Competitive pressures and other factors have made it impossible for the rugged individuals of the Fourth Estate to come to a consensus on reforms.

Thus, the great technological changes that have taken place in the setting of the press conference, the damaging effects of its scheduling in recent years, and the lack of other agreed-upon responses to these developments all led the members of this Commission to believe that they could make a contribution to the current discussion of presidential-press relations by collectively advancing some suggestions.

THE PRESIDENTIAL PRESS CONFERENCE: A STATE OF DISREPAIR

"If there is ever to be an amelioration of the condition of mankind," John Adams observed in 1815, "philosophers, theologians, politicians, and moralists will find that the regulation of the press is the most difficult, dangerous, and important problem they have to resolve. Mankind cannot now be governed without it, nor at present with it." While the First Amendment to the Constitution specifically forbids any law "abridging the freedom . . . of the press," and while such freedom is one of the glories of our heritage and our history, the problem about which Adams expressed concern one hundred sixty-five years ago, long before the birth of radio and television, is no less difficult, dangerous, and important today. It is difficult not only because government is far more complex but also because the news media have become truly mass, both in the pervasiveness of their message and in the multitude of those who spread it (2,661 news gathering organizations in Washington alone). It is dangerous because despite all their numbers, despite all their technological magic, news organizations right now have a standing with the American people, as one distinguished commentator has observed, somewhere between that of undertakers and used car salesmen; freedom of the press is less cherished and fear of the press more widespread. It is important because the security of our institutions and the survival of our liberties depend, perhaps more than ever before, on a well-informed public.

The dimensions of this persisting problem are vast, and it is neither the desire nor the duty of this Commission to examine them all. We do feel, however, that one of the most important avenues of communication in this land runs from 1600 Pennsylvania Avenue to the rest of America, from the White House to

Main Street. We further feel, and with good reason, that this avenue has, in recent years, been beset by detours, pocked with potholes, and cluttered with rubble; hence it is currently in a state of distressing disrepair.

Yet this state need not be permanent. On the contrary, ours is a most favorable time to commence the work of repair. The heat and passion of an election year have subsided, a new president has been elected, and the climate is propitious for new ideas, new initiatives and new departures. Moreover, there is every indication that the American people, however great their alleged cynicism and distrust of government, long for a restoration of confidence. Clearly the people are looking for leadership in which they can have belief, faith and hope. And at the pinnacle of American leadership stands the president.

There are, of course, many ways in which a president can *exert* leadership. Equally important, a president must *express* leadership. Surely, one of the best means for such expression is the presidential press conference, where the chief executive has the opportunity to answer questions directly, somewhat as a British prime minister does during the traditional "question period" in the House of Commons. Since an American president, unlike a British prime minister to the Commons, is not answerable to the Congress, the press conference is a significant process of communication: it not only offers the expression of leadership; it also serves the people's right to know. Still, if the people have a right to know and the press is the means by which they can gain that knowledge, members of the press, in turn, have a responsibility to conduct themselves with dignity and decorum. This problem is compounded by the fact that "the press" is not a monolithic institution. It has no hierarchy, no chain of command by which standards of behavior may be enforced. Yet the issue of the behavior of participants in the press conference must be addressed. Otherwise, the process, a delicate one at best, breaks down; and the interests of all—the president, the media, and the people—suffer accordingly. That breakdown has occurred in recent years.

No one party in particular is to blame for this breakdown in communications, yet all involved share some of the guilt. Too often, particularly in the Vietnam and Watergate years, the president has appeared to many observers devious and distrusted in his relations with reporters. Some reporters, their numbers swelled to record proportions, have on occasion demonstrated more an instinct for the jugular than for journalism. Under these circumstances, in an atmosphere of mutual dislike, rather than providing any clarity about the issues of our time, press conferences have sometimes conveyed only confusion; despite their positive features they have at times collapsed into a babble of sound and fury informing nobody. Finally, the public's expectations have been too great. A presidential press conference, however long and however frequent, cannot answer all the questions or solve all the problems, much as many Americans seem to expect.

What then can be done to improve the present precarious condition of the presidential press conference? Obviously, as a physician must "heal thyself," so the healing here must be largely done by the president, aided by the press secretary and the reporters assigned to cover the White House. But there may be a role in the healing process for a group of outside, objective and qualified observers, and that is the reason for this Commission. Asked to serve by the White Burkett Miller Center of Public Affairs, itself charged with the study of the presidency in all its aspects, the Commission's members do not consider themselves strangers to public affairs—or to the White House itself. James Rowe, for one, has a history of public service dating back to his years as a member of Franklin D. Roosevelt's staff. Carroll Kilpatrick, for another, was a White House correspondent during a period spanning the administrations of Roosevelt and Gerald R. Ford. Douglass Cater, for a third, was the Washington editor for *The Reporter* magazine before becoming a special assistant to Lyndon B. Johnson. The Commission's cochairmen are, respectively, a former Virginia governor and assistant secretary of state, Linwood Holton, and a former NBC White House correspondent now vice president of RCA, Ray Scherer. Julius Duscha and Robert Pierpoint are old hands on the Potomac beat, while Felicia Warburg Rogan has long been active in journalistic and community endeavors in New York City and Charlottesville.

The Commission began its deliberations at the outset of last summer and has since held a series of meetings in Washington and Charlottesville. The purpose of these meetings, some of them daylong, was to explore the whole question of the president and the news media with past and present White House correspondents as well as several past presidential press secretaries and staff assistants. Each meeting was taped, and the transcripts of the tapes run to more than four hundred pages. Additional research material and assistance were provided by the staff of the Miller Center under the able guidance of its director, Kenneth W. Thompson. At its penultimate meeting in Charlottesville in early October, the Commission decided to limit its recommendations to the press conference alone, without getting into such matters as the media's varying requirements (e.g., those of a news magazine vis-à-vis a wire service or a television network, dinners for selected reporters like those in Eisenhower's time or one-on-one TV interviews a la Cronkite, Chancellor, and Walters). Two points should be emphasized: 1) the Commission is not acting alone from the vantage point of some lofty ivory tower; it has had the generous assistance and advice of those who have participated in White House press conferences since the administration of Calvin Coolidge; and 2) the Commission does not offer its recommendations as the be-all and end-all solutions to the conduct of presidential press conferences, but rather as suggestions as to how the conduct—and accordingly the product—of such conferences can be improved. A final point is this: we are not so naive as to think our recommendations will be received with reverence but we would trust that our report will be given the care and consideration which went into its making. We offer our suggestions fully cognizant that the press conference is the president's prerogative. There is nothing in the Constitution which directs him to meet reporters. He can lay down any rules he wishes. He can even choose to hold no press conferences at all. We are not directing him in this report to do anything. Again, we ask only that it be considered. Before offering our recommendations, however, we believe that a short history of the presidential press conference is in order, and it constitutes the next section of this document.

THE PRESIDENTIAL PRESS CONFERENCE: A BRIEF HISTORY

The presidential press conference is an institution whose long and distinguished history has given it a prominent place in the American political firmament. Although earlier presidents may on occasion have had casual meetings with editors and reporters, the press conference as such is a phenomenon of the twentieth century. For eighty years presidents have, in one forum or another, answered questions from reporters in an effort to communicate with both the news media and the public at large. Theodore Roosevelt first brought groups of reporters into the White House for interviews from time to time—often while he was being shaved in the morning. After a four-year lapse during the Taft administration, the press conference returned in 1913 to Woodrow Wilson's White House, where it has since remained. Wilson introduced the practices of regular meetings with the press and equal access for all accredited reporters to conferences. Warren Harding, Calvin Coolidge, and Herbert Hoover continued these sessions, although they required that questions be submitted in writing to them in advance.

With the presidency of Franklin Roosevelt, the press conference entered its most productive, and perhaps most colorful, era. Roosevelt's conferences contained very little that was wholly new; submission to a spontaneous question-and-answer period, a willingness to speak off-the-record and provide extensive background information, and the availability of direct presidential quotes to reporters were all devices that had been used previously by one president or another. But Roosevelt's skillful mixing of all these elements when he met with one hundred or so reporters gathered around his desk gave the press conferences of his day a distinctive flavor—informal yet informative—which they had not enjoyed before and which they have rarely recaptured since.

Over the past thirty-five years, the press conference as an institution had continued to evolve, responding to continuing changes in communications, most particularly the advent of television, and in the American political system. With the United States emerging as a superpower from World War II and Washington becoming the capital of the so-called Free World, the number of reporters attending White House press conferences increased enormously. As a result, Harry Truman had no choice but to stand before the assembled reporters rather than speak to them as they clustered about his desk, and much of the Rooseveltian air of intimacy was lost. Radio taping and, to a greater extent, television filming for delayed airing inaugurated under Dwight Eisenhower, made it more difficult for presidents to provide extensive background information off-the-record. They also became more reluctant to speak freely, fearful of being caught in a slip of the tongue. The decision to televise press conferences live, made by John F. Kennedy, accelerated these trends. Projected in black and white, later in "living color," a president was directly in the public eye and seemed to feel that he could neither seek a delay for more information nor say, "No comment." Kennedy's immediate successors only contributed to a worsening in relations between the president and the members of the Fourth Estate (or what one member of this Commission has called "the Fourth Branch of Government"). What many in the press regarded as deceptions, as with Lyndon Johnson's reports about the Vietnam War and Richard Nixon's duplicities about Watergate, raised a curtain of distrust between the president and the press. If the role of the news media in their relationship to the White House had hitherto been adversarial, it now became downright antagonistic.

Meanwhile, the presidential press conference turned into a shouting contest among reporters for the president's eye. Although reporters had clamored for attention before, the presence of television added a new dimension to the turmoil of the press conference. And such conditions continued to prevail, for the most part, under Gerald Ford and Jimmy Carter, with reporters jumping and yelling for attention like children on a playground. Thus *Broadcasting* magazine was prompted to headline its September 29, 1980 story announcing the formation of this Commission, "Trying to Create Order Out of Chaos."

THE PRESIDENTIAL PRESS CONFERENCE: RECOMMENDATIONS

Creating order from chaos does not have to be a monumental undertaking, provided there is a willingness on the part of both parties, the president and the news media, to agree a) that the status quo is unacceptable and should not be continued, and b) that some give-and-take from each side is required to make the necessary innovations and/or improvements. We believe that such a willingness may exist, and we therefore trust that our recommendations will not be consigned to that great dustbin of unread proposals. Our proposals may seem almost too simple at first glance, but they can, we unanimously believe, be of benefit to all concerned — the president, the media, and most of all, the American people.

The key to the success of any presidential press conference relationship is frequency. The more often a president meets reporters, the greater the interchange, the less chance there is for communication breakdown. We are encouraged by President-elect Reagan's declaration at his November 6 post-election Los Angeles press conference to "do our best to have them on a fairly regular and consistent basis."

Our recommendations are these: 1) the president should have a *regular monthly* press conference available for live television coverage and open to all reporters; and 2) in addition, the president should have weekly informal meetings with reporters in a setting of his choice, with or without radio and television equipment. Here we reprint with commendation the opening remarks made by Franklin Roosevelt at his first presidential press conference on March 8, 1933:

THE PRESIDENT: It is very good to see you all. My hope is that these conferences are going to be merely enlarged editions of the kind of very delightful family conferences I have been holding in Albany for the last four years.

I am told that what I am about to do will become impossible, but I am going to try it. We are not going to have any more written questions; and, of course, while I cannot answer seventy-five or a hundred questions because I simply haven't got the time, I see no reason why I should not talk to you ladies and gentlemen off the record in just the way I have been doing in Albany and in the way I used to do in the Navy Department down here. Quite a number of you, I am glad to see, date back to the days of the previous existence which I led in Washington.

And so I think we shall discontinue the practice of compelling the submitting of questions in writing before the conference in order to get an answer. There will be a great many questions, of course, that I won't answer, either because they are "if" questions— and I never answer them—and Brother Stephenson will tell you what an "if" question is . . .

MR. STEPHENSON (Reporter): I ask forty of them a day.

THE PRESIDENT: And the others, of course, are the questions which for various reasons I do not want to discuss, or I am not ready to discuss, or I do not know anything about. There will be a great many questions you will ask that I do not know enough about to answer.

Then, in regard to news announcements, Steve (Early, Assistant Secretary to the President) and I thought that it would be best that straight news for use from this office should always be without direct quotations. In other words, I do not want to be directly quoted, unless direct quotations are given out by Steve in writing. That makes that perfectly clear.

Then there are two other matters we will talk about: The first is "background information," which means material which can be used by all of you on your own authority and responsibility, not to be attributed to the White House, because I do not want to have to revive the Ananias Club. (Laughter)

Then the second thing is the "off the record" information which means, of course, confidential information which is given only to those who attend the conference. Now there is one thing I want to say right now about which I think you will go along with me. I want to ask you not to repeat this "off the record" confidential information either to your own editors or to your associates who are not here; because there is always the danger that, while you people may not violate the rule, somebody may forget to say, "This is off the record and confidential," and the other party may use it in a story. That is to say, it is not to be used and not to be told to those fellows who happen not to come around to the conference. In other words, it is only for those present. (*The Public Papers and Addresses of Franklin D. Roosevelt.* 13 vols., New York: Random House, 1938), 11:30–31.)

We believe that these ground rules provide the best opportunity for the two types of press conferences to serve their somewhat different purposes. The formal conference lets the president communicate directly with the people of America and of the world; it also serves the important symbolic function of displaying a president's continuing mental and physical vigor, as shown by the ability to handle a series of unrehearsed and probing questions with the nation as witness. The informal weekly conference is an opportunity for more reflective, candid discussions of issues and events. It allows the president to educate the public indirectly; and, by providing reporters with the necessary background on important topics, it enables them to ask more for informed questions which better protect the public's right to know.

To the argument that weekly informal meetings and at least one large televised conference a month are too much of a demand on a president's time, we might point out that Roosevelt—hardly an inactive executive, and president during the difficult Depression and war years—met the press twice a week. And both Truman and Eisenhower regularly held sessions once a week; it is only in the past twenty years that the frequency and regularity of press conferences have declined. Furthermore, meeting reporters more frequently and more informally might give them a better comprehension of what the president is seeking to attain and the president a better idea of what issues concern the public. More frequent meetings might also help the president to better understand the demands on the media and the media to better comprehend the demands on the president, thereby retaining the traditional adversary relationship between government and the media without so much antagonism getting involved.

The manner in which presidential press conferences are presently conducted on live television—with reporters jumping up, waving their hands, and shouting, "Mr. President! Mr. President!" in an effort to gain the president' eye and the opportunity to ask a question—is what so many viewers (and participants) find appalling. The easiest remedy for this requires little more than an exercise in presidential leadership: the president could enforce order by refusing to, acknowledge or answer any reporter who shouts. He answers only those who raise their hand and allows follow-up questions.

Another option which might be considered would be to have the questioners at a televised press conference chosen by lot. This has worked well on presidential trips out of Washington. Reporters desiring to ask a question would submit their names—but not their questions—in advance of the conference. Those chosen in a system of random selection would be listed in the order picked and the list posted, with a copy going to the president, who would then call those on the list and allow each questioner a follow-up question. At least two exceptions could be made: the Associated Press and the United Press International correspondents would retain their traditional right to ask the first two questions.

To those who say the president benefits in the eyes of the public from what is now perceived as a confrontation with the arrogant and obstreperous behavior of correspondents, we would offer an eloquent rebuttal made by British author Godfrey Hodgson in his new book, *All Things to All Men: The False Promise of the Modern American Presidency.* In his chapter on the president and the media, entitled "The Electronic Mephistopheles," Hodgson concludes: "The media's interest in the President seems increasingly tinged with cyncism. The public seems increasingly skeptical and indifferent. A cycle of diminishing returns seems underway, perhaps irreversibly so."

Although we believe the last, best salvation for a modern president is the exercise of effective leadership—and leadership he clearly enjoys exercising—we cite Mr. Hodgson to show that the president has something, in fact a great deal, to gain by getting away from the circus-like atmosphere of today's press conferences.

There is much to be said for renewing the informal gathering of correspondents that took place during the 1930s and 1940s. We realize, of course, that the size of the present news corps precludes gathering around the president's desk. But we see no reason why the president cannot have a weekly informal meeting with reporters. In some circumstances, the president could speak for attribution but not for direct quotation—"The president said." Reporters would, though, have the right to check with the press secretary in certain instances to see if the president would permit a quote.

So we hold that these innovations, a minimum of one monthly live TV conference, with a better method of questioning, and weekly informal meetings, can have a substantial and significant benefit.

We hope these recommendations will be received as we have endeavored to formulate them—thoughtfully, thoroughly and sincerely. We do not offer these proposals as though they were engraved in marble and not subject to further contemplation and change; nor do we assert that the ideas which underlie them are wholly new or original. We do offer them secure in our belief that if there is a will to explore them, there is a way to turn them into realities.

THE PRESIDENTIAL PRESS CONFERENCE: AN AFTERWORD

We opened this report with a quotation from one of America's founding fathers. We close with a quotation from another, one intimately involved with the institution of which the Miller Center is a part—the University of Virginia. For that institution, the Virginian who is so much its father had many great expectations. And one of the expectations Thomas Jefferson envisaged for his university was this: " . . . here we are not afraid to follow the truth wherever it may lead, nor to tolerate any error, so long as reason is left free to combat it." That, we submit, is the standard to which all involved in the presidential press conference must adhere.

Linwood Holton, cochairman
Ray Scherer, cochairman
Douglass Cater
Julius Duscha
Carroll Kilpatrick
Robert Pierpoint
James Rowe
Felicia Warburg Rogan

CONCLUDING OBSERVATIONS

The present volume contains cogent presentations in four of the most crucial areas involving the future of the American presidency: the president as political leader; organizing approaches to policy-making; the president, communications and the public; and the president and the international setting. By inviting serious dialogue on key issues in the four areas, the Miller Center hopes it may contribute to constructive improvements of the presidency. It has also seemed appropriate that a copy of the important report of the "National Commission on Presidential Press Conferences" be included. The report provided the basis for the Reagan administration's initial approach to press conferences according to press secretary James Brady. It has been widely discussed in the national press and on the educational and commercial television networks.

Each of the *Virginia Papers* carries a particular message or theme: Bartlett's that the six-year single, single presidential term merits study; Donovan's that there are limits as well as marginal possibilities of the special advisor's proving helpful; Powell's that presidential press conferences should be keyed to important national issues; and Johnson's that both strength and flexibility are required in Soviet-American relations. All four of the *Papers* are rich in insights on contemporary government and provide a kind of working text on the living Constitution. They bring the educator closer to the realities of politics; they offer guidance and pointers to new leaders who have just assumed official responsibilities. Above all, they continue the Miller Center's commitment to the reunion of theory and practice in public affairs.

IV

Presidents As Communicators

The President as Communicator

THOMAS RESTON

INTRODUCTION: Mr. Thomas Reston is Deputy Assistant Secretary of State for Public Affairs. He is a graduate of the Law School; he organized and directed the Student Legal Forum. Upon graduation, he was Secretary of the Virginia Democratic Party. It is a pleasure to have Mr. Reston with us this afternoon.

One of the six main themes of our Forums is the President as Communicator, the President and the Public. So far the missing chair in our discussions on this aspect of the presidency has been someone speaking from responsibilities inside government. We've had the media perspective from Sander Vanocur and Ray Scherer. But we have yet to have a representative of the government's approach to communicating with the public. So, it is a very special privilege to welcome Tom Reston back to his own University.

MR. RESTON: Thank you, Mr. Thompson. It is indeed a great pleasure for me to be back in Charlottesville at the University. This is a very special place in terms of American education.

I have not prepared any particular thoughts for you on this subject. I think I prefer to just take your questions because I am not sure what aspect you would like me to dwell on. If you take me in the direction that you want to go, I think it would be better for all of us. So I'll do my best in terms of trying to explain the somewhat difficult job which we have in trying to put our point across to the American people.

I think that, if nothing else, we learned during the war in Indochina that if your foreign policy doesn't have a pretty broad consensus of support among the American people, then you can have pretty much of a disaster on your hands. It is difficult for us to communicate with the public, especially difficult in terms of foreign policy when up until early November of last year foreign policy was not uppermost on the minds of the American people. Since then we've faced a couple of pretty extraordinary situations in Iran and Afghanistan, and the mind of the country, or at least the frustration of the country, is now resting upon foreign affairs to a much greater extent than it was for the first two and a half years of this Administration.

QUESTION: I would like to ask you a question about adversarial relationships from your vantage point. Many years ago when I was a student I interviewed your father at some length. He was chief of the Washington Bureau of the *Times* then and he expounded on the adversarial relationship between press and government, thinking it was a good thing. The first question is, does this seem more or less so to you from your current vantage point, if that's a correct characterization?

Another relationship that sometimes appears to be competitive if not adversarial is that between the White House's foreign office and the State Department's foreign office. I wonder if you would confirm, deny, or amend either of these propositions from the viewpoint of your working experience.

MR. RESTON: Well, first on the relationship between the government and the press, it is an adversarial relationship. It should be. It's proper that it should be. It's proper that the press should not really entirely trust what I am telling them. It's proper that they should go digging around and try to trap me in any inconsistency or some half-truth. That is their role, to keep a check on the government. I have no problem with that at all. And it is very much viewed that way both by me, Hodding Carter and others, and by the press itself. It's not to say that we make a point of fighting with the press; we don't. But I am paid to represent the interests of the government and the Administration.

I also have a contradictory kind of role which I perform in private and which is, in a way, a far more difficult role for me to play. This is privately to represent the interests of the press to the government, for example, to Vance. I go in and say, "Sir, they keep asking me this question and we keep refusing to answer it. In my judgment the government ought to come forward with an answer and now is the time we ought to do it. Let me go tell them what the answer or what the rationale for the policy is instead of just stonewalling them." The business of trying to drag information out of the bureaucracy is almost the hardest part of my job. It is ultimately adversarial and it should be.

Now as for relations between the National Security Council and the State Department, anytime you get two competing bureaucracies who are more or less charged with having an influence over a single policy, I think you're going to get inevitable disagreements which can on occasion turn into bigger bureaucratic hassles than they need be. There is not a great deal of difference between how Mr. Vance sees the world and how Mr. Brzezinski sees the world. They do have differences. Brzezinski is inclined to beat up on the Russians much more than Vance is. Brzezinski is a theoretical man who thinks in theoretical, conceptual ways about the world. Vance is kind of a practical, ad hoc lawyer who sees a controversy and says, "Now what are the practical things we have to do in order to compose this controversy?" There are two different ways of thinking about the world, it seems to me, reflected in different views of policy between the two men.

Obviously there are other players in this too. The vice president is a player in the game. Andy Young, while Andy was still with the Administration, had a particular view of the world and an enormous influence on the policy. So there will be clashes. There is competition between the State Department and the White House. It is often fed more by the people around the two principals, Zbig and Vance, by their staffs, you know, pushing their man so that the hassles become more blown up than they should be. But of course it exists and there are a lot of other bureaucracies in town.

QUESTION: Do you think that's equally healthy as the one between the press and the government?

MR. RESTON: Not when it gets out of hand. Not when people start telling personal stories on the other or essentially trying to backstab each other.

QUESTION: That brings up another related question. How is it determined whether the White House or the State Department, or any other press office releases information to the press? Who's going to get the credit? And that's not an easy decision because in the Hodding Carter case, with regards to Iran, it may be better to decentralize the information transmission on a daily basis. Another one is, who has the expertise? Can Jody Powell handle the daily briefing for the press? Clearly there needs to be a coordination function so that perhaps State is the reservoir. And finally who is going to be able to give the clear signal?

MR. RESTON: Well, every morning, there is a conference call between State, Jody Powell's office, the NSC, Defense, sometimes the Arms Control Agency and also the vice president's office. We talk about just this thing, who handles what. Now there are certain logical things where if you're talking about the deployment of U.S. forces, carriers steaming into the Indian Ocean, and that sort of thing, it is done by the Defense Department because it is a logistical thing.

I sometimes think that there is a rule of thumb working that if it's a political triumph, Jody get's to do it and if it's a disaster I get to do it! That may be the bottom line here. Generally the White House will do more political things. Generally the White House will do anything which directly involves the person of the president. If the president is meeting with the prime minister of Italy at the White House, the White House will do that because it's a state visit. While I was making a bit of a joke about a political triumph gets the White House and a disaster gets the State Department, I think that in a way that may be a principle that does operate. I know that on several occasions if there is something good going on, I have called Jody and said, "Well, why don't you announce it over there?" Sometimes when the State Department really has the lead on something as we have had on Iran, most of the action on Iran has been with Vance and the career people at the State Department, then it will only be logical that the spokesmen, Hodding or I, should do it because it is what our people are doing as opposed to what the White House is doing. I'm not suggesting that the White House is not involved in the Iranian thing. It is very involved. But nevertheless, we do the day-to-day stuff.

QUESTION: I would assume you would need to be very careful in terms of choice of language, response to specific questions; and that the presidential press secretary whose real expertise, at least in Powell's case, is politics, especially electoral politics, just doesn't have that foreign policy expertise. So I assume there is a self-conscious decision on the part of the foreign policy advisors that you will take care of that. And I'm curious that you would characterize that as a disaster because, in a sense, I think it's been a very positive accomplishment.

MR. RESTON: Well, the most positive accomplishment would be to bring these folks home safely. But, Jody is a very good press secretary. Jody is very good precisely because he understands President Carter; he understands how his mind works and what motivates him. Jody is also more than a press secretary in that he is a substantive policy advisor on megapolicy issues so that the press over there knows that when they deal with Jody they are dealing with somebody whose fine hand is very much in the policy decisions. Jody didn't have a background in foreign policy, extensive service, but he's a very quick study and to a large extent the job of a press secretary is the job of being a quick study.

Hodding and I didn't have extensive backgrounds in foreign affairs either when we came to the State Department. We knew something about foreign affairs. It wasn't as if we were totally ignorant. But we did not have years and years of study of international relations as a constant preoccupation. I was lawyer, politician and newspaperman, albeit a foreign correspondent; Hodding was a newspaperman and a politician by profession.

QUESTION: It seems from your answer that there may be two ways in which the State Department and other people involved in communication follow up on presidential statements. One might be a rationale that is directly developed out of what the State Department defines as the intention and meaning of the president. But another might be to create a rationale and then teach the president that that's in fact the best position to have.

MR. RESTON: We've done both things. Sometimes the president will make mistakes. He made a mistake on the "Meet the Press" program. He misnamed Afghanistan and Pakistan. He got it mixed up. So sometimes the president is wrong and "misstates" the policy. And while we never like to contradict the president, we would go straight to Jody in that instance and say, "Jody, he just got it wrong, and you've got to go in and tell him he was wrong." Because sometimes the president will say something when he hasn't really thought about it and it's a "mistake" in terms of being a departure from past policy which he hadn't really meant to make. But, it's such a minor kind of thing we will go scurrying around saying, "Yes, the president has thought this out and this is what the policy is now and this is the rationale for it." It depends on a case-by-case approach as to how we handle it. We discuss whether we should say he was wrong or whether we should back him up.

Now obviously in every instance in which it makes sense and it's not a complete disaster your constant instinct is to try to back the president up. Now I'm speaking as a political appointee of the Administration here, but I would think, by and large, it holds true for the career—foreign and civil—service as well.

QUESTION: Without dealing with personalities, how does domestic politics and foreign policy mix? Can anyone who speaks for the president give primacy to foreign policy, or alternatively, give primacy to domestic politics? Or is there a mechanism which operates, in your opinion, effectively to bring these two issues together in a successful way?

MR. RESTON: I think the mechanism which operates to bring the two types of issues together is the November election in 1980. We are acutely aware that foreign policy is going to have an important role to play. I think the Iran crisis has operated domestically on the president. It has changed the public's image of the president. Everybody had been saying he's not a leader, and this has given him an opportunity to show, at least in most people's minds, that he is a leader. It has erased, I think, the main stumbling block for Jimmy Carter because as of the end of last summer or the beginning of last fall you could hardly find a politician anywhere in the country who gave him a chance to get reelected.

Also, I think that you have to look at the issues. There are many issues in foreign affairs which have their domestic constituency groups. It's not as if the secretary of state and the president sit down and make foreign policy. You proceed on the margins by little increments. Your latitude for movement is not very great. For instance, on a question of whether we should stay in the International Labor Organization or not, nobody in the Administration would draw a breath on that without talking with the AFL-CIO or the pro-Israeli lobby, which would have figured in that decision very greatly as well. Yes, they do tend to get mixed up.

Now, I think that the career officers of the foreign service act somewhat as a brake. The career foreign service by and large doesn't know very much about this country and sometimes regard the intrusion of domestic political issues into our foreign policy as somehow unprofessional, or not to be taken account of. They resist those kinds of pressures. So the foreign service operates to insulate these foreign policy decisions from the crasser domestic political considerations, like how many votes will it pick up in Cleveland if we beat up on the Russians today.

QUESTION: When you were saying that the mind of the country wasn't on foreign policy, I was thinking that one of the great successes that Carter had was the arrangement of bringing together Begin and Sadat. As far as the president as communicator is concerned, there was a great deal of condescending and anxious comments in the newspapers and the media generally before he finally got an agreement. Then it seemed to me that there was a public relations triumph that had a tremendous success and that went beyond the interests of special groups; and it was interesting to me that he lost so much after that. A number of papers came out and said they were surprised he succeeded. The point is that an administration doesn't have much control over what happens, that a lot is done by the media themselves, not necessarily intentionally, but as they pick up a story.

MR. RESTON: I think that's right, but to a certain extent we can control it. Obviously, if you bring Begin and Sadat to Washington to sign a treaty on the White House lawn, chances are you're going to get a few photographers around.

But there is a phenomenon I think in Washington journalism of "pack journalism." They all might be writing about Camp David one week, but if something else comes along suddenly they'll all start writing about that. An example, although a somewhat more murky example, is the issue of the hostages being so prominent for so long, then the Afghanistan crisis happened and there was very much less written about the hostage situation in the newspapers and seen on the evening news programs.

I think to a certain extent the Camp David success was dissipated rather fast. I'm not exactly sure why that happened. I know that the president's support was so far down in the groups which have traditionally supported Israel that by the time he produced the Camp David agreement, it was politically only a kind of stanching of a wound by then.

QUESTION: For about two weeks when he was quietly at Camp David the press reported every night on the television that nothing was happening.

MR. RESTON: That's right. We closed down that operation completely. I think some of the funniest briefings which were ever given in Washington were given by Jody Powell trying to report, saying nothing on what the president was doing out at Camp David. They were even more ridiculous briefings than Hodding Carter's and my briefings at the State Department, which are pretty amusing in themselves in that they don't say very much.

NARRATOR: Would you be willing to say just a word about staffing in both State and the White House? We have been exposed to a whole succession of statements from other visitors to the Miller Center to the effect that recent administrations, particularly this one, have been governments by children. And the focus of the criticism has been that young people suddenly elevated to high positions within this and other administrations are tempted to prod cabinet members, and even the president, on behalf of their own constituency saying that: the secretary or the president asks you to do so and so. More experienced and mature people might not press this point.

The main criticism, coupled with the gratuitous comment about age, is that the White House and various other agencies are over-loaded with staff and that you have had a movement away from an earlier pattern where departments ran their affairs—State, Treasury, Defense. And now the White House intervenes at almost every level to shape decisions. Lower level people speak on behalf of the president in ways that cabinet members, including those who have come here, found quite intolerable.

MR. RESTON: Leaving aside the question of age—it's really a question of judgment—I think "White Houses" are more prone to do the type of thing that you're suggesting than other agencies of the federal government would be. But there is nothing more irritating than to have somebody from the White House on the phone saying: I am speaking on behalf of the president; you must print this speech; or, the president wants you to mail something to 15,000 college professors all over the country. People, regardless of their age, who don't have good judgment, don't have good judgment.

And there are some arrogant people and there are some people who are not arrogant. Some of that goes on, the playing of the top sergeant by White House people when reasonable and rational conversation would do the job. Yes, I've run into that. I've even run into it from people who do not work for the government. So it happens and it's always unpleasant when it happens. You never know whether the president really does want you to mail out those 15,000 letters.

Just today we had something like that in our staff meeting where the president apparently decided that the State Department should send one person to the White House to help answer the mail. Now frankly I don't believe that the president makes decisions like that. If he does we are in much more serious trouble than I think. But there was a call from the White House which said: the president wants you to send one person to help answer this flood of mail at the White House. It's an example of that type of thing. And we're going to send him on the off chance that maybe the president did make the request.

QUESTION: There's one thing that comes to mind when I'm watching Hodding Carter make his announcements over TV. Is he told what to say? To what extent would his own judgment enter into it?

MR. RESTON: Our press conferences run generally about an hour. Out of that hour I suppose we would be reading a prepared statement maybe about three minutes out of the hour. All the rest is give-and-take, and it's Hodding's words that he's making up as he goes along. Now obviously he is not running the State Department, but he knows what the policy is. When I am doing the briefing, for instance, I see the secretary of state about four times a day. If I need to see him more than that I can always get through to him. He knows that if I've got a problem it's something that I think he has to deal with; it's a potentially serious problem and so we can get through. One of the virtues of having this job is that it affords me complete access to everybody at the State Department if I need it. I don't make a practice of barging in on the secretary of state when I don't need to see him, but we have access to people who can tell us what the policy is. So while it may be Hodding's words or my words, it is still within the policy.

The great nightmare of spokesmen is that they will "misspeak" the policy or say something which is wrong, which could have instantaneous ramifications of enormous proportions. Take for instance the Iran situation. Iran is kind of strange to a large extent because we are not able to deal privately with the Iranians. To a large extent these negotiations have been going on in public. Hodding will say something, the terrorists at the embassy will respond, we will respond to what they have said, and to a large extent it is carried out in public. But you can think of all kinds of missteps that a spokesman can make in this very tenuous, turmoiled situation which could have serious implications for the safety of those people.

QUESTION: I think one of the virtues of the things you've said here, and I think it probably comes from your particular foreign policy perspective, is that communicating with the public can often run counter to the necessary things that governments do. I wonder if you could expand a little bit on your role of keeping quiet sometimes, and why that is sometimes necessary?

MR. RESTON: I think the operating principle there is that everything somebody says in public becomes a rigidly defined position. So that if we take a position on something it is very hard for us to climb down from it. Therefore, if we say nothing—and much of the time I say nothing about our various initiatives which are going on—it allows us to retain private flexibility over what our position will ultimately be. But if we take a position publicly, we're much much less inclined to change it subsequently. That is the reason why you will often see Hodding or me on television making the most ridiculous, silly kinds of nonentity statements. It's because we mean to be choosing our words very carefully and saying that meetings are fruitful and not really talking about what went on in the meeting. It's just because we don't want to say anything because we want to retain our flexibility.

QUESTION: Do you think there would be any virtue in addressing that topic? In other words, instead of just making up things to distract reporters from the questions they want to ask, saying straight out: here's the case for flexibility; we can't tell you the details of a particular situation, but we can give you some indication of why we just have to have this discretion. Would that ever be an appropriate . . .

MR. RESTON: Oh, yes. I do that all the time.

QUESTION: But don't you often strain to try to give them something to put in the first paragraph?

MR. RESTON: Yes, but there are many subjects on which I'll say: I can't talk with you about that.

QUESTION: Isn't it true that in communicating you hope people abroad will take your words to mean one thing, and sometimes you try to tell our people something else — you used the word mood. Now I expect that one of the major things that you are trying to do in the Afghanistan situation is to create a mood here at home of concern and danger and threat; and certainly all the people who believe that that exists, whether Afghanistan does or not, are quickly jumping on the wagon and questions like the draft are coming to the fore. At the same time, it seems to me that while you're doing that, you're looking abroad to tell them that this is what we want you to see. We want you to see these people getting mad so that you will think that our will is now mobilized. I'd like to learn a little bit more about how you juggle those kind of issues. Once they get loose, aren't they very tough to back off from?

MR. RESTON: We're talking, as you say, both to the American people and to people abroad, which is another reason why often the statements sound murky because you're trying to address two audiences at the same time. Yes, we are trying to create a mood here in the United States. We are trying, to a certain extent, to identify ourselves with a preexisting mood in the United States, a kind of mistrust of Russia's motivations in terms of some of the actions that it has taken lately. So to a certain extent we're trying to build a national resolve to get tougher on defense, to show the Russians we will not tolerate Soviet expansionism and that there is a will in the American people to pay the price, to sacrifice, for taking tough action.

And this is one thing I think that hasn't really dawned on the public yet. But if you are going to penalize the Russians, we here in this country are going to pay a price for it. And the farmers are going to pay a price, the athletes are going to pay a price, the people who want to look at a famous Russian art collection in Minneapolis are going to pay a price because it is not going to be coming to the United States. I think that that is part of the education that we are trying to produce as well, to educate the public as to what it is going to cost them to take this tough posture.

QUESTION: One of the things that troubles me a little bit is that hardly anybody thinks that you're really dumb on television and most of the people expect you to be murky and understand that sort of thing. We know it comes with the job. But I think we do try to understand what you're trying to have us think or what you would rather have us believe so we could talk over tables like this more knowledgeably than those people who just think you're dumb. What I wonder is, has anyone been looking at the possibility of trying to achieve some of the president's domestic purposes, energy conservation being one, and of trying to use reports to the people as a bully pulpit? We contemplate going to war, but we can't contemplate a fifty percent increase in gasoline tax or rationing. Do you all sit down and try to find some way of getting people to sacrifice at home so they don't have to think about war abroad so much?

MR. RESTON: The president thinks about that quite a bit, specifically energy. And it was one of his great frustrations, and he would express frustration about this in private, that when he goes on television and talks about the moral equivalent of war, people don't believe him because the one thing politically that people in the United States are not prepared to do is either to conserve energy or pay exorbitant prices for it. In my judgment, we're going to get to the point where we will be paying exorbitant prices for energy. We are going to be conserving ultimately because it's going to be too expensive to go on wasting energy as we do. We are, as everyone knows, the most wasteful society with energy in the world. The Energy Department is pumping out government propaganda all the time about how we must have an energy program and how everybody has to conserve energy. Such appeals are meeting with enormous individual resistance among individual Americans.

QUESTION: I can understand that. In one sense, patriotism that would call for a general sharing of energy conservation might make more sense than just putting it on the athletes or the farmers.

MR. RESTON: Well, if you listened to the president's State of the Union message, he said 1980 must be the year of energy conservation.

Somehow, because the message is so unpalatable to the American people, I think that they are just tuning it out.

QUESTION: George Ball, in a recent article in *Foreign Affairs,* wrote that sometimes you have very sensitive and secret meetings at the highest level of the State Department and the White House which everyone knows are privileged. Yet as soon as the meetings are over, someone leaks information to the press. He argues that these leaks really are against the wishes of the participants. What's your position as a spokesman; and what is the State Department's position?

MR. RESTON: Well, in a way it doesn't really matter what my position is. The point is there will always be leaks because there is always going to be someone who is unhappy. What is going to happen even if you have the most closely held meeting at the White House, with only five or six people very high up, they'll come back and tell their deputies or their staff aide and then in order to lord it over somebody at a cocktail party that night, the staff aide will say, "Guess what, we're going to war with Russia tomorrow." The word will get around and it will come out. So I think there always will be leaks.

Some leaks are officially sanctioned leaks. I leak classified information to journalists all the time but I do it because an official says, "You know, you had better sit down with the *New York Times* today and explain to them how this policy, even though it looks like a disaster, is a brilliant success, and mention this aspect of it," which was previously secret. That's one kind of authorized leak. I generally do that when I'm talking on background so that I'm not identified as the spokesman of the State Department. I'm a "senior State Department official" which makes me giggle a little bit because I think about Jimmy Carter and his teenage diplomats, which I'm sure is what the foreign service thought of me when I came in.

But then there are the leaks which are the result of fighting policy battles; generally being leaked by the guy that is losing the policy battle. Then too you have leaks which are completely unauthorized but are very healthy leaks. I think the Administration in recent memory which leaked the most was the Nixon Administration because there were a lot of people in the Nixon Administration who were horrified by what was going on and they would leak things in order to get it on the public record. There will always be leaks. Whether I approve of them or not is irrelevant.

QUESTION: Would you give us a general evaluation of what you think the quality of network and newspaper reporting on foreign affairs is? I ask the question because we've had many people come to the Miller Center and tell us the media is very influential, and probably detrimental, but they don't explain what the real problems are. I wonder if some of the things that you mentioned today, for instance, over-reporting of today's crises, exaggerating bureaucratic differences within the Administration, are systematic distortions by the press that occur all the time.

MR. RESTON: The trouble with journalism is that it is like a bathroom. You have hot and cold running water. The State Department either has scored a triumph or the State Department has plunged us to the brink of war and disasterous humiliation for the American people. Things are always more complicated than they seem in the media. But to a large extent I think that the people in the profession have been trained to exaggerate or simplify a complicated story so that their readership or their viewership can understand it. If you had to explain the Iran story in thirty seconds on the CBS Evening News, it would be very difficult to give a simple picture of the situation; it's an enormously complicated story. The frustrations which the government has in dealing with Iran are enormously complicated. But you cannot bring out all that complication in thirty seconds on television.

Now having said that, by and large, I think that the diplomatic press corps which covers the State Department is a pretty fine press corps. People like Marvin Kalb are very thoughtful and sophisticated people who have enormously good sources in the Department and throughout the government, and really know what they are writing about, by and large. Now sometimes Marvin gets it wrong but that's because Marvin is human just the way you and I are human. But by and large I think it's a pretty good press corps. Like other press corps it tends to take on the coloration of the people it covers so it tends to be a more restrained press corps because the foreign service is extremely cautious and restrained. You can go—or you could until these recent crisis were upon us—to a place like Milwaukee and pick up a Sunday paper, a great huge thick Sunday paper in Milwaukee, Wisconsin, and not find a single word about foreign affairs, not a single word in the Sunday paper. Now that's a pretty sad commentary on what is getting through to most of the people in the United States, which is zilch. And then something happens like Iran which people don't understand and they have no background through their peers to understand what's going on.

QUESTION: You think that's a recent development? I remember when I was growing up—of course it was during World War II—that the *Chicago Tribune* had better than two dozen foreign correspondents, and in the late fifties they had four. There's a tremendous reduction of foreign correspondents in American newspapers.

MR. RESTON: Well that's certainly true and that's an unhealthy sign, and the reason, I'm sure, is economic. It is enormously expensive to have a foreign correspondent in London. It is just enormously expensive. To put one person in London or Rome, to do European stories, leaving aside Africa or the Middle East, it could cost over a hundred thousand dollars a year, or maybe as high as two hundred thousand. The dollar has gone down so drastically and costs to travel in Europe—airfare and hotel bills—are extraordinarily high. You've got to have a secretary for the correspondent and rent office space and that's very expensive. I'm sure that's the reason why papers like the *Chicago Tribune* don't have that many foreign correspondents anymore.

NARRATOR: I'm sure I speak for all when I say thank you Mr. Reston.

Presidents I Have Known

RICHARD STROUT

NARRATOR: I'd like to introduce the Forum we have been hoping we could have for several years and which, thanks to the former publisher of the *New Republic,* Robert Myers, now has come about. Not many journalists are legends in their time but Richard Strout certainly is. His famed TRB column has provided a steady diet of political education for many of us. He received his A.B. from Harvard, his M.A. and Litt.D. from Brown. He began his newspaper career with the *Sheffield Independent* in England. He wrote in this country initially for the *Boston Post* and then, beginning in 1921, as a columnist with the *Christian Science Monitor.* He served as a lieutenant in the infantry in World War I and as a war correspondent in World War II. He is a recipient of the George Polk award for national reporting, the journalism award of the University of Missouri, the Sidney Hillman award, the Fourth Estate award of the National Press Club, and a Pulitzer Special Citation award. He is author with E. B. White of *Fairwell to Model T,* editor of *Maud,* and editor of *TRB: Views and Perspectives on the Presidency.*

We've billed him as opening a discussion on the Presidents he has known. We thought we'd ask if Richard Strout would begin the discussion and then he knows that many of you have questions. It is an honor to have him with us.

MR. STROUT: It is hard to know where to begin. I think I'll begin with the Model T Ford and say that I was sent down to Washington in Harding's administration. It took me three days to get there in that wonderful car and I loved it beyond any other apparatus I know. I was ushered into my first press conference. And I was in actual touching distance of the President of the United States, Warren G. Harding! He was the handsomest President since George Washington. And he was in plus fours, though they hadn't invented the term then, I think. There was this group of I suppose about thirty newspapermen around his desk and they were asking him hateful questions. They were asking him mean questions. He held up his hand and he said, "Gentlemen, gentlemen, please be gentle with me today, I want to go out and play some golf. Let me go." And they did.

I had then the feeling that you people would have, I think. There was the President of the United States and when I looked at him I could hear subconsciously the "Star Spangled Banner." He was my President, and on the other hand he was a politician. So what does a journalist do? And that is the ambivalent kind of a world in which a Washington correspondent lives. Ultimately, I suppose you would say we take our Presidents for granted and get what we can out of them. They are trying to guard the sheep and we're trying to steal the sheep. We try to get the news and they try to give us the news that is appropriate as they see it.

In my time I've seen twelve Presidents. You've got me down to Mr. Nixon, I think. The greatest President of all, of course, was Franklin Roosevelt. He had altogether just under a thousand press conferences and I suppose I covered most of those. With the exception of four or five I was there physically in the room watching him.

Harding, you all recall. The best description that was given of him was simply that he was a nice, amiable fellow but he was a slob. I think that remark was made by Mrs. Alice Longworth. Nothing more appropriate was ever said about him and you sympathized with him. His great tragedy, of course, was that he was inadequate to the job and knew it, poor fellow. One time—I know this happened; the Press Club then was in the Albee building in Washington and they were playing cards there one evening—an agitated waiter came in and he said, "Please, President Harding is outside and he wonders if he could come in and play a little poker?" And they said they wouldn't object at all. Ah, those were the happy, bygone days when there was "a little Green House, on K Street" and other little houses around and today you go and ask the superintendents of apartments there if they realize what historic mansions they are working in and they've never heard; they didn't know anything about it. They used to deliver liquor—the secret service used to come up with armed guards and deliver liquor to the home of one of these friends of Harding's and he would play there and get away from the Duchess. Those were happy unsophisticated days. There was corruption, yes. After Harding died, it was brought out by Paul Y. Anderson and others but it was a kind of innocent corruption. The cooks were stealing money, they weren't stealing power. Under Nixon it was power they were after.

Harding was succeeded by Coolidge. I never knew any of these Presidents well. I liked them, all except one. My friend Tom Stokes told me one story about Coolidge. At Thanksgiving somebody always sends the President a live turkey and this one came in a hamper. Coolidge actually put the White House cat in the hamper with the turkey—to see what would happen. Nothing much did, I believe. At another time Coolidge was at his great desk alone, surrounded by buzzers, and he pressed them all, all the alarms, and then he got behind a curtain. Crowds of alarmed secret service men came rushing in. He came out from the curtain and they asked why he did it and he said he just wanted to see what would happen.

You know the stories about him better than I do so I won't try to repeat them. Once they asked what the minister had preached about at church? "Sin," Coolidge answered laconically. And what did he say? He "was against it," Coolidge replied.

Then along came poor old Hoover. Hoover was secretary of commerce and we all went down to see a novel device that had just been invented. You could actually watch what somebody was doing in a distant city. I went along as a guest of the secretary of commerce and I got him to sign the program afterwards. It was of course the first unveiling of television and the man at the other end was in New York and he was about the size of a postcard and there he was, you could see him. And the next day the *New York Times* on its front page, in the bank of columns about television said "Commercial Value in Doubt." I prize that very much.

Poor old Hoover was a great tragedy. I liked him. I think I voted for him. He was a victim of the anti-hero plot in a Greek tragedy. He didn't know what had hit him. The gods had turned on him. Once he had been the greatest benefactor in the world, a great person who saved lives in Belgium, and then his world collapsed and he had no idea what to do. He said, "We ought to balance the budget." And he actually put in a tax increase right in the height of that awful collapse. The Depression came just as I was attempting to buy a house in Washington. I remember those dreadful days very well.

And then along came Franklin Roosevelt. I think the thing that astonished me, and I still haven't quite understood it, is why the public did not realize the paralysis that bound him down. I would see him wheeled across in front of the White House to his desk in the morning. He was always jolly and the press would go in and see him twice a week. He'd be behind his desk when we went in. There would be fifty to one hundred reporters and he always had his cigarette holder and smile and would begin "What's the news, boys?" And we would respond, "Why we came here to find that out." Once he looked down and said, "What's that great big fellow from the UP doing there — three people can't see around him. Fred, sit down. That's your seat from now on." And that was Fred Storm of the UP and from there on he always sat there while the rest of us stood. There was a sort of club-like atmosphere. He learned as much from us as we did from him.

People didn't realize how much of a cripple he was. I've wondered if that was the fault of the newspapermen or if we should have dwelt on it more or if what we did was appropriate. But I'd go out with him when he was running for the presidency and he would have to be aided up to the back platform of the presidential special train. It was painful to watch him. He'd take these slow steps. He had iron braces on his hips and he would go up and I can recall the absolute silence that would fall on the crowd as they watched this man, the President of the United States, who could barely walk, and then he would get up to the lectern or back platform and he'd give a big wave, perfectly unaffected, completely natural. And the tension would snap and you could hear the sigh go through the crowd; they would often applaud.

I read books now in which they reproach the journalists for having concealed that and in a sense I think perhaps we did conceal. But after you've said that the President is a cripple for about six months you can't stress his inability to walk every time. I discovered his condition when I first met him. Paul Leach of the *Chicago Daily News* and I were taken to the rear of his special train — where would we have been going, could it have been to Charlottesville, where he made his famous "stab-in-the-back" comment about Mussolini? He interpolated the phrase. It was not in his prepared text. I was there in 1940. The reporters were all seated together. There was a massive crowd of academic types and some as I recollect had gowns and robes. Suddenly there was a commotion among the 50 or 100 newsmen at the press table, "What did he say?" we shouted. Our excitement was communicated to the crowd. He had said something startling and it was flashed round the world.

There are so many of these recollections; it's hard to tell them all. There came a telephone call from a friend who said, "Have you heard what's happened at Pearl Harbor?" I said, "Where's Pearl Harbor?" "The Japanese have attacked us." "What? What?" That was on Sunday afternoon, December 7, 1941, so I went to the White House which as a journalist I had to do. And the press room was in wild turmoil. It was like an ant hive that somebody has kicked. Reporters rushed around. They had actually attacked us at Pearl Harbor. I remember one young reporter. He was in journalistic rapture. He'd sent out three bulletins and one stop-press already. He had never sent a bulletin in his life before. Steve Early was there. Then we gradually accommodated ourselves to the fact that we had been attacked. I and about a dozen other reporters went on to the portico of the White House after dark under the colonnades and waited there. Imagine passing the night of Pearl Harbor under the colonnades of the White House. Pretty soon limousines came up and they were the Senate Foreign Relations Committee and they came in silently and somberly and none of us asked them a question which showed how awed even reporters were. The great isolationist William Borah had died but Senator Hiram Johnson was there, and we didn't ask him a question. And later on they came out again. Johnson had argued before Pearl Harbor that the war was over there in Europe, "Let's leave it there, we can't possibly be attacked," he insisted. But here it was and inside the White House Roosevelt was telling his plans, and next day he made his speech before a joint session of Congress, denouncing a "day that will live in infamy."

At great moments a little crowd always collects in front of the White House. It's always there. It's a stage property and that crowd was there at eleven o'clock at night. All the other scenic properties were there too: there was a skeleton moon seen through the bare branches of the trees. It was a clear night. At the end of it the little crowd down below tried to sing "America the Beautiful," and they couldn't sing "America the Beautiful," and my eyes grew moist.

A week later, I guess it was, we went to a White House press conference and Roosevelt introduced us to Winston Churchill. He had come over—he didn't fly over, he came over on a boat—and there we were in the same room with Franklin Roosevelt and Winston Churchill. What did we do? We shouted, "We can't see you, we can't see you!" I don't know whether we said "Winnie." He stood up in a chair. And what did this man have we wondered that made him a leader of the free world? He looked sort of cherubic. He looked a bit like a Kewpie doll. He began to talk and suddenly used the word "Nazi." His jaw stuck out and he got intimations of loathing and contempt into the word that made us suddenly realize this was actually Winston Churchill. He and Roosevelt got on well and it was a godsend for the free world that they did so.

Harry Truman was next after FDR. I knew his people and his friends. Charlie Ross was a particular friend.

After him came Ike. Everybody liked Ike. America likes a military hero for its President, particularly after the war. But I regretted one thing. I was aboard his special train out in Wisconsin when he omitted a passage praising General George Marshall and he omitted it because Senator McCarthy was on the platform with him who had attacked Marshall as a traitor. I loathed McCarthy. Oddly enough that was the only time I ever got any publicity as a journalist. Somebody ghosted a book for McCarthy and at the beginning he gave an anecdote which was wholly false. McCarthy wrote that as he looked down the committee room in one of his famous hearings he saw Strout of the *Christian Science Monitor* reaching across the table and shaking hands with a correspondent of the communist *Daily Worker*. Well, it wasn't true. I mean it was just a made up story out of spite and it could have done me great harm. I had never been subjected to malice of that sort or believed such could happen in my innocence. There is a new book on McCarthy just out by John Adams in which he shows the statements that he would make and comments of that sort. And McCarthy, we got rid of him thank God, but I think always that McCarthy was a failed demagogue in that basically he had no ideology. He was against communism as a political issue but didn't know what to do with it. He could make these amazing charges! He never arrested a communist. He finally died of alcohol.

Then John F. Kennedy with his Camelot. That was a lovely, glamorous time but it was tragically short.

Lyndon Johnson—I interviewed him one time, I got into an argument with him. He wanted total acceptance; if he was talking to somebody he was not satisfied just to have the man agree, he wanted total approval. As we talked he chanced to say, "I'm not a babe in arms." And he suddenly shot up out from his great chair in the ornate Capitol Hill suite and walked up and down the room as if pacing with a babe in his arms. It was just natural for Johnson to do that.

Nixon—he made the greatest political speech, with the exception of one other, that I ever heard and that was the Checkers speech. A magnificent political speech. He told about "the Republican cloth coat" his wife wore, a Republican cloth coat and little Checkers. It was utterly corny and a complete success.

Ford didn't leave a lasting impression; and then, of course, Carter . . . we all know, both Carter and Reagan.

I come now to my phobia which I bring out about this point every time I speak—that I think we have a terrible government. I think it is a dangerous government and it's going to cause us trouble sometime. I don't know when the trouble is going to come but I think things are speeding up. The danger is greater than it has ever been before. If you go down and enumerate some of the things that we don't do, we haven't had a balanced budget since 1960 with one exception. We have two successive deficits ahead of two hundred billion dollars each. We can't seem to balance the budget. The public, I think, is uneasy. We have had no President who served two terms since Eisenhower. We are going through another interminable presidential elections which lasts—well, you can say they last three years but it is often longer than that. Tomorrow in England they have an election. An election there lasts about six weeks.

I live in Washington, but it's hard to say who's running the government. You can't tell. Is it Congress? Is it the Democratic House? Is it the Republican Senate? Is it the President? Is it his Cabinet? Is it the bureaucracy? If you can't balance a budget, I don't know how you can run a country that way! I'm trying to put it as harshly as I can to stir you and, I trust, challenge you. But Margaret Thatcher gets elected tomorrow. If they change so much as a sentence in the budget that she submits, she will call another election and they will have a prime minister who can pass a budget. We have been trying to balance the budget for two years. We are still trying to balance the budget. We don't have a budget yet.

QUESTION: I think that the press handled Mr. Roosevelt's handicap just right and that I wish we'd see more of that now. I wonder whether the modern press writes more about gossip because its easier to write about gossip or is it a matter of competition among them? Are there too many? Are they trying to get ahead of each other? What's going on?

MR. STROUT: That's worth an hour's talk. The press has changed enormously in my time. When I came to Washington back in 1933 I entered the room one time, the *Christian Science Monitor* office, and I said, "Bob, have you heard about the scurrilous new anonymous book that has just been published that's called *The Merry-Go-Round!*" And he didn't give me a direct answer but a minute later I could hear him pound down the corridor of the 12th floor of the National Press Building, and around the corner to the office of the *Baltimore Sun* where Drew Pearson worked, and he was telling Drew Pearson that the book was out. He had written the book, of course, Drew Pearson and Bob Allen, and that started me off about the press. In those days the press was controlled by the imperial publishers, Hearst and McCormick and Patterson and so forth, and I know this happened again and again. They would get directions from home to attack FDR and they would write it.

Reporters had less freedom of judgment than they have now. But news reporting has become more impersonalized. The press will not be told by the publishers at home what to write but there is a new thing now. You have what I would call the trivialization of the news on television, we're all getting accustomed to short items and bulletins. The newspaper *U.S.A. and World Today* specializes in that. I like news analysis myself.

As to Roosevelt's health I think that the press's obligation is to tell the public what the physical condition of the President is. Whether he is smiling or has a headache or isn't up to his job. But how you go about it, I'm not sure. It's a delicate thing.

QUESTION: By 1940 Mr. Roosevelt was very ill. McIntyre kept giving you bulletins that he was in great shape. Steve Early of course hushed everything up, including getting Hoover in on it to find out where the leak was. Why in 1940 did you not tell the world he was sick?

MR. STROUT: I've asked myself that same question and I don't know the answer to that. I was present at his last inauguration which you remember was held on the balcony of the White House. And there his physical condition was such that he actually had to be lifted up by his son, Jimmy, and the White House guard and put before the lectern and then instantly when he was before the lectern the magic happened. The miracle right before my eyes. And I've asked myself this question because Roscoe Drummond, my friend and my colleague, said, "We all knew he was going to die." And I said, "Did we know that?" I wasn't sure. I thought he was immortal. He had been elected four times.

QUESTION: But you all knew it and didn't report it.

MR. STROUT: No, I didn't know that he was going to die. I didn't know he was that bad, that sick. My testimony is I didn't know and I was deceived.

QUESTION: You see, my point is simply this. There is a tremendous responsibility of the press but there is also the problem that McIntyre had and of course Lord Moran because Churchill had his coronary at the time you are talking about right in Washington. And what's the responsibility of the physician, what's the responsibility of the press?

MR. STROUT: I don't think the physician has any responsibility. I think the physician's responsibility is to the patient but the press certainly has a responsibility for letting us know.

QUESTION: And also the same thing was true of Wilson that the public was fooled about his health.

MR. STROUT: They were fooled about Wilson and again you touch a chord. I was a young man. He had a stroke, though. That cleared the thing up so that then his condition was concealed by his wife.

QUESTION: Did his wife conceal it or did the press conceal it?

MR. STROUT: The story didn't come out in the press but I don't think it was a conscious concealment. I think the press was bewildered and deceived itself.

QUESTION: In your opinion why did President Roosevelt select Senator Truman to succeed him.

MR. STROUT: He thought he was a good man. I take it by your question you disagree with that.

QUESTION: No, I don't.

MR. STROUT: I thought Truman was a very good President.

QUESTION: I think so too.

MR. STROUT: Roosevelt picked Truman to succeed him. He had Marshall in the military and he had two or three other superlative people. His appointments were superb, I thought. I don't want to argue about Truman. Truman made his mistakes. You'll probably recall some of them. He had a good press conference.

QUESTION: Why do you think Truman was so underrated while he was President?

MR. STROUT: I don't know the answer to that. There is a cycle in the public estimation of any President. Roosevelt partly escaped that cycle. A President is elected who is a myth. He doesn't exist. In normal times it takes about two years to discover that this man we've elected President isn't the man we thought he was, and then he goes down, often in the second year. Then about the third year he may reach a stationary point and then the fourth year he comes up again. That was true of Truman. I think Jimmy Carter would be President today if it hadn't been for Iran; and you are going to have the same forces for Mr. Reagan.

QUESTION: What would be your suggestion in improving the political conditions, organizationally or structurally? You've suggested that we have a pretty sorry condition now. What, from your experience, would be a better alternative?

MR. STROUT: I'm awfully pessimistic about this thing. I don't think there is very much we can do except things I know we won't do. But I would have a parliamentary system. Every other successful democracy has a parliamentary system. It isn't a panacea. It won't cure all our problems but I think it will eliminate a lot of dangers. There are organizations that are trying to get this. We don't trust ourselves enough to have a constitutional convention. "Why," they say, "we might have a king!" It's better to keep what we have and we've gone two hundred years under our present system.

Then you get Nixon who is betraying us. And we were defeated in Vietnam! Some other misfortune might come. The Constitution gives the President every power, every military power if we are in some sort of disaster and then I don't know what will happen. I leave it to you. I'm more pessimistic than most: I fear that within eight or ten years we are going to have a demand for blackmail by some terrorist group who is going to say we have the atomic bomb. What are we going to do then? I don't know.

QUESTION: How do you feel about the televising of press conferences?

MR. STROUT: Well, naturally I've thought about it a great deal because I've seen them from the very beginning. The Roosevelt press conferences were quite spontaneous and they were wonderful because we would ask a question and then he would answer and then we would ask a follow-up question. It's the follow-up question that always gets the news. It was more like the parliamentary system where we had an interchange between the questioner and the President. Then there came radio and then finally television. I was against introducing television but it was inevitable, I guess. These breakfasts in Washington that I go to now, they are generally two or three times a week and we've had a lot of talk about handling the news. The breakfasts are informal and pleasant and there are cabinet members sometimes. It's been suggested to the White House that they could get a degree of informality by doing something that they are experimenting with now in which they have a panel of six or eight reporters who ask questions and the direct exchange is piped out to the larger audience in the press room so they follow it and make notes. So that is a sort of a marriage, a compromise between the two. They are experimenting with that. I don't know whether that will work.

I don't think anything compares with just having the opposition party sitting across from Maggie Thatcher and asking her questions and having her give replies. I was in London last summer looking down as a veteran Washington journalist and the exchange was thrilling. You see the same thing in Ottawa or you see it in Scandinavia. You see it anywhere else today, the parliamentary system. They ask polite but harsh questions. I can't think of any comparison to make in America, but for a Washington journalist to look down at this thing [parliament] rouses deep envy. It's the greatest show on earth.

QUESTION: Mr. Strout, I noticed in your opening remarks as soon as you got to Jimmy Carter you began to talk about the system. That was your first mention of the system. Is it Jimmy Carter that particularly makes you feel that way?

MR. STROUT: I always liked Jimmy Carter and my relations with him were quite good. Perhaps friendly is the word. I think he was a man who was trying very, very hard to be a good President, and who had the attributes which would have made him a terrific member of a Cabinet in the parliamentary system but his mind was filled with detail. He lacked those qualities of making people laugh and saying the appropriate thing and winning over a crowd, something that some other Presidents have had but he wasn't a success in that way. But I think some of the things he did, his Panama Canal Treaty was a splendid thing. The Camp David effort was a splendid thing. I wrote a eulogistic piece in the TRB column in the *New Republic* about this, about the coming together of Camp David, and he read it and he invited me to the White House. Alas the accord didn't work out but it broke down some barriers.

QUESTION: Is it possible to reduce the influence of presidential advisers like Baker and Meese and transfer that power to the actual Cabinet?

MR. STROUT: I think my answer would be a brief no. But everybody has tried it and everybody says they are going to. Carter said he was going to re-establish the Cabinet system of government. I've heard that half a dozen times. They are all going to do this. But I think that by the time you run against the power of Congress, or the power of the bureaucracy, the Cabinet will not have that power.

QUESTION: On Monday, we heard a strong argument to the effect that Eisenhower had Cabinet government. Do you think he did?

MR. STROUT: Well, I would argue that either way. He listened to his Cabinet more. I think he was more deferential to his Cabinet. He had strong members in the Cabinet. I suppose when you say Cabinet government, it's a Cabinet which proposes policies and then the President accepts them or rejects them. Yes, I think it was possible to give Eisenhower outside stimulus as to what he should do and he would take it. On the other hand, there were plenty of times when he didn't ask for advice or initiate policies.

QUESTION: Mr. Strout, some very serious students of the presidency including some from this Center have suggested that if the presidency is to be effective the President is going to have to retreat from such an overpowering involvement with day-to-day management of the government and center on a handful of really super important issues and devote his attention and time to managing those issues. My question is if a President came into office with this concept of leadership do you think the press would support him in this effort or would the press's insistence on making him accountable for what happened yesterday in the Office of Management and Budget or the Department of the Interior bring him to his knees if he made the effort?

MR. STROUT: Well, that requires an hour long answer. I think Eisenhower is an example of a President who tried to do something of that sort. On the whole I would say no, I don't think the President can disassociate himself from his other powers. He is the leader of the armies, he makes a budget, and he does all these other things. He has six or seven roles. I don't think he can drop them. Now you singled out the press. I think the question itself shows a misconception. I don't think it's the press that would spoil that. The press would simply report what was going on and then the man in the street would say: do we want the President to devote himself just to one thing and not do another thing? I don't think the public wants it. I think what the public would want perhaps would be a President who was a ceremonial master of state, not master of government, but master of state, and he would sit there and the flag would float behind him and there would be the Lincoln bed and all this would be a shrine and we would be proud of him. Then over here would be the political leader who might be the prime minister or have some other name and he would handle the politics of it. That is the association they have in the parliamentary system. One is political head of government, the other is ceremonial head of state.

QUESTION: By coincidence I did run across a sentence from one of the TRB columns. In 1964 there is this sentence: "It seems to us after long and patient observation that Mr. Johnson has many qualities of greatness. Now it remains to be seen whether he has greatness itself." Would you like to pick that up there?

MR. STROUT: No, I think that's a damn good statement. Who could have put that more succinctly? Well, I can't answer any of these questions without going back and taking a running leap at it. I sat in the press gallery over Johnson's head when he addressed a joint session of Congress and I have all my written notes. It was his famous civil rights speech and I poured my thoughts out on this scrap paper and about the third or fourth page it just says, "I like this President, I like this man." It was the speech he ended with, "We shall overcome." That was his high point as far as I was concerned. I was a liberal and I thought it was magnificent. They applauded that speech forty times. And then of course he made his mistakes. Vietnam was one of them.

How would I rate him? I think this latest book about him is unfair and unjust, Caro's book. I know nothing about Johnson's life. I think under normal times if he hadn't had war on his hands he probably would have done pretty well.

MR. DUMAS MALONE: I personally have been around longer than Mr. Strout.

MR. STROUT: Impossible!

MR. MALONE: I was not living in Washington at the time but I was in Washington during the Harding regime.

MR. STROUT: Who was your first President?

MR. MALONE: The first President that I knew?

MR. STROUT: That was in Office when you were aware of him, was it Wilson?

MR. MALONE: Oh no, it was Theodore Roosevelt.

MR. STROUT: Oh, really?

MR. MALONE: The first political view I remember ever seeing was the election of 1904, the Roosevelt landslide. I was 12 years old.

MR. STROUT: In 1904 I was six years old and my father had me distribute throwaways at the Avenue C station of the Brooklyn

Rapid Transit railroad about Roosevelt. Vote Democrat or vote Republican or vote something or other.

MR. MALONE: When I was living in Washington later on, I belonged to what was known as The Literary Society. I don't know if you ever heard of it. And one of the members of the Society was a cartoonist, Berryman. The father of the more recent Berryman. He went back to the days of Harrison and Cleveland. Once at a meeting of The Literary Society he gave an illustrated speech on "The Presidents I Have Known." And they said of all these Presidents you have known which one was the nicest guy, which one did you like the best? And he said, "Harding."

MR. STROUT: That would be justified. He was also a newspaper publisher and he felt a professional feeling there, I guess.

MR. MALONE: I share your great concern about the state of our political mechanism. I think it's terrible. I think we are ripe for a constitutional convention but nothing would terrify me more. I would be scared to death of what they would do and wouldn't know what to do.

MR. STROUT: Would you vote for it or against it?

MR. MALONE: I think I would vote for it but I would be scared to death and I wouldn't know what in the world would happen to it after they got through. If they did what they ought to do, I don't know whether the public would accept it or not. So I'm awfully depressed about the possibility.

MR. STROUT: A continuation of this argument will appear ultimately in Bill Moyer's not yet published series of interviews with thirty public people of whom I am number two.

MR. MALONE: Speaking in terms of the immediate situation I wish you would make some comments on the Reagan revolution.

MR. STROUT: I think a sitting journalist is not required to make comments about the President in office. I can say there are things I like more and things I like less about him. I can attest to the things I like more in his personality. He is a very pleasant, nice fellow. On his political philosophy I often disagree with him. But as a sitting journalist I think I can't go beyond that.

MR. MALONE: I was thinking about the effect of his attempts to reduce the functions of government.

MR. STROUT: Oh, I don't think that can be done. No I've been here long enough so that I think the tide is the other way. I've been here long enough and you have, too, just to see that opposite thing going on all the time and you say can it go any further than it has and I think yes, it can go further.

NARRATOR: We thank all of you very much, not least our friends who voted for Theodore Roosevelt or Woodrow Wilson.

Woodrow Wilson and the Press

GEORGE JUERGENS

THOMPSON: Professor George Juergens is a leading historian at Indiana University. He is undertaking a major review of the presidency and the press and has published a first book on the progressive presidents. He is continuing his work with a second volume on Franklin D. Roosevelt. He has had grants from a number of foundations, including the Rockefeller Foundation. We thought since we may not have done Woodrow Wilson justice, or the period he represents, that it would be good to start out with a discussion of Wilson and the press.

JUERGENS: Thank you, Dr. Thompson, and thank you for inviting me to participate in this session at the Miller Center. It's a pleasure to be here.

In discussing Woodrow Wilson's dealings with the press, it seems to me that we have to balance contradictory themes. On the one hand, he was a brilliant publicist, someone whose effectiveness in advertising himself and his causes made him a dominating political presence in the Progressive era. In the sense of using publicity as a vehicle for power, he easily belongs with Theodore Roosevelt and Franklin Roosevelt as one of the giants who laid the foundation for the modern presidency. On the other hand, throughout his public career Wilson was handicapped by an inability to adjust to the demands of popular journalism, and even by a blindness as to what the role of the press is in a democracy. For a long while he succeeded in compensating for those weaknesses. In the end, as I will argue, they contributed to his defeat on the issue he cared about above all others: American involvement in the League of Nations.

What caused the abrasions between Wilson and reporters? How did he manage to adjust? Why did the abrasions matter in the long run? These are the questions I propose to address in the time available to me. I hope in our discussion later my comments will have some bearing on the presidency of today.

A way to start is to say that in one sense the problem between Wilson and the press was as complicated as human personality itself. Bear in mind that we speak about a figure who had been involved in politics for barely a year when he set out to win his party's presidential nomination. A lifetime spent as a college professor and college president—and at Princeton, no less, hardly one of your places for the *hoi polloi*—was not the best preparation for dealing with reporters whose police court origins were not that far behind them. They were a down-to-earth lot, even boisterous on occasion, who looked for the common touch in the men they covered. They admired colorfulness more than dignity, horse sense more than high-flown wisdom. Wilson had never met their kind at Princeton and didn't know quite what to make of them. Part of the reason he and the press clashed is that they were strangers to one another.

Their differences could easily have been bridged, however, but for the more serious problem of Wilson's austere personality. He was a man of enormous reserve, one who without intending it gave the impression of somehow being apart from the rest of humanity. Even at his best moments, the quality of remoteness was always there. As one historian has pointed out, Wilson enjoyed great popularity as a teacher at Princeton, but for his ability in lecturing to large groups, not in handling the give and take of small classes. As a political leader he moved audiences with his eloquence; he rarely warmed them by his presence. The contrast between Americans calling Theodore Roosevelt "Teddy" (a nickname he detested, by the way) but Woodrow Wilson seldom "Woody" conveys the difference. He was not the sort of person newsmen would naturally take to, nor the sort who would even try to win them over.

Compound personal differences with clash over news values and the problem deepens. The disagreement took many forms. In its most mundane aspect—but no less deeply and bitterly felt for all that—it had to do with coverage of the Wilson family. The issue, of course, is a perennial one in American life. Presidents, like anyone else, want some privacy; at the same time public interest in the family that fills an almost symbolic role has the press constantly digging for more information and, when the information is not freely given, making do with speculation about what might be. The result is invariably tension between presidents and the press. In Wilson's case, however, the tension reached unprecedented heights because of the kind of man he was. His reserve and high sense of dignity would have made this aspect of public life an ordeal even if he alone had been in the spotlight. He nearly cracked upon seeing his beloved wife and daughters subjected to the treatment. Wilson, after all, was a Southerner. He worshiped women in the old-fashioned way, thinking of them as innately pure and finer creatures to be shielded from the world outside. It was almost more than he could bear to have what he regarded as the coarse and ill-mannered denizens of the press hounding his ladies, and as if that were not enough, speculating about their personal affairs in public print.

The troubles began immediately after Wilson's nomination when a horde of reporters descended on his summer home in Sea Girt, New Jersey, looking for human interest material on the candidate's wife and daughters. The Wilsons, all of them, were pathetically unprepared for the persistence and brazeness of the questioning. As the President's middle daughter, Eleanor, recalled,

> We, who had been taught to be closed-mouthed about our family affairs, found this prying into our lives strange and annoying. They did not hesitate to question us about any and every detail of our lives. What were our favorite colors, occupation, sports? Did we like to dance? Were we in love or engaged? Did we intend to marry and, if so, when?

The loyal Eleanor traced her father's troubles with the press to the trauma of those first interviews. As she wrote, "He resented almost fiercely the attempts to pry into family affairs and tried to protect us as much as he could. I've always believed that the first rumors of his 'aloofness' and 'unfriendliness' were the result of his annoyance at this first onslaught upon us." Perhaps, and then again, perhaps not. The important point is that the onslaught never stopped, and Wilson—who had to suffer in coming years through press coverage of two daughters' engagements and weddings, the concert career of a third daughter, the illness and death of his wife, the courtship

of Mrs. Galt and controversial marriage to her—never got over his
bitterness against prying reporters.

Wilson's misunderstanding, or perhaps it was stubbornness,
about another way in which journalism works caused still more
tensions between him and White House correspondents. He thought
of news as the announcement of a decision made or a step taken,
which it was the responsibility of the press to convey without
comment or interpolation. Reporters, as far as he was concerned,
had no business speculating about what might happen, or printing
information before it had been officially released. Of course newspapers run on that basis would be little more than bulletins for the
administration in power. The responsibility for keeping the public
informed assumes that stories will often be published that government leaders would prefer to remain under wraps. It also assumes
that reporters will enter the picture while decisions are being made
so that the people can have some voice in the process, rather than
always being presented with a *fait accompli*. Wilson was hardly
unique among presidents in wanting the press to be little more
than a conveyor belt passing along his statements as provided. But
he more than most chose to make an issue of the matter, and in the
process deepened the chill in his relations with reporters.

Again, the troubles started even before the inauguration. Wilson
was enraged, for example, to the extent of blowing up altogether at
a couple of press briefings because of the attempts by newsmen to
ferret out the names of his cabinet appointees before he was ready
to make the announcement. Indeed, like Lyndon Johnson decades
later, he gave the press something of a veto power over who found
places in the administration—an unwelcome power, I might add—by
refusing to follow through on appointments if newspapers got wind
of the names first.

Still another area of contention—one that may have mattered
most of all—was the sense among reporters that Wilson's word
could not be trusted. They felt early on, and became more convinced with the passage of time, that the things he said to them
were often calculated to deceive. Not that he typically engaged in
outright lies. Wilson's usual tactic when he wanted to throw up a
smokescreen was to respond with the truth, but the truth expressed
in such a way that listeners could easily be fooled. "It was impossible to rely on anything he said," a *New York Times* reporter
wrote (incidentally, the reporter happened to be a Wilson admirer).

"I do not mean he lied. I mean that he took such an intellectual pleasure in stating a thing so as to give an opposite impression to the fact, though he kept strictly to the truth, that one had to be constantly on the alert to keep from being misled." The problem with playing Wilson's kind of "intellectual" game is that it made him too clever by half in the eyes of the press. Reporters then as now are likely to put up with any number of peccadillos in public figures, and perhaps even be amused by them. What they cannot accept is a politician, particularly when he is President of the United States, whose word cannot be accepted at face value. Wilson struck them as such a man.

All of which is to say that by the time of his inauguration in March 1913, Woodrow Wilson was thoroughly disillusioned with the press, and the press thoroughly disillusioned with Woodrow Wilson. Indeed, I can think of no twentieth century president—with the obvious exception of Richard Nixon, in all things a story unto himself—who entered office more estranged from working reporters.

It is ironic, considering that one of his first steps as President was to institute regular press conferences at the White House, an innovation that did much to enhance the status of Washington correspondents, and that for decades afterwards provided the mechanism for frequent contact between presidents and press. The further irony is that he took the step in large part because of how he felt about reporters.

The seeming contradiction is easily explained. Wilson was much too shrewd a student of government to underestimate the importance of publicity for the person who presides in the Oval Office. Long before he entered public life he had made the point in several scholarly works that leadership in a democracy depends on the ability to influence public opinion. At one time he assumed that the legislative branch, being closer to the people, could do it best. His thought changed, largely under the influence of Theodore Roosevelt's presidency, when he recognized the unique opportunities available to a president to get his message across. As he wrote in *Constitutional Government in the United States,* published in 1908, " . . . that part of the government which has the most direct access to opinion has the best chance of leadership and mastery; and at present that part is the President." With his own election the moral was inescapable. To be a strong president he would have to rally the people behind him, explaining to them what he was trying to accomplish in order to win their support. And since the newspaper represented his primary medium of communication, it made sense to do what he could to influence what appeared about him in newspapers.

By the same token he also knew that he couldn't manage his press relations in the way Theodore Roosevelt had, by seeing reporters almost every day, either individually or in small groups, for personal chats. Aside from the physical strain, and Wilson had never been a robust individual, it seemed silly to have to repeat his points over and over again in individual conversations. He might have felt differently if, like Roosevelt, he had enjoyed the company of newsmen. In that case, seeing them could be a welcome break in the daily routine. But since he didn't like most newsmen, he needed a different way to stay in touch with them while minimizing the aggravation they caused him. The press conference, an idea most likely suggested to him by his secretary, Joseph Tumulty, provided the answer. He would strive to lead public opinion by meeting regularly each week with reporters to answer their questions, which presumably were the questions on the minds of the citizenry. At the same time, he would keep reporters at least somewhat at a distance by seeing them all at once, and pretty well restricting his availability to these formal and, he hoped, businesslike sessions. Respect for the people he would be meeting with had nothing to do with the decision. If anything, he made the move despite his feelings about journalists.

All things considered, perhaps it is not surprising that the conferences never worked well. Wilson was appalled by the petty, personal, uninformed questions many reporters asked. In fairness to him, he dealt with a press corps far less educated and qualified than Washington correspondents of today, and he often had good reason to be upset. So did he resent the attempts by newsmen to badger him into making information available before he was ready to do so. They never seemed to learn that he intended to be the one to decide what news got out and when. He felt particularly strongly on the matter in foreign affairs, an area where as far as he was concerned the press could only cause mischief, and therefore had no business intruding. It didn't lead to notably fruitful exchanges in the conferences.

There was always a very cool reserve, (a former associate wrote) and Wilson gave the impression that he was the best judge of what was proper for the newspapers to have. He was saving mankind, and he would let the world know about it in his own good time. He certainly did not believe in government by newspapers, and it was his policy that the newspapers should not know of any transaction until it was accomplished.

If the President's failure to be forthcoming hardly endeared him to the press, his air of aloof superiority did nothing to help matters. To their annoyance, the reporters felt like schoolboys apprehensive about being in the presence of a haughty headmaster. Worse, they got the sense (reading Wilson correctly as it turned out) that he didn't regard them as particularly bright pupils. It is one thing to be treated with chill formality, and another to be cast as a dullard. Wilson had a way of doing that, to the discomfort of experienced journalists as well as those just starting out.

Perhaps the fundamental problem, underlying all others, was that Wilson had little sense of how to structure the conferences to serve his publicity purposes. He rarely used opening statements to generate news and suggest a line of inquiry for reporters to follow. He didn't plant questions with cooperative newsmen. By and large he didn't excel at turning questions around to hold forth on what he really wanted to discuss. His press conferences belonged mainly to the reporters to do with as they liked. When he didn't approve of the direction in which they wanted to go, which was most of the time, he simply clammed up.

Considering the hard feelings these sessions caused for all concerned, it is little wonder that they came to a limping end. Wilson started out by meeting the press twice a week. Twenty-one months into his administration, in December 1914, he cut back to one conference a week. Seven months later, in July 1915, seizing on the *Lusitania* crisis as an excuse, he abandoned the experiment altogether. The press conferences lasted less than two-and-a-half years out of the eight years of Wilson's presidency. After dropping them he met with reporters in a body on only three occasions in the second term to urge support for the League of Nations.

My point is not to minimize the significance of Wilson's experiment. He established a precedent that his successor in the

White House came back to, and then the next president, and the president following. By the time Franklin Roosevelt had completed twelve years in office, holding to a remarkably consistent schedule of two meetings a week with reporters, the conferences had ceased to be an option available to presidents and developed as an important institution in their own right; an institution that many observers, incorrectly I believe, went so far as to compare to the parliamentary question period in Great Britain.

The fact remains that Wilson, the president who started it all, derived little publicity benefit himself from the conferences. If anything, they may on balance have been a liability in exacerbating his already strained relationship with reporters. This human dimension in the dealings between presidents and the press should not be ignored. What I'm about to say might be challenged later, but it seems to me that while a personally popular president may receive rough treatment at the hands of journalists (Harry Truman is perhaps an example), the chances of a personally unpopular president receiving favorable treatment are much more remote. In those cases the judgments about performance in office are colored, necessarily so, by the dislike for the sort of man he is. For the great majority of reporters, Wilson's conferences succeeded mainly in confirming how much they in fact disliked him.

And yet for most of his years in office he received a good press. What did he have going for him? It didn't hurt that he came to office at a time of relative prosperity, and presided over a popular program, and succeeded with great political skill in getting that program enacted. William Howard Taft, by contrast, lost enormous credibility in the first months of his administration by failing to deliver on the promise of tariff reform. Wilson showed he was made of different stuff by barely settling into the Oval Office before he had taken on the lobbyists and pressured Congress into passing the Underwood Tariff, the first significant reduction in duties since the Civil War. It is extremely difficult to take potshots at the man in the White House when the people are happy with what he is doing, and contented with their own lot in life.

Wilson's formidable skills as an orator provided a further source of strength. Through the spoken word he was able, at least to an extent, to reach out directly to the public and pretty well require that the press pay respectful attention. Particularly when he did something so dramatic as revive a practice that had been abandoned since John Adams by appearing periodically in person to address the joint houses of Congress. It was impossible not to give such speeches saturation coverage. The country was fascinated. And once he had the attention of the national audience, Wilson demonstrated time and again his ability to elevate the spirit through noble thoughts eloquently expressed. Reporters, even if they disliked him could do little against that kind of clout.

During the first term, before his fall from influence, Joseph Tumulty also helped a great deal. Part of the reason is that reporters liked Tumulty just about as much as they disliked his boss. In almost every respect he was Wilson's opposite as a human being (which is odd considering the close bond between the two men). To a legion of admirers, Tumulty summed up everything best in the stereotypical figure of the warm-hearted Irishman. He was funloving, witty, marvelous at telling Irish-dialect stories, generous, compassionate. Tumulty performed many publicity functions for the President. He conducted daily briefings for the press, and with great skill. He knew how to pace the news, how to build up forthcoming events, how to float trial balloons, how to milk all the drama out of a human interest story. Wilson used him as a sounding board for his speeches, and relied heavily on his deft reading of trends in public opinion. Perhaps his foremost contribution, however, and also the one most difficult to pin down, was simply in making friends of Washington correspondents. As a surrogate the secretary could only accomplish so much, but he was able to say, in effect, to reporters, "Come on, the old man's not so bad," and have some influence. So the correspondents recognized, themselves, in the words of one of them who covered the White House at the time, "There is no use denying that 'Joe' puts over many a thing that [would be treated differently] lacking the power of the personal equation."

Finally, American involvement in World War I gave Wilson an enormous publicity advantage. It was not simply that national leaders tend to be beyond criticism when the wars they preside over are going well, although that factor weighed heavily enough. With the establishment of the Committee on Public Information to handle government propaganda, the executive branch did something that had never been done before, and that Congress would specifically forbid the Office of War Information from trying again during World War II. Under George Creel, the Committee pitched its message about American unity and idealism and purpose around the figure of Woodrow Wilson, Commander-in-Chief. Boy Scouts were enlisted to distribute millions of copies of his speeches door to door. Every teacher in the country, 600,000 of them, received a biweekly newspaper from the Committee with suggestions on how to incorporate the theme of Wilsonian idealism into the school curriculum. The so-called "Four Minute Men" delivered over one million talks on the same theme at movie houses and churches and social clubs, reaching an estimated total audience of four hundred million people (which is not bad considering that the population of the country at the time ws only one hundred million). For nineteen months of war Woodrow Wilson symbolized the goodness and inner convictions of America. Which is to say, he stood above politics on a plateau hitherto reserved for presidents safely dead. You can't ask for better publicity than that.

And yet, in the end, publicity—or more precisely, estrangement from the working press—contributed to his downfall. By the time he went to Paris to negotiate the treaty that he hoped would end all wars, many of the old sources of strength were gone. At the insistence of Congress the Committee on Public Information was forced to rapidly dismantle its operations. Joseph Tumulty had long since been stripped of his publicity function, and if the second Mrs. Wilson and Colonel Edward House, the President's chief aide, had their way, he would have been forced out of the administration altogether. (Mrs. Wilson regarded Tumulty as common and vulgar; not the sort of person a refined man like her husband should have as a close associate. She also bitterly resented that Tumulty had urged the President to put off remarrying until after the 1916 election.) At this juncture not even the magic with words offered much of an advantage. Wilson obviously could not address his countrymen from three thousand miles away, and in any event by 1919 the years had taken their physical toll and he was no longer the orator he had once been.

The moral was inescapable. To win support for his cherished League of Nations the President had no choice but to put old animosities behind him and work closely with reporters, explaining to them the importance of American involvement in the League so that their dispatches might, in turn, educate the country. This he failed to do. Instead, he acquiesced in the news blackout that poisoned the atmosphere at the Peace Conference, and encouraged a drumbeat of negative dispatches back to the United States. His aides recognized what was happening and pleaded with him to repair the damage by making himself available to the press. He refused, partly because time in Paris was precious and the strength for any extra chore just about nonexistent, and partly because he thought that if necessary he could rally the country by going on a speaking tour once he returned home.

It is a nice question whether minds are won that easily, but we never found out. You all know what happened. Wilson suffered a stroke on the tour that forced him to cancel his remaining engagements and rush back to Washington. A second massive stroke a few days after his return crippled him. During the long ratification struggle in the Senate, many reporters got their revenge against a president they resented by cooperating actively with the Irreconcilables in lobbying against the treaty. Public opinion, which had started out cautiously in favor of the League, slowly turned. In November 1919, the Treaty and the League it encompassed were decisively rejected. The education conducted over many months in newspapers that might have made the difference never took place. Wilson's tragic inability to work at first hand with reporters finally mattered.

KILPATRICK: I'd like to say I thought it was a superb paper. I thought I knew a little about Wilson but I certainly didn't know anything about his press operation. I thought that Lyndon Johnson and Wilson were the two most opposite presidents in every way, and now I find that there is a great parallel.

JUERGENS: There are certain parallels, although I think of Lyndon Johnson as a rather crude man and, whatever we would say about Wilson, he wasn't crude. One of the problems we have is that the transcripts of the conferences are not complete. They are more like minutes than verbatim transcripts, so it's difficult to say exactly who asked what and how he was answered. But as you read through those transcripts, it's remarkable to what extent in conference after conference virtually nothing of substance was said.

SCHERER: He didn't use it to make news? He didn't come in with announcements?

JUERGENS: No, and that's an important point. I happen to believe that the first president who knew how to do that, and he remains perhaps the all-time champion at the art, was Franklin Roosevelt. But Wilson knew nothing about using opening statements as a way to make news and to influence what questions he would be asked. Now, I don't think we can speak in black and white terms. There were one or two occasions where he did use the press conference effectively. One occasion in particular comes to mind, although I think it's revealing that it was very early in his presidency, in the first six to eight weeks. Some reporter asked him about the revolution in Mexico, and on this occasion Wilson had the good sense to respond, "Look, why don't you ask a good question? Why don't you ask a question about something closer to home? Ask me a question about all these lobbyists who are descending on Washington trying to defeat tariff reform. You can't throw a brick without hitting one of them." He then held forth on the lobbyists and generated good news. That's a case of his using conferences the way they could be used, but there were only a few such occasions in his presidency.

SCHERER: What was the physical setting? Was he seated at his desk in the Oval Office?

JUERGENS: He sometimes received the press standing behind his desk, but he also used the East Room.

LATIMER: Were there any ground rules about direct quotes?

JUERGENS: You couldn't quote him directly unless he gave formal permission, and then he preferred the quote to come in a written release. In this regard, his practice was very close to Franklin Roosevelt's. On the occasion with the lobbyists, for example, when the reporters asked for permission to quote him, he said, "Well, I'll give you something in a little while." He wrote out the answer and had Tumulty issue it as a release. Otherwise the correspondents had to use indirect attribution. But at least they could cite the President as their source. The "White House spokesmen" euphemism didn't come along until the Coolidge years.

LATIMER: How big were these conferences? About how many people were there?

JUERGENS: The first two conferences drew an enormous number of people—well over a hundred, getting close to two hundred— which was remarkable considering the size of the press corps in 1913. Many reporters, including some who were close to Wilson, said that he seemed to be almost appalled by the size of the turnout. He gave the impression of being taken aback at seeing all of those people present. Of course, as the conferences became what they became, attendance dropped precipitously, and toward the end you'd have maybe twenty people showing up.

SCHERER: I'd like to pose the question of whether Wilson would have been more effective if he had had radio or television. The new technology, would it have made a difference? He seemed to have a particular animus toward the writing press and looked down his nose at them.

JUERGENS: Of course there's no way of knowing, but there are historians who argue that if he had had radio rather than having to go on that speaking tour, it might have made a difference regarding American involvement in the League. After all, he was a marvelous speaker, and for purposes of argument we can assume that he would have been as effective on radio as he was on the public platform. I don't know. Here I must defer to you gentlemen, but I tend to be dubious. It strikes me that you don't change minds overnight. I think that a selling campaign, particularly on something as profound as America changing its whole history by entering the League of Nations, would have required more than three or four radio talks. And he couldn't have done more than three or four without dissipating their impact. I think the job was something that has to be accomplished over months. After all, he had to deal with senators who are elected for six years. Even if Wilson impressed some of their constituents back home, senators have a certain staying power to resist constituent pressure. In order to win, Wilson would have had to start the selling campaign early in 1919; instead, he waited until the end of the summer.

SCHERER: The curious thing that comes out in your presentation is how this mutual personal animus was apparently heavily reflected in what they wrote, and they actively got in league with the opposing senators. He then began to look on the press as an enemy.

JUERGENS: I gather that when American reporters went to Paris, although there was the long history of animus between them and the President, for reasons of simple patriotism they were ready to write pro-Wilson articles. All the more because when they got there they saw a French press that struck them as a captive press.

From the beginning they yearned to be spoken to so that they could present the American side. That in a way compounded their disillusionment; they wanted to help and they couldn't. Of course there was also the disillusionment in taking the first of fourteen points literally. It was probably naive of them, but they thought that Wilson literally meant "open covenants openly arrived at." They seemed to think that somehow the press would be covering secret conversations between Lloyd George and Wilson. So there was a sense of betrayal. Far from having open covenants openly arrived at, the conference was closed down to them. Whatever news came out, came out through leaks. The results were reports from Paris that in effect said—and I think this hurt—"It's not a brave new world; it's the same old thing of secret diplomacy for selfish gains." What I am trying to suggest is that Wilson needed publicity on the theme, "We're in the process of building something that mankind has never attempted before, an international organization." Instead he got news reports that told America, "It's the same old game."

BLACKFORD: But in fact, that is what it was. It was Smuts who said that the Treaty of Versailles is the peace that passeth understanding.

JUERGENS: I think it was also a peace treaty that fell between every considerable stool. I think that Wilson undoubtedly was trying to build a new world—

BLACKFORD: Lloyd George and Clemenceau weren't.

JUERGENS: No, they weren't, but of course he tugged them and they tugged him, and that's how you ended up between stools.

THOMPSON: Do any of his press conferences show what Keynes and others were later to criticize him for on the Peace Treaty, lack of interest in detail? Was that any problem with reporters?

JUERGENS: Bear in mind that he had only two or three conferences in the second term, so there were only two or three that would touch on the Treaty at all. One of those conferences he held just before he sailed back to the United States for a visit midway through the conference. He met with reporters at the dockside, and responded rather flippantly to a question of enormous emotional significance at the time. He was asked about the freedom of the seas point, and he said in a kidding way,

Well, I suddenly realized when I got here that the joke's on me. The freedom of the seas issue is irrelevant because you only have to worry about freedom of the seas when you don't have an international organization, and we're going to have the League of Nations. So freedom of the seas isn't a problem.

Someone asked him if the British gave him that line, a sort of hostile question, and he laughed and said, "No, I thought that one up all by myself." The point is that the dispatches about the press conference suggested that on an issue of enormous importance to most Americans—after all, we'd gotten into the war because of freedom of the seas—Wilson was being a little cavalier.

BLACKFORD: I have an essay by John Milton Cooper called "Woodrow Wilson: The Academic Man" in which he points out that Wilson really didn't have all that much interest in detail, that he was not of the real Johns Hopkins/German school of scholarship and he did not really like working with graduate students. I was wondering if this academic background could have any effect on his later relations with the press?

JUERGENS: Well, I think it did from the point of view of making him excessively cultured in the eyes of the press. But you're quite right; I also think there's a great myth about Wilson. We think of Wilson the intellectual, Wilson the scholar. That's not altogether so. He wrote his doctoral dissertation on Congress while at Johns Hopkins, in Baltimore, and in the writing of it never once went to Washington to research on the spot what Congress was actually about. He wasn't interested in that sort of detail. When the book was published, his fiancee—who became the first Mrs. Wilson—wrote to him saying, "You should feel triumphant. Why are you so depressed?" And he wrote back to her, "I don't want this. Scholarship doesn't interest me. I want to lead people." Theodore Roosevelt was in many ways an intellectual; he read voraciously and widely. Woodrow Wilson pretty well confined himself to detective novels.

SCHERER: Did the relationship between Wilson and the whole press corps go sour? Did he not have one defender? One single columnist?

JUERGENS: Yes. Here, once again, in the short time available I'm making things too one-sided. There were certainly people who respected him. Richard Oulahan covered him for the *New York Times,* and there was sentiment on the paper that he should be relieved of the assignment because he struck some editors as excessively pro-Wilson. Walter Lippmann and Wilson also respected each other. Wilson regarded Lippmann as a bright man. He didn't think of all newsmen as nincompoops, and several of the correspondents respected Wilson in turn.

KILPATRICK: But Lippmann at the time was not an active correspondent; he was really working for Wilson most of that time.

JUERGENS: He joined the government in World War I.

THOMPSON: Then he broke.

KILPATRICK: He was a great admirer and then he broke. Would you agree that in talking about Wilson's not taking the press into his confidence while he was in Paris, his contempt for the press was one factor, and another was his feeling that he could always go out on the stump and sway the people with a great speech? He could get home and he could turn things around.

JUERGENS: That was a major factor, and something I didn't hit hard enough, a third factor is that Wilson believed that the press had no business covering a subject until the decisions had been made. He felt particularly strongly in that regard when it came to foreign affairs. Right along he felt that all the press can do in writing about foreign affairs before the agreement is made is muck things up. So if he kept reporters at arm's length, one of the reasons is that he thought it would be poison to bring them in.

KILPATRICK: Or the Senate into it.

JUERGENS: Or the Senate.

KILPATRICK: That was the fatal error.

JUERGENS: That hurt a lot.

DONOVAN: May I ask a question? How much influence do you think the second Mrs. Wilson had in Paris, in keeping him away from the press?

JUERGENS: I think she had a certain influence, because bear in mind, he may have suffered a stroke in Paris, and was certainly dreadfully ill. Several accounts describe as almost pathetic the scene of him emerging from the working sessions. Lloyd George would stalk out hale and hearty, while Wilson could barely make it to a couch before he had to sit down to catch his breath. My point is that Mrs. Wilson was concerned first of all with protecting her husband's health. It wasn't only the press. She wanted to keep everybody away from him as much as possible, including key members of the American delegation, so he would have a chance to rest. I think that was a factor.

JONES: I wondered whether he viewed the magazine people any differently from the newspaper people, or were these the same people at this time?

JUERGENS: They were essentially the same people, and I'm not sure that he viewed them differently.

THOMPSON: We've been told that Teddy Roosevelt called the reporters in from the rain, and that began the press conference. Is there any substantiation of that in Wilson's explanation of where he got the idea?

JUERGENS: No. He seems to have hit upon the idea independently, with Tumulty perhaps providing a nudge. I think, though, that Theodore Roosevelt had an enormous influence upon Wilson. The two men were great rivals and Wilson chortled any time he came up with something that Theodore Roosevelt hadn't thought about. But what Theodore Roosevelt did teach Wilson was that if you're imaginative you can own the headlines. And owning the headlines means power. Theodore Roosevelt redefined for Wilson the nature of American government in demonstrating the publicity powers of the presidency.

Franklin Delano Roosevelt and the Press
CHALMERS ROBERTS

\

THOMPSON: Now let's begin discussion of the other Roosevelt. FDR did quite a bit toward demonstrating the publicity powers of the presidency, too. Chalmers Roberts is one of America's foremost journalists, a columnist for the *Washington Post* and author of a number of books.

ROBERTS: Thank you. On Tuesday, May 18, 1937, President Roosevelt began his 367th press conference by saying,

> I am going to ask you for a very few minutes to resolve ourselves into a Committee of the Whole. Off the record, wholly off the record. I wanted to tell you a story that I think you ought to know because it does affect the press of the country. I think you will all agree on that, when you hear what I am going to read. As you know, I have always encouraged, and am entirely in favor of, absolute freedom for all news writers. That should be and will continue to be the general rule in Washington.

What FDR went on to say was this: The McClure Syndicate circulated to some 270 newspapers each week a pink sheet containing information for editors, a sort of confidential news tip sheet. This was in addition to so-called white sheets, stories intended for publication. The President then read from the latest pink sheet, to wit:

> Unchecked. A New York specialist high in the medical field is authority for the following, which is given in the strictist confidence to editors: Toward the end of last month Mr. Roosevelt was found in a coma at his desk.

185

Medical examination disclosed the neck rash which is typical of certain disturbing symptoms. Immediate treatment of the most skilled kind was indicated, with complete privacy and detachment from official duties. Hence the trip to southern waters, with no newspapermen on board and a naval convoy which cannot be penetrated.

The unusual activities of Vice President Garner are believed to be in connection with the current situation and its possible developments. "Checking has been impossible."

Roosevelt then read a second item, also from the syndicate. It concerned a private dinner in New York at which an official of American Cynamid had called the President "the paranoiac in the White House," and had gone on to declare that, "a couple of well placed bullets would be the best thing for the country, and that he for one would buy a bottle of champagne as quick as he could get it to celebrate such news."

There followed some give and take between FDR and the reporters during which the President said that the editor of the offending syndicate was one Richard Waldo. At one point a reporter asked: "Isn't that second one (the second item) actionable under law?"

To which FDR replied: "You know, that does not make any difference at all. The President of the United States does not sue for libel and the Department of Justice does not proceed for libel."

After taking up about half the press conference time, that is, about fifteen minutes I would estimate, FDR reiterated that, "It is all off the record; all strictly in the family and nothing else." And finally he said, "The Committee (of the Whole) will now recess." Whereupon the President went on to talk about and take questions on the topical issues of the day.

To the best of my knowledge all of the two hundred or so reporters—and they included a few, very few, women—observed FDR's off-the-record rule. Nothing appeared in the public prints or on radio newscasts. This was pretelevision, of course. Everybody in town naturally soon heard all about it by word of mouth. Some indignant members of the press struck at Richard Waldo, the offending editor, by having the National Press Club's board of governors call on him to show cause why he should not be expelled for insulting a fellow member—FDR. Waldo appeared—and here I quote from Oliver Clapper's 1946 book—

and threatened each board member with libel action, declaring that their homes, savings, et cetera, would be seized if he won. The board members naturally hesitated. No formal action ever was taken but Mr. Waldo nevertheless went out of the club.

I assume he resigned.

I have cited this incident in some detail because I think it tells us a great deal, in retrospect, about the relationship between FDR and the press.

My premise today is that FDR was the best presidential communicator—to use the current term—in modern times. His honeymoon with the press lasted about two years, an extraordinary length of time. But the honeymoon did end and the normal press-president adversary relationship came into play. The approach of World War II sharpened antagonisms prior to Pearl Harbor; afterwards, both a sense of patriotism and military censorship widened the gap between press and president until his death.

In reflecting on FDR and the press, I think it is vital to go back to the beginning of his first term. I did not come to Washington until October 1933, seven months after his inauguration, but the mood I describe here was instantly evident to even a cub reporter just out of college earning fifteen dollars a week on the *Washington Post*.

You must remember that by 1933, as historian John Morton Blum has put it, "... the presidency had lost the stature that Theodore Roosevelt and Wilson had given it." In the Harding-Coolidge era of the 1920's, New York, not Washington, dominated the nation. The Great Depression brought demands for federal action, largely resisted by President Hoover. By the end of Hoover's term, with the depth of the Depression, relations between president and press were absymal, just about nonexistent. So when FDR moved down from Albany his opportunity to change that relationship, and to do so to his advantage, was immense—and he seized that opportunity.

At his first press conference a few days after his inauguration each of the two hundred or so who crowded into the Oval Office was introduced to the President, who shook hands. Some he recognized from Albany of the campaign and he called them by their first names. You must remember that he was seated behind his desk which made it difficult for those in the back to hear, and just about impossible to see him. I know because at times I stood in the back rows, in 1933-34.

That first day FDR announced that he would divide what he wanted to say into (1) statements attributable to him but only in indirect quotation, (2) material for direct quotation which was relatively rare and usually on request of reporters to use, in quotes, some striking phrase, (3) background information that showed up in print under such euphemisms as "the President is known to think that . . . " and (4) off the record information ranging from the incident I have cited to comments on individuals or nations that often subtly colored the reporting about both.

All of this was such a switch from Hoover that at the end of that first press conference the reporters broke into applause. I don't believe that has ever happened again.

Why did they applaud? Because the reporters knew they were going to have access to news, the meat and potatoes of their profession. And because, as it turned out, that access was extensive and continuous. Despite the war, FDR, in just over twelve years in the White House, held 998 press conferences, a sea change from his predecessors and a record unmatched by his successors. They usually were held on Tuesday mornings and Friday afternoons, to give a time break to afternoon and then morning papers. As Frank Luther Mott, dean of historians of journalism, put it,

> He knew what newspapermen recognized as a good story, and he knew as well as they did how and when to 'break' it. Moreover, he was genial to the point of exuberance, and it was clear that he thoroughly enjoyed the give and take of the mass press conference.

And of course FDR had a facility of phrases: the "horse and buggy" Supreme Court of the Nine Old Men, the "garden hose" to help the allies like helping a neighbor, the shift from "Dr. New Deal" to "Dr. Win the War."

The White House was much more open to the press in those years, especially the pre-war years. In some previous administrations the press, or some of them, had been invited to one or another of the rather formal annual White House receptions along with the top bureaucrats, the military and/or the diplomats. FDR gave the press its own annual reception. I remember them well. He sat in a chair in the East Room smiling up at us as we came up to shake hands. Eleanor was at his side. There was punch and snacks and dancing in both the East Room and outside on the top of the adjoining portico to the east wing. I relish a story about George Bookman, one of the *Post's* White House reporters. He and his date were still enjoying one such party at two o'clock in the morning when Mrs. Roosevelt said sweetly: "Isn't it a little late for ice cream?"

FDR's sense of humor was a winner with the press. One day, when he was laid up in bed with a cold, the *Post* pulled a classic typographical error. The page one headline read: FDR IN BED WITH COED. Hardly had that early edition reached the White House than a *Post* reporter picked up the phone to hear: "This is Frank Roosevelt. I'd like 100 copies of that first edition of the *Post*. I want to send it to all my friends." Alas, the circulation department had scurried out to recover all the papers from the corner stands and destroy them. FDR never got his 100 copies.

Roosevelt, as that veteran reporter Richard L. Strout recently put it in an interview, had charm and magnetism and an ability to think quickly. John Gunther wrote that in twenty minutes FDR's features "expressed amazement, curiosity, mock alarm, genuine interest, worry, rhetorical playing for suspense, sympathy, decision, playfulness, dignity, and surpassing charm." He knew how to answer and how to dodge. He knew how to play on particular egos and how to tell the reporters it was not they, he was sure, but their Tory bosses, the publishers, who wrote such terrible things about him and his New Deal.

But the honeymoon could not last. After all, the issues are what count with reporters. When the New Deal began to run out of steam and when FDR took on the Supreme Court some reporters grew critical, others outright hostile. Occasionally FDR would tell a particular reporter to go stand in the corner with a dunce cap for asking what he considered a silly or dumb question, but that seemed mostly to be in jest. With the coming of the bitter pre-war struggle over possible American participation in World War II some press relationships grew extremely hostile and some of this continued after Pearl Harbor. At one point FDR awarded a hypothetical Iron Cross to a reporter. It happened this way. John O'Donnell, who wrote for the *New York News* which had been bitterly isolationist, reported that the army was issuing contraceptives to the WAC's, the new women's army corps. He had gotten the story, I'm told, from Clare Luce who was no FDR admirer. Roosevelt knew it was true but he took the tack that to say so in print was unpatriotic. O'Donnell, himself, avoided Roosevelt press conferences so at the next one FDR asked Earl Godwin, one of the front row regulars known as a Roosevelt fan, to give the Iron Cross to O'Donnell. Whether a medal actually was handed to Godwin, let alone O'Donnell, I don't know—I doubt it—but the incident left a sense of bitterness against the President even among journalists who thought little of O'Donnell himself. It certainly was one of FDR's least admirable moments.

That Roosevelt had reason to dislike—yes, hate—some of the barons of the press in that pre-TV era is evident from another incident. In 1935, as the honeymoon was ending, he got hold of an international Hearst empire message from a Hearst executive to its news service, saying,

> The Chief [as William Randolph Hearst liked to be called] instructs that the phrase Soak the Successful be used in all references to the Administration's tax program instead of the phrase Soak the Thrifty hitherto used; also he wants the words Raw Deal used instead of New Deal.

James MacGregor Burns recounted that an indignant FDR wanted to make the message public but that more prudent counsel prevailed. Anti-Roosevelt publishers used to complain that FDR had hypnotized their Washington reporters with his charm and misled them with his propaganda, as Leo Rosten put it in his 1937 book on *The Washington Correspondents.*

One of the reporters who had come down from Albany with Roosevelt was Ernest K. Lindley who had written the first FDR biography. But when Lindley wrote something FDR disliked about a New York political fight, the President demanded, at a press conference, that the reporter apologize. On another occasion he denied a Lindley story that FDR had picked Secretary of State Hull to be his successor in 1940 and that he had vetoed Jim Farley because he was a Catholic. At the next press conference Roosevelt said the story was made of whole cloth but that, as the *Post* next day put it in paraphrase, he considered Lindley's to be " . . . one of the most respected columns that he considered only about twenty percent wrong, as against other columns that are eighty percent wrong." Incidentally, reporters then had no access to the White House transcript of press conferences and the tape recorder was not yet born.

When the President is an activist the press tends to play him up as an individual. Witness Kennedy and now Reagan. In FDR's case, as Reston put it in 1937,

> The Washington correspondents had propagated the impression that Franklin D. Roosevelt was a paragon of talents and a repository of supreme political skills. Events which shattered this idea released that iconoclasm which is the successor to faith.

Something akin to that has been happening in Washington this fall.

It is always easier for historians, especially in such a lovely setting as we are in today, to look back, read the now available printed record, reflect and then discern the strands of greatness or of failure in any presidency. Roosevelt's unprecedented twelve years in the White House centered on two of the most cataclysmic events of our national existence, the Great Depression and World War II. And we still argue about the economics of the former and the causes of the latter.

The press in those great events was a conveyor belt between government and public. The correspondents who crowded into those 998 press conferences were the technicians for that process. On occasion individual journalists did influence the course of history or deflect government from its course. But even such occasions were incidental to the conveyor belt function. Then, as now, the messenger—to change the metaphor—often brought unpleasant news and the recipients of the news, the public, cried out for the head of the messenger. Remember Watergate.

What was the lasting role, the historical role, of the press in the age of Roosevelt? Did it go beyond the role of the messenger, the function of the conveyor belt that applies to all administrations?

Yes, it did, and it did so just as FDR's four administrations have affected our nation for almost a half century since that first inauguration day. In time, many of the New Deal measures have been altered, watered down, strengthened, or otherwise changed. But the central point—that the federal government has basic obligations to its citizenry—remains, though it clearly has been, and today still is, under challenge. Nonetheless, I do not think we are going to see a return to the states' rights, or to the county poorhouses, of pre-FDR eras.

Those of us in the press who came of age in the FDR years could no more escape being influenced by him and his New Deal and his internationalism than could the nation as a whole. And the influence has been just as lasting. I believe that only the influence on the press of the American Revolution and of the Civil War have matched that of FDR and of his stewardship of the New Deal and his direction of the allied effort in World War II. More than one generation of newsmen and women in Washington—and indeed all across the land—have reflected that, myself included. Many were isolationists in foreign affairs and believers in states' rights, or at least in state responsibility, in domestic affairs. It is true, as many conservatives have been contending for some time now, that the press, most especially the Washington press, tends to be liberal in its outlook, probably more so than the public as a whole. And that is true not only of those remaining few of us who were here in Washington with FDR in 1933 but most of those who arrived prior to Pearl Harbor. Those who came to the Capital in, say 1939, right out of college, are today the most senior among the current crop of active journalists. Nor should we neglect the effect on a second generation of journalists who were in grade school, or not even born, during the Depression and who now can vividly recall their parents' accounts of FDR and the New Deal, just as the oldest among us still can recall tales of the venerable Civil War veterans of our own early years.

It is worth mentioning, too, that the FDR aura is still remembered by our political leaders, notably by Ronald Reagan. His obeisance to the New Deal he remembers from his youth is evident in what he calls the social "safety net." That net may be getting ragged nowadays but before FDR there was no net at all, as Reagan well remembers. Perhaps Lyndon Johnson's Great Society today is being dismantled in large degree, but FDR's New Deal at home and his internationalism abroad remains very much central to this nation, and journalists by and large reflect this.

Today it is hard to imagine a Washington press corps all crowded into the rather small Oval Office. It is hard to imagine a president who never appeared on television, for whom the radio was a rather sparingly used device to go over the heads of the antagonistic press lords to the voters, and for whom the twice weekly press conference was thus so vital a means of communication and influence. But all that was true of FDR and even to recall it is, to me, both a stimulating exercise and a refreshing reminder that this nation, the press very much included, is far better off today for Franklin D. Roosevelt having passed this way.

John F. Kennedy and the Press
CHARLES ROBERTS

Charles Roberts began his career in journalism as editor of the University of Minnesota Daily during his undergraduate days. He went on to write for a variety of newspapers over a ten year period, then for *Newsweek* for twenty-two years. He served for fifteen years as White House correspondent during the Eisenhower, Kennedy and Johnson years. He was on the first press bus under the assassin's window in the fateful shooting of John F. Kennedy in Dallas. He was present at the swearing in of Lyndon B. Johnson aboard Air Force One. Only he and Merriman Smith were the reporters on Air Force One returning to Washington. He has received numerous awards including Newspaper Page One Guild award for investigative reporting in the *Chicago Daily News*. He became widely known and much respected for his byline in *Newsweek*. His paper on JFK and the Press reflects a breadth of view and thoughtful criticism blending with sympathetic understanding.

THE BEGINNING OF A 'NEW ERA IN POLITICAL COMMUNICATION'

Although it happened only a generation ago, few Americans remember or realize what a stir was created by the first presidential news conference to be televised "live" from Washington. It happened on January 25, 1961, just five days after John F. Kennedy took his oath of office.

A record crowd of 418 reporters, bathed in bright TV lights, participated in the dinner-hour show. That was 106 more than had ever before gathered for a presidential news conference.[1] An audience of 60 million watched in living rooms, dining rooms, and bar rooms across the country as the new, young President dramatically announced before 11 TV and movie cameras that the Soviet Union had released two captured U.S. airmen—a possible "break" in the cold war—and then gracefully fielded questions from 31 reporters who managed to get recognized. The show lasted 39 minutes—10 minutes longer than his aging predecessor had allowed his conferences to run—and JFK's fast-paced performance was almost flawless.

From my assigned seat, second row center in the cavernous auditorium of the then-new State Department Annex, I sensed from the moment the President walked onstage that the presidential news conference would never be the same again. It had not only become "show business"—confirming the dire predictions of recalcitrant writing reporters—it had also, as *Newsweek* noted in its next issue, opened "a new era in political communication."

News magazines, trying to give an extra-dimension to a well-covered story, are often guilty of hyperbole, but *Newsweek's* description of that conference as "momentous" and "historic" has stood the test of time. Kennedy's decision to go "live" changed the presidential press conference (as it was known before TV) more than any other single innovation in the 80-year history of scheduled meetings between journalists and the chief executive.

In an administration that was eventually accused of managing the news and taking reprisals against correspondents who refused to be cheerleaders, Kennedy's innovative news conference was the most successful of his many approaches to the media, so we will examine it first and then look at his other relations with the press.

THE NEWS CONFERENCE

Since some may argue that Kennedy and his press secretary, Pierre Salinger, simply adapted to the electronic age, it may be useful to look back on the conference as it existed before JFK crossed the New Frontier. President Eisenhower's press chief, Jim Hagerty, had permitted radio taping of Ike's press conferences since December 12, 1953, and filming of those conferences since January 19, 1955. In each case they were recorded for broadcast at a later hour, and Hagerty reserved the right to edit them.

In practice, Hagerty did little or no editing, but because the "canned" conferences lacked any sense of immediacy when aired several hours after the event, the networks, by 1960, were using only brief excerpts, or "highlights," of Ike's often-dull encounters with the press.

Hagerty had permitted one hastily-arranged Eisenhower press conference to be televised live. That was at the Republican National Convention in San Francisco in 1956, when Ike announced that Harold Stassen was abandoning his "dump-Nixon" drive and would second Richard Nixon's renomination for vice president.

Eager to get that harmonious word out to the delegates in a hurry, Hagerty permitted live cameras to carry the announcement and a brief question period that followed. After that the White House resumed its ban on live cameras at news conferences.

Throughout the 1950's, a decade of tense relations with Moscow, the most powerful argument against the President going on the air while actually jousting with reporters was the widely-held belief that a slip of the tongue might cause international repercussions. Kennedy's two top foreign policy advisers, McGeorge Bundy and Dean Rusk, were among those who thought that this risk outweighed the putative advantages of a live telecast.

It was just about a month before his first news conference—while he was still president-elect—that Kennedy decided to run that risk. JFK, Salinger later told me, was not only confident that he could handle foreign policy questions, but realized that *if* he slipped he could fire off a correction or clarification by the same fast medium that aired his blunder.[2]

Like many White House correspondents who had covered Eisenhower, my "beat" became President-elect Kennedy immediately after the 1960 election. (Because *Newsweek* thought Nixon would win, I was in Los Angeles, rather than Hyannis Port, that long night the votes were counted.) Salinger informed us of Kennedy's decision to go live with his press conferences at a briefing in Palm Beach, Florida, a few days after JFK had entertained us at a Christmas party in his father's oceanfront home. Despite a prevailing mood of bonhomie, print reporters—comprising the vast majority of the press corps—objected vociferously to the idea of making a "TV spectacle" out of the news conference.

Most of the correspondents summoned from poolside at the Palm Beach Towers that day had been around Washington much longer than Salinger, if not Kennedy, and thought they had a better feel of how a White House press conference should be run. Some argued that the new format would destroy the informal give-and-take of the conference—Truman had called it "rough and tumble" —while others complained it would make "actors" out of honest newsmen. This ignored the fact that many Washington correspondents had already moved in that direction with the installation of movie cameras at the Eisenhower conferences.

In Palm Beach and at a subsequent pre-inaugural working lunch with Salinger at a hotel in Washington, many of us also objected to Pierre's proposed abolition of the rule—dating back to Truman—that a reporter should identify himself before asking a question. Salinger insisted that many correspondents sought presidential recognition at Ike's conferences just to get "free advertising" for their networks or publications. There was a germ of truth to this charge; many correspondents for provincial papers *did* feel their jobs were more secure when their names appeared with regularity in the transcripts of Ike's news conferences in the *New York Times.*

Reminding us not too tactfully that it was the *President's* conference, not ours, Salinger rejected all efforts to preserve it in *status quo.* He then went about the business of setting up the 35th President's first news conference, including arrangements for new, supersensitive "shotgun" microphones to pick up reporter's questions at long range and the assignment of 58 reserved seats for White House "regulars"—23 more than Hagerty had set aside in the old Indian Treaty Room. The rest, as they say, is history.

The live cameras transformed the "bully pulpit" of Theodore Roosevelt, the first president to meet regularly with journalists, into a podium far more powerful than anything envisioned by TR. They gave the President the upper hand forevermore in his verbal bouts with the press. And they also enabled Kennedy's successors—via satellites that were launched later—to address the chancelleries of the world, instantly and without any ambassadors as middlemen.

But, most important, the live cameras handed the President a platform from which he could speak, literally, over the heads of reporters and editors, anchormen and commentators—what JFK called the "hostile press"—directly to the voters on any issue at almost any time.

"We couldn't survive without TV," said Kennedy's special counsel, Ted Sorensen, who had also opposed the move, once he saw the implications of this breakthrough. Kennedy put it in earthier terms to a friend from the print media. "Well," he told Ben Bradlee, then my boss as Washington Bureau Chief of *Newsweek,* "I always said that when we don't have to go through you bastards, we can really get our story out to the American people."

In a euphoric mood, Kennedy clearly felt he had solved the problem posed by Bryce when he wrote at the turn of the century: "To catch and hold the attention of the people is the chief difficulty as well as the first duty of an American reformer." In fact, Kennedy liked his invention so much that he held 20 news conferences during his first year in office—in contrast with President Reagan's six during the same period.

That the American people also liked the televised sessions was documented in a survey conducted for the White House by Young & Rubicam, a New York ad agency. In June of 1962, Y&R researchers found that 95 per cent of the people they interviewed thought watching a JFK press conferences was a "worthwhile experience." Among the reasons given: The conferences were "informative" and "educational" and gave "a feeling of democracy." Surprisingly, some respondents who thought Kennedy was not doing a good job as President took a favorable view of his news conferences.

Franklin D. Roosevelt, made a similar breakthrough, from the presidential point of view, when he invented the radio "fireside chat" as a means of bypassing the press to reach the people in the depression-ridden 1930's.[3] But the televised news conference is a far more effective vehicle because, in good times or bad, a spontaneous, unrehearsed encounter with reporters will command greater attention. And although TV networks can and have refused to provide free time for presidential speeches, they are less likely to turn their backs on live news conferences, which underline their importance as purveyors of news.

Kennedy and his successors have avoided wearing out their welcome at the networks by not conducting many news conferences in prime time. Shortly after the Y&R survey, Salinger told me he had not scheduled evening conferences since JFK's debut because (1) any news the President made would miss all the morning papers and (2) it would cost the networks a lot of money in lost advertising. At that time, after 18 months in office, the audience for the President's news sessions, held mostly in the afternoon, had leveled off at about 6 million homes.

Had a president with less charisma than Kennedy first faced the press on live TV, it is possible that the televised conference would not have become a part of the presidency—a custom that all presidents are obliged to respect. But Kennedy's quick wit and facile tongue made press conference watchers out of many citizens who had never read (and never will read) transcripts of White House news conferences. Five administrations later, it is almost inconceivable that a future president, no matter how inept on camera, would risk the wrath of the media and the voters by refusing to face the press and public simultaneously on the "box."

Re-reading the transcripts of Kennedy's conferences after 20 years, one is reminded of the saying "that everyone laughs at a rich man's jokes." Some of JFK's fast rejoinders that rocked the room with laughter—even when they were designed to evade embarrassing questions—are not that funny when read today.

But it was a growing infrequency of press conferences, rather than a lack of humor in them, that brought about the first criticism of Kennedy's press relations. That was the fall of 1961 when—after weathering the Bay of Pigs fiasco and the Berlin Wall crisis—the President went from August 30 to October 11 without facing the media. Correspondents noted that this did not comport with his campaign statement of August 20, 1960, at Independence, Mo., where he said: "I would think that whoever was President would see the press at least once a week."

By November he had fallen behind Ike—who was criticized by the Democrats for eight years for the infrequency of his news conferences[4]—and I was noting in a memorandum to my editors in New York that "many reporters feel he is now less responsive to questions than President Eisenhower was. . . . The transcripts of his conferences are full of evasive filibusters."

Yet, when Bob Pierpoint, who covered the presidency for CBS for 25 years, asked a group of past and present White House correspondents to rate seven presidents—from Eisenhower through Reagan—on their press conference performances, he found that collectively we gave Kennedy the best "report card," and that JFK scored higher than the other presidents in two areas—"compative skill" and "humor."

Here is Pierpoint's survey as it appeared in the January, 17, 1982, issue of *Parade* magazine, with each president rated in each category on a scale of 1 to 10:

	Eisenhower	Kennedy	Johnson	Nixon	Ford	Carter	Reagan
Candor	8	5	2	5	7	8	6
Informative Value	7	6	3	6	5	7	4
Combative Skill	4	9	6	8	4	6	8
Humor	3	9	4	4	6	7	8.5
Total	22	29	15	23	22	28	26.5

Was Kennedy himself satisfied with his press conferences? In one of his last meetings with reporters, after invoking poet Robert Frost, he expressed doubt that some proposed changes would improve the format that had evolved. This was the exchange:

Q. Mr. President, have you given any thought to some of the proposals advanced from time to time for improving the presidential conference devoted all to one subject or to have written questions at a certain point?

A. We . . . , I have heard of that, and I have seen criticism of the proposal. The difficulty is—as Mr. Frost said about not taking down a fence until you find out why it was put up—I think all the proposals made to improve it will really not improve it.

I think we do have the problem of moving very quickly from subject to subject, and therefore I am sure many of you feel that we are not going into any depth. So I would try to recognize perhaps the correspondent on an issue two or three times in a row, and we could perhaps meet that problem. Otherwise, it seems to me it serves its purpose, which is to have the President in the bulls eye, and I suppose that is in some ways revealing.

The date of the 61st conference, with its ironic reference to having the President "in the bulls eye" was September 12, 1963, just a little over two months before the President was murdered at Dallas with a rifle mounted with a telescopic gunsight.

PRESS RELATIONS

Although it is the most visible part of a president's relations with the press, the news conference is by no means the end-all, be-all in that relationship. Kennedy cultivated the media in many other ways and broke new ground in some of his dealings with the journalists who chronicled the New Frontier. His overtures to the press included:

- Allowing reporters greater access to members of his White House staff than had been granted by previous administrations.
- TV "specials," including in-depth interviews with network correspondents and a tour of the White House with his wife, Jackie.
- Similar exclusives for print media, including magazine picture spreads and stories on "a day in the life of the President."
- Backgrounders at which, on a not-for-attribution basis, he revealed his thinking and described to White House "regulars" his options on major problems confronting him.
- White House luncheons for editors and publishers from the hinterlands.
- More "perks" for journalists, including invitations to lunches, state dinners, and other social functions.

Of these devices for getting a better press, the granting of access to White House staff and the TV specials were the most innovative. White House correspondents, I can testify, were most grateful for the Kennedy/Salinger decision to let reporters probe behind the walls of the lobby in the West Wing, to which we had been virtually restricted in Eisenhower's day. Where, under Ike, no reporter could see a White House staffer (Chief of Staff Sherman Adams excepted) without first "clearing" it with Jim Hagerty, under JFK it was possible to talk to key members of the Kennedy team in their offices or at lunch.

This was a break for those correspondents who wanted to go beyond the handouts distributed at Salinger's twice-daily press briefings to find out how and why presidential decisions were made. (Some newsmen who had actually slept in the lobby's overstuffed chairs during the Eisenhower Era continued to doze under Kennedy.) McGeorge Bundy (on foreign affairs), Kenneth O'Donnell (on politics), Lawrence O'Brien (on legislation), and Ted Sorensen (on JFK's mood and thinking) were invaluable sources whose names rarely appeared in the informed reporting they made possible.

The TV specials were a stunning success, from the President's point of view. At the first of them, in December of 1962, JFK got mostly friendly, or "softball" questions from three network correspondents who were apparently so grateful for their "Conversation with the President" that they entirely forgot about the adversary relationship between journalists and the chief executive. Walter Cronkite and Chet Huntley got exclusive one-on-one interviews when their CBS and NBC evening news shows switched from 15 minutes to a half-hour format, and ABC was allowed to tape a close-up of the President in his command post during his battle with Gov. George Wallace over integration of the University of Alabama.

But the real *coup,* in which the medium was used to the maximum advantage of the First Family, came when Jackie Kennedy took CBS and millions of TV viewers on an hour-long tour of the White House in 1962 to see what her "restoration" had accomplished. This show got such a build-up that ABC and NBC demanded that they be allowed to air it along with CBS. Salinger acceded to this unprecedented plea and the CBS-originated show appeared simultaneously on all three networks.

The idea of unattributable background sessions for White House "regulars" did not originate with Kennedy—Eisenhower tried them during his second term—and the two that he staged produced mixed results for JFK. Both were held on an invitation-only basis at his father's Palm Beach home during the Christmas holiday season with the idea of providing reporters with material for year-end "think pieces."

The backgrounders were divided into discussions of foreign and domestic policy. Each produced a rash of stories reflecting Kennedy's thoughts on current issues, deviously attributed to "sources close to the Administration" or "persons who have talked to the President." These circumlocutions did not fool sophisticated readers or editors, but they did produce a rash of complaints from papers that were not invited.

The luncheons for editors and publishers, invited to the White House in state and regional groups, generated some editorials that reflected a greater understanding of the President's problems. But they, too, produced some unwanted side-effects. At the lunch for Texans, E. M. (Ted) Dealey, publisher of the *Dallas Morning News,* teed off on Kennedy for being "soft" on the Soviets. He read a 500-word prepared statement calling for "a man on horseback to lead this nation," adding: "Many people in Texas and the Southwest think that you are riding Caroline's tricycle."

The White House response to this newsmaking violation of JFK's 100-proof hospitality came ten days later when Charles Bartlett, then Washington correspondent for the *Chattanooga Times,* wrote a story quoting at length from what he said was Kennedy's reply to Dealey at the luncheon. "I'm just as tough as you are, Mr. Dealey," Kennedy said, according to the Bartlett story. "And I didn't get elected by arriving at soft judgments."

Wire services that picked up the Bartlett story noted that he was a close friend of the President. He was, in fact, the man who introduced JFK to his wife, Jackie.

Dealey and several other Texas publishers denied that Kennedy made the speech Bartlett attributed to him. But, whether Dealey or Bartlett was right, the exchange illustrates another facet of JFK's relations with the press: Kennedy had more close friends among the working press in Washington than any president in memory—and he did not hesitate to use them in defense of the New Frontier.

The new President made it clear he would not turn his back on his prepresidential journalist friends when he dropped in at the home of columnist Joe Alsop in the wee hours following his inauguration and on *Newsweek's* Ben Bradlee, a former Georgetown neighbor on his first Sunday morning as President. Among his other good friends in the press were Stewart Alsop, then Washington correspondent for the *Saturday Evening Post,* and Rowland Evans, then with the *New York Herald Tribune.*

These friendships proved mutually beneficial when JFK wanted to put out an "inside" story with the assurance that it was in friendly hands. For example, Bartlett and Stewart Alsop wrote for the *Saturday Evening Post* an all-but-authorized behind-the-scenes account of how the Cuban missile crisis was handled. Bradlee and I, with access to FBI files, collaborated on a *Newsweek* piece that put down what we called the "John's other wife" story—a widely-circulated rumor that JFK had been secretly married to the thrice-married Newport socialite before he met Jacqueline Bouvier. The

Newsweek story was far more effective than a White House denial would have been.

But the Kennedy's close friends in the press were not the only journalists to benefit by his presidency. Because of greater access to him and his advisers, all of us were able to write more authoritatively during the early days of his administration. And during the Thousand Days of Camelot, reporters were romanced with invitations to glittering state dinners, luncheons, and receptions at the White House on a scale unmatched by previous administrations.

Unlike the Eisenhower days—when Ike talked to us like supply troops, a sort of necessary appendage to his command—there was almost a spirit of camaraderie among White House staff and press, particularly during the first-year "honeymoon." This is a dangerous position for journalists to get in; it can numb their critical faculties. However, JFK was our age, knew a lot about our business[5], and seemed genuinely interested in our work and our families. None of us regarded his friendliness as phony or his hospitality as a mere gambit to get a better press. The first strains in this relationship occurred a few months into the new administration when it became apparent to some of us that Kennedy was not only the friendliest, but the most thin-skinned of presidents. Although JFK and his aides were quick to compliment a reporter on a "good story," i.e., one favorable to the administration, they were intolerant of any criticism. What was worse, reporters who wrote stories that annoyed the White House suddenly found that their sources of information were drying up. Those staffers who had been so accessible were suddenly too busy to talk. Phone calls went unreturned.

"You are either for us or against us," is the way Kenny O'Donnell, the President's appointments secretary, put it to me.

What the White House wanted in the press room, obviously, were cheerleaders, not skeptical reporters. The carrot and stick treatment extended even to such presidential friends as *Newsweek*'s Bradlee, who, for example, was chewed out first by the President and then his brother, the Attorney General, for a story that the administration was preparing to put a Massachusetts political hack (who had worked for the Kennedys) on the federal bench. The story was true; what the Kennedys resented was that it was embarrassing.

The UPI's Merriman Smith, then the "dean" of White House

correspondents, marvelled at how the White House could spot an unfavorable paragraph in a paper of 3,000 circulation 2,000 miles away. "They must have a thousand little gnomes reading the papers for them," said Smitty.

The public first became aware of JFK's hypersensitivity, I think, when the story leaked out in the spring of 1962 that the President had cancelled the White House's daily order for 22 copies of the *New York Herald Tribune,* a staunchly Republican paper that had carried several less-than-flattering stories about the Kennedys. One was a story about their lavish entertainment at Mt. Vernon for the president of Pakistan. The emphasis of the story was on the cost rather than what a grand party it was. Another was the *Trib's* handling of the Billie Sol Estes case, a grain storage scandal in Texas.

It was in the wake of this petulant move that Kennedy was asked at his May 9 press conference about his attitude toward the press and replied that he was "reading more and enjoying it less." He added, with apparent resignation, that reporters were "doing their task, as a critical branch, the Fourth Estate and I am attempting to do mine, and we are going to live together for a period of time and then go our separate ways."

The story of the White House press corps' disenchantment with Kennedy broke into the open three months later when *Look* magazine, in a spread entitled "Kennedy vs. the Press," reported that 25 or 30 Washington correspondents had been reprimanded by members of the Kennedy family or White House staff or been questioned by the FBI or Pentagon security officers. Several complained that the White House had put "the freeze" on them for stories that did not pass the test of friendliness.

In fairness, *Look* reported that of about 100 correspondents it questioned, about half took a "lighthearted view of the Kennedy administration's knuckle rapping of the press." The rest saw it as a serious attempt to pressure them. Still, *Look,* which had its share of favors from the Kennedy White House, concluded that the press had taken "almost as many lumps in 19 months of Kennedy rule as in the previous three administrations put together."

The situation got worse that fall when for several weeks in the aftermath of the Cuban missile crisis officials at all levels of the White House, State Department, and Pentagon became totally uncommunicative. To make sure they remained uncommunicative, the Pentagon and State Department ordered their officials to report in writing on any contact they had with reporters.

No reporter I know faulted Kennedy for managing the news while he and Soviet Premier Khrushchev were "eyeball to eyeball" at the brink of a nuclear war over the question of Russian missiles in Cuba. But when the embargo on *all* information concerning negotiations with Moscow and the U.S. blockade of Cuba continued long after Khruschev had agreed to remove his missiles, the press perceived, as the *New York Times* put it, that it was "being used more often than informed."

This feeling was reinforced when the Pentagon's chief spokesman, Arthur Sylvester, told an interviewer that "the generation of news by the government becomes a weapon in a strained situation," and then added in a subsequent speech that the government had a right "if necessary, to lie to save itself when it is going up in a nuclear war." Both of Sylvester's statements were arguably true, but they did not improve Kennedy's relations with the press.

Arthur Krock, the venerable Washington oracle of the *New York Times* and a onetime mentor of JFK, wrote: "A news management policy not only exists, but in the form of direct and deliberate action, has been enforced more cynically and boldly than by any previous administration in a period when the U.S. was not at war."[6] At his next press conference following the missile crisis—his first in ten weeks—Kennedy seemed to concede that his administration had gone too far down the road of news management. He defended, of course, the close-mouthed handling of troop movements and intelligence data, but promised to "see if we can get this straightened out so that there is a free flow of news to which the press is entitled and which I think ought to be in the press, and on which any administration really must depend as a check to its own actions."

Apparently, the press's critical reporting of the Washington news blackout had served as a check on the President.

REQUIEM

The bullet that killed President Kennedy made him a hero, posthumously, to all but the most dyed-in-the-wool Kennedy haters. His martyrdom assured him, at least temporarily, a better niche in history than he might have earned by serving out his first, and perhaps a second, term.

Now historians and biographers are taking a harder look at his brief tenure. They are finding, in many cases, that his rhetoric was better than his record. They are also finding character defects. His celebrated war record and his sole authorship of two books are questioned. It is revealed that he lied about the state of his health and that he taped phone conversations with unwitting White House callers, including newsmen. Worst of all, there is persuasive evidence that he was a compulsive—and indiscriminate—philanderer.

These disclosures raise some troubling questions for journalists. If Kennedy's shortcomings were known or suspected—as many were—why weren't they reported more effectively? Was Arthur Krock right when he charged that JFK managed the news by "selective personal patronage" and "social flattery" of Washington correspondents and commentators? Were we the victims, rather than the beneficiaries, of briefings and contacts with JFK that left us in a "state of protracted enchantment evoked by the President's charm and the aura of his office?"

Most reporters who covered Kennedy would, I think, acknowledge that these questions are valid, but argue that to pose them now—particularly the problem of Kennedy's peccadillos—is to ask them out of context. In the pre-Watergate days of Camelot, most reporters on the White House beat, I believe, thought that what a president did in his spare time was his own business—if he wanted it that way, and provided his extra-curricular activities did not impair his effectiveness as chief executive. Some also lived by the Biblical injunction: Let him who is without sin cast the first stone.

As for Krock's charge, there is no denying that Kennedy flattered and charmed the press by his attentions. What is debatable is the extent to which we were rendered uncritical. The fact that reams were written about JFK's attempts to manage the news is certainly evidence in mitigation of the charge. If we were captivated, we at least protested profusely while the seduction was in progress. But most of us now reaffirm what we knew then: that an arms-length relationship (such as we had under Ike) is better for both the journalist and his readers. Whether it should also be an *adversary* relationship is a topic for another day.

The irony of what is happening now is that as estimates of Kennedy's presidency go down, his marks for skillful handling of the press must be revised upward. If his presidency is to be branded as mediocre—if his administration got a much better press than it deserved—then he must be acknowledged as the greatest manipulator of the media since FDR and an even greater communicator than Ronald Reagan. One thing is certain: Whatever his motive, his distinction as the first president to admit the public via television to the White House press conference is secure. He did open "a new era in political communication."

NOTES

1. 312 reporters jammed the Indian Treaty Room of the old Executive Office Building on Feb. 29, 1956, to hear President Eisenhower announce whether he would run for a second term.
2. Kennedy did, in fact, bobble a foreign policy question at his first conference. He said he looked forward to a resumption of atomic "tests" when he meant atomic "talks." There were no repercussions.
3. FDR used the "fireside" format sparingly, making only four such talks during his first year and only eight during his first term as President.
4. With 64 news conferences in 34 months, for an average of 1,882 conferences per month, JFK finally finished behind Ike, who held 193 in 96 months for an average of 2.01 per month. Both finished far behind FDR (998 in 12 years and 3 months, 6.789 per month) and Truman (324 in 7 years and 9 months, 3.483 per month.)
5. He was a reporter briefly for Hearst's International News Service following World War II and a voracious reader of newspapers and periodicals.
6. *Fortune* magazine, March, 1963.

Ronald Reagan
HELEN THOMAS

MR. THOMPSON: I want to read a bit from someone who very early in the Reagan administration wrote the following column:

> President Reagan has managed to keep his domestic program of massive federal spending cuts on center stage but in the foreign policy field he still is feeling his way. The policy so far has been marked by ambiguities and contradictions with no apparent overall direction. The current line vis-à-vis the Soviets appears to be the hallmark but even that seems vulnerable to other pragmatic requirements.

That piece written by Helen Thomas stands up rather well.

Helen Thomas was born in Kentucky; attended Wayne University; has honorary degrees from a number of institutions; served as wire service reporter in Washington beginning in 1943; White House bureau chief, 1974 to the present; was president of the White House Correspondents Association, 1975–76, the first woman president; was the recipient of the Woman of the Year in Communications Award by the *Ladies Home Journal;* was the first woman elected to the Gridiron Club of Washington; has been a member of the Women's National Press Corps and its president; has been a member of Sigma Delta Chi's Hall of Fame; Delta Sigma Pi's honorary membership; is the author of *Dateline: White House* and, finally, is one of the most respected figures in the American field of journalism. It's a privilege to welcome you to Virginia.

MS. THOMAS: I'm honored to be here at the University founded by a great defender of freedom of the press, Thomas Jefferson, though he may have wondered himself at times what hath God wrought. I'm particularly proud to be on the same platform with two great reporters who know so well the byzantine manipulation of information at the White House through the years. For as all presidents learn, information equals power. Press relations with any president always run a predictable course—downhill. And it may be ever thus as long as we are the watchmen at the tower.

I've always considered myself greatly privileged to cover the White House. Each day is an education and of course we have the proverbial ringside to history, instant history. It's true, of course, inasmuch as some may think otherwise, we are mindful that human beings live in the White House with their joys, their sorrows, their insecurities, their arrogance and their rare nobility. The obvious inevitable prognosis for relations between any president and the press seems to go from bad to worse, though not in the beginning when every president is accorded a honeymoon. That was best typified when the *Washington Post* cartoonist, Herblock, gave Nixon a clean shave after he assumed office. Many years earlier dating back to the McCarthy era, he drew Nixon in the most sinister terms. In the full flush of an inauguration presidents are twelve feet tall and all is right with the world. The press, too, is caught up in this uncritical moment that goes along with learning that, in those first euphoric days of Gerald Ford's accession, Ford toasted his own English muffins. Then there is the mood, perhaps in the press as well as the country, to give him a chance as his style and his actions come into focus.

Ronald Reagan had a longer honeymoon than most presidents. The attempt on his life coming so soon after he had moved into the White House produced an understandable brief moratorium and bought him some time, even as his aides spoke of a "safety net for the poor" as social programs were being slashed. As time went on, the press was accused of not laying a glove on Reagan and some of their peers like Anthony Lewis wrote that reporters were being too soft on the President and were giving him a free ride. Since we see ourselves as factual reporters, I don't think a day has passed that we have not faithfully reported Reagan's moves to dismantle the programs from the New Deal to the Great Society, or at least to curb them radically. From that aspect Reagan has been true to his philosophy. He is a rigid ideologue and only rarely does he beat a strategic retreat.

In the early days of the Reagan administration the promise was, as it is with every president, an open administration. I can only say—that will be the day, not only for this administration, but all the others we've covered. Press access to Reagan during his 1980 campaign was extremely limited, more a case of hit-and-run with aides closing in before a reporter could toss a follow-up question. The *modus operandi* continued at the White House. Then reporters were treated to an affable, genial, nice president—very friendly, seemingly willing to answer any question during brief so-called photo opportunities in the Oval Office. His top aides, Edwin Meese, James Baker, Michael Deaver, all neophytes to the national government—except Baker whose own experience was limited— became apopleptic when Reagan would deliver an off-the-cuff answer. Reagan himself could not resist an answer. But it appeared that his aides protectively and perhaps with some smug superiority on their part felt that he should not be questioned, that they were really smarter than he was and that some of his answers were not programmed or screened enough.

Since the picture takings were the only point of access to Reagan, reporters tried to make the most of it. I recall one day when Reagan was meeting with a head of state, the "thundering herd," which is what we're called, rushed into the Oval Office. The time was ten forty-five a.m., fifteen minutes before the eleven o'clock deadline that Reagan had set for firing the air traffic controllers. It was an opportunity not to be passed up. I asked Reagan while picture-taking was going on if he was indeed going ahead with his plan to fire the controllers. He said he was and we ran to our electronic computers, not the telephone as often any more. Within hours his top aides decided that they had had it with impromptu questions to the press and they laid down the law that Reagan was not to be questioned when he was with a foreign leader for decorum's sake. We agreed to nothing and never do, but we did not push our luck with heads of state. Then, heady with a bit of success in putting us in our place, the Reaganites decided that all questions to the President during such sessions should be verbotten. We defy those rules all the time but in their frustration they devised a system whereby once a week Reagan would answer questions in a quicky ten minute encounter on their own terms and whenever they decide.

Access to Reagan is very limited and under the most controlled circumstances. He's had nine news conferences so far, a far cry from FDR and some of his predecessors. FDR held two a week even in wartime. Being human, presidents do not relish the idea of meeting the press, particularly when there's nothing to brag about. When Jim Brady was on deck, he managed to keep the atmosphere light and to deflect hostility. It no longer is the Gulag that we once knew in the Nixon era. His deputy, Larry Speakes, who presides at news briefings came up through a tough school. He had worked in the White House in the Nixon era as spokesman for Nixon's chief Watergate lawyer. Speakes, White House Communications Director David Gergen, and the big three advisors huddle every day to decide what story they will feature, what story will land Reagan on the front page in the best light, of course. They decide what activity of the day involving the President we can cover. Days can go by when we do not see him, even when he has a full official schedule on the record. The term "managed news" coined in the Kennedy era has been developed to a fine art. Reagan's aides even have trained him to say, "I can't comment, it's a photo opportunity." It's all on their terms and they calculate what will do them the most good, imagewise.

And yet one wonders at times, because sometimes it gets away from them. For example, last Friday when the highest unemployment rate since the Great Depression was announced, Reagan, togged out in his lovely riding britches, came out on the South Lawn, denounced the Democrats for demagoguery and went off like the playboy of the western world on a helicopter to go riding in the Virginia countryside. And then he was very stubborn imagewise when his aides told him that the economy was so bad and the picture was so bad that he really shouldn't take a vacation in Barbados and stay at the home of Claudette Colbert seeming to be wallowing in the rich atmosphere that he's often identified with. He insisted that he was going, so they immediately started putting on some official meetings, had him stop overnight in Jamaica where he could be treated as a head of state and have official talks on the Caribbean. Then, when he went to Barbados, they did have a meeting with some of the smaller Caribbean nation leaders. Then for three days he had his vacation. Well, the AP, unfortunately not us, did the story saying that it cost the taxpayers 3.5 million dollars for Reagan to have his vacation in the Barbados, which he insisted on doing even though his aides had told him, imagewise, it's not so good. Then he made a speech, one of his regular Saturday radio speeches and he started out by saying, "Well, I took the day off on Good Friday like everyone takes off and I'm going to church on Sunday," and it was so defensive. But he did have his vacation. It isn't "Let them eat cake," but I think that he calls his own shots even though they try to manage and program him.

In recent months Reagan has lost some of his initial affability with the press. But not all. He has fallen into the presidential syndrome of displaying anger over leaks from time to time. Washington is one giant ear, he has complained. He also says he is convinced there are bugs in the chandelier in the cabinet room. Many of the reforms that grew out of the nightmare that was Watergate have been eliminated or will be if Reagan has his way. The drive has been systematic to cut down legitimate access to news in the foreign policy field. New regulations have been devised to tighten the circle of those with access to top secret documents. The Freedom of Information Act is under siege, and Reagan's forces seek to legitimatize domestic spying by the CIA.

Worse yet is the atmosphere of darkness at noon with lie detectors being used to nail the leakers. When a colonel was accused of leaking the report that experts believed that defense spending would rise dramatically to a trillion dollars, he was informed that he would probably lose his job, although it's still under investigation. "We want to make an example of him," said one Pentagon spokesman. *Deja vu.* No plumbers on the scene so far as we can tell. But the atmosphere is conducive. There is little or no room for devil's advocates in this administration and it's doubtful that Reagan gets a variety of opinion except for the bickering that was often exposed between then Secretary of State Alexander Haig and Defense Secretary Caspar Weinberger. The people are not in on the take-offs, only the landings.

I remember when they started the whole focus on El Salvador. Ed Meese appeared on "Issues and Answers." It was February, one month after Reagan had taken office and we were practically drawing a line in El Salvador. People didn't know what was going to happen next. And Meese went on the air and under questioning said, "We will do whatever is necessary in El Salvador." And we heard this program had been taped so he got on Air Force One with us coming back from Santa Barbara to Washington; he came back to the press area and we said, "What do you mean, whatever

is necessary? What exactly? Will you be a little more specific?"
And I said, "After all, when do the American people enter into this
dialogue on what is our foreign policy, and whether they fight and
not?" He said, "They come in every four years when they elect a
president."

MR. CORMIER: A lot can happen in four years.

MS. THOMAS: The people's right to know is coming under attack by
some elitists in the press and the press is always under attack. But
we know too well how much is suppressed under the stamp of
national security, and the price of such secrecy. Exposure of the
bombing of Cambodia for fourteen months in the *New York Times*
sent Nixon and Henry Kissinger up in smoke, and spotlighted their
long deception in that Vietnam war and other war moves.

Of course the lack of credibility at that time was not restricted
to Nixon. The Johnson era is replete with such stories. Reporters
will not soon forget Secretary of State Dean Rusk, angered over
the line of questioning on the Vietnam war, asked reporters, "Which
side are you on? I'm on our side," he said. Inevitably, it becomes a
matter of self-protection for those running the show, badly or not.
And then there was the Kennedy era when Pentagon spokesman
Arthur Sylvester contended that the government had the right to
lie in national security matters. I saw two presidents bite the dust
because they were no longer believed, and without credibility they
could not govern: Lyndon Johnson and Richard Nixon. And it was
not without some incredulity that I watched six press secretaries
take brief nostalgic turns at bat at the White House podium recently.
All but one, Jody Powell, maintained that they had never lied to
the press. Ron Nessen did admit that he had deceived the press on
one occasion as to the reason why President Ford wanted to take a
trip to Florida. Later he said it was for a golf match. Powell
couched his only fib in the cloak of national security, naturally. He
said he had lied about the ill-fated hostage rescue mission in Iran.
Unfortunately, I did not have a Bible on hand to rush up to them
and ask them to play it again and raise your right hand.

I do not, and never have, underestimated the difficulty of
speaking for a president. Few have ever done it well and it can only
be with fear and trepidation. And then there are people like LBJ
who could hardly stand having a White House mouthpiece. As a
consequence he had five of them and none excelled at the job. LBJ

was his own press secretary for better or for worse. My ideal press secretary wears two hats. He is indeed the voice of the White House but he also has a responsibility to keep the American people informed and to maintain the accountability of a president. Few have filled the bill well. Perhaps James Hagerty for Eisenhower was above par; Pierre Salinger was good for Kennedy because he was tuned in, and for one brief shining month we had Jerry ter Horst for Ford. He quit when he was deceived in the White House about the Nixon pardon. I think it should also be remembered that press secretaries are paid by the taxpayer. They are government servants not to be confused with publicists hired to do a public relations job for the president, even though they don't see it that way.

And then there is the image. Reagan has been appalled and admits being very disturbed over the perception that he is Scrooge, cutting school milk and food stamp programs, college tuition loans, disability, and so on. He has become particularly irate when the television networks feature programs about the poor, victims of cuts in benefits. "Anytime anyone gets laid off in South Succotash he gets interviewed on television," Reagan complained. Counselor Edwin Meese at the Sperling breakfast accused the networks of running up and down the street trying to find someone out of work to portray the bad effects of Reaganomics. "TV reporting is so downbeat it is hurting the economic recovery," says Reagan. But their complaints do not hold water. Reagan cannot say that he does not get ample television exposure anytime he chooses. As for his advisors, turn on any TV any morning and especially on Sunday talk shows and try not to find one of them being interviewed on the major network programs.

Like his predecessors, Reagan has found late Friday afternoon, when there are few reporters around, is just the right time to drop the touchy news such as financial disclosure statements of top aides on the table, and income tax returns. And when it came time to reveal Reagan's order to the IRS to give tax exemptions to schools with known discriminatory policies, of course it was put out late Friday. Every day the White House turns out a bunch of releases, mostly appointments, including U.S. marshals, for various reasons. Trivia for most reporters but for wire services we do carry them because we are covering the whole country. Yet, when the administration decided to ask Congress for a new multi-billion dollar civil defense program, it was released by the Federal Emergency Management Agency, put out on a quiet wire without any fanfare with only alert reporters finally catching up. One has to ask why. Surely a program affecting the safety of every American should have been announced at the White House. But perhaps the White House wanted no close identity with a program that informs Americans that they've got eight days to get out of town in the event of a nuclear war.

I know that in the eyes of some the role of the press is dubious. We are self-appointed watchdogs, annointed by none, feared by some, and guided, we hope, by one main ethical goal: to pursue the truth wherever it leads. If government servants are watched, well, we are, too. We reporters get a report card every day. Every day we are tested for our accuracy and our profound responsibility to the American people. And I must say that there would be no covering of the White House if the White House didn't have a lot of rope. People will never know how physical is such a job and how demeaning in many ways because we never cover a president except when they put a rope around us. We're corralled like cattle. The Secret Service now has taken over our lives in the protection of the president, whether valid or not. More and more they've discovered helicopters—he rarely travels in public, his access to people has become almost nonexistent except on occasion when everything is very sanitized.

But the whole question is that reporters are some sort of a necessity yet this is the way we are treated. Our credibility is also at stake and is much more quickly exposed for all to see in any newspapers, on any television. A Supreme Court Justice once said that a constant spotlight on public officials lessens the possibility of corruption. And in the words of Justice Brandeis, if the government becomes a law breaker, it breeds contempt for the law. The importance of a free and robust press cannot be underestimated, but that we are a thorn in the side of government officials and others in public life is obvious. We know it's not our role to be loved or even liked—respected, we hope, and even by presidents, for being fair.

Each president has had his troubles with the press, going back to George Washington. We have a photograph of FDR in our press room which is inscribed to the White House reporters from their "devoted victim." "When the press stops abusing me, I'll know I'm in the wrong pew," said Truman. "Reading more and enjoying it less," said Kennedy. What LBJ said is unprintable. Nixon had his enemy's list and, once when the press walked into the cabinet room for picture taking, Nixon looked up at the press and said, "It's only coincidental that we're talking about pollution when the press walks in." Carter always seemed to be saying, "Lord, forgive them, for they know not what they do." As for Reagan, well, it's like being in those silent movies. He thinks we should be seen and not heard.

But I thought that Amy Carter kind of summed up the attitude when her mother escorted her to a public school, first day in class after they moved into the White House. Reporters and cameramen had been alerted in Washington that they could record this historic moment and promise never to bother little Amy again. And so the reporters and photographers flanked the walk to the school door. Amy looked at the press, her hand was held by her mother and she looked up at her mother and said, "Mom, do we still have to be nice to them?"

And I'll go with Jeff Carter, the former President's youngest son during the first Christmas in Plains, Georgia. We were standing across the street from the family home keeping an eye on Carter who had come out on the porch, playing with his grandchildren, grandstanding, we thought, on the porch for our benefit. A television cameraman asked Jeff, who strolled across the street, if he didn't feel sorry for his father hounded by the press, clocking his every move, and Jeff said, "No, he asked for it." And I guess that's the way I feel about presidents. They ask for it, knowing the press tries to be ever vigilant, ever present to keep an eye on the person who has life and death, pushbutton power over all humanity today, to keep the people informed and democracy alive. Thank you.

MR. THOMPSON: Do you think it's numbers that threaten presidents? If there were not as many reporters following them, if there were three of you, say, or ten more, would some of these historic attitudes of aversion toward the press be as deep-seated?

MS. THOMAS: You mean in terms of how we're treated?

MR. THOMPSON: Well, yes, and in terms of the negative attitudes toward the press.

MS. THOMAS: In terms of the public or the White House?

MR. THOMPSON: Well, in the early press conference days people talked about the fact that Roosevelt could fit the reporters into the Oval Office. Now if a graduate student at American University has made a contribution to President Carter's campaign he can get into a press conference.

MS. THOMAS: I don't think there's any question that the magnitude of the press corps now magnifies the problem. But I maintain that sometimes when we're only a pool of three or four reporters the Secret Service still continues to push us around because it's become a built-in syndrome. You cannot believe that if you're wearing a pass, if you have been cleared by the Secret Service, that you shouldn't even be in the White House if you're any kind of threat, and yet they continue to draw a line on every step you take.

MR. LATIMER: Did that then accentuate during the Reagan administration or was it just as bad under Carter and the others?

MS. THOMAS: It gave the Secret Service a chance for a quantum leap. They would just as soon keep him in a little capsule and. . . .

MR. DEAKIN: What you're saying is that this jump started after the assassination attempt?

MR. LATIMER: That's what I was wondering.

MS. THOMAS: It's all relative.

MR. CORMIER: It was not to this degree by any means, not at all.

MR. LATIMER: Does this seem to be the personal decision by Reagan himself? I mean, if left to his own devices would he do all this?

MS. THOMAS: Oh no, no. He's a friendly, nice man. There is no question about it. He likes people; I think he perhaps is not as affable as sometimes he appears but he certainly is a good politician. He knows people are important to a politician. But of course the press is in the role that you can't defy security because, indeed, they may be right or maybe they know something you don't know. But I am saying that people will never understand what it takes to get information. One day I was on a helicopter six times just covering the President to make sure that while he is in public nothing happens. I know it's macabre but that's the way it goes.

MR. CORMIER: It goes to ridiculous lengths. This is almost off the point but I can't forget it. Paul Healy borrowed a book from Nelson Rockefeller when he was vice president and the security in the old Executive Office Building in Washington, at least prior to Reagan, was much more stringent than at the White House. And so Paul had an appointment to see Rockefeller to return this book. The police stopped him, wanted to know what he was doing and he explained, and they made a call to Rockefeller's office: yes, he had the appointment; and the police said, "You can go in but the book stays here." It becomes pretty damn oppressive.

MS. THOMAS: At the same time the press offices also do not want us to comment—well, in terms of image this is a very interesting thing. You're always challenged on your own scepticism. Are you being fair? Every reporter does the same soulsearching every day. I've seen the Reagan administration make many end runs around civil rights laws, trying to cut them down and so forth. There's no question about it. Then the President picked up the newspaper, as they tell it later, and reads about this one family in College Park, Maryland right outside of Washington that had been harrassed; they've had a cross burning five years ago, crank telephone calls and garbage dumped on their lawn. He is struck by this horror and he comes in waving his newspaper in the Oval Office and he asks his aide, "What can we do about this? This is terrible, I'd like to go see them."

So the aide proceeds to put everything in place, get in touch with the family's lawyer and so forth and six hours later Larry Speakes comes running out. We have fifteen minutes to get on a helicopter because the President's going to go visit this family. He says the President did not want to take any press with him. He just wants to go tell this family how sorry he is, but we have talked him into having the press there—with the four thirty and the six o'clock news, you've got an hour and a half to make good—but we insisted, we told him that he had to. So anyway the President gets on the helicopter on the South Lawn and we go practically to the Washington Monument to get on another helicopter, fly to another spot, motorcade through the rush hour to get to this family. The President and Mrs. Reagan go into this home to talk to the family. The family had been alerted, the little girl was in her Sunday best and so forth. Every neighbor—I mean, at least 150 neighbors who were supposed to be maltreating these people and I'm sure they had been—were there, every television station had sent a cameraman and reporter. It's a good local story as well as for us, it was very good. But three or four times we were told the President absolutely did not want any press but that they had convinced him that it was necessary because he would be in public. He spends about 20 minutes inside the house, then comes out and a reporter asks a question, He is from here to the wall and one of his aides said "No further, this is the line." This is Andersonville. They drew the line. We were part of a pool, we had traveled with him and so forth. So you still find yourself almost shouting and he obviously wants to talk.

Then I think: am I so cynical that I think that maybe they wanted the press? They are embarked on an image change in terms of blacks, women, whatever and yet, I said, maybe he legitimately did not want the press, so you are confused as to where the truth is. Anyway, my feelings did not get into my story. I wrote it as factually as possible, pulling out all the stops on how the neighbors felt and so forth. Reporters do their own soul searching and I'm a cynic with hope.

Well, they did make the evening news, indeed they did in a very positive way.

MR. DEAKIN: Can I make a comment on the subject of bigness? What you're really asking, I gather, is: Are the American people offended and do they grow irritated and suspicious when they see this tremendous quantity of coverage, the number of people surrounding the president? You've got television people and cameras, and the president and the press are all jockeying for position and so forth. In a way you dealt with this in your commission report— the shouting, the waving hands and so forth.

Two points: In 1937, when Leo Rosten wrote his book on the Washington press corps, he found that there were six hundred accredited correspondents in Washington. He did this simply by counting up the number of reporters and photographers who were accredited to the Congressional press galleries. Today the figure is at least 4,300. So the press corps between 1937 and 1982 grew at least sevenfold, from 600 to 4,300, and probably more. And somehow people have the idea there's something wrong about this. Some of them are simply offended by the undignified spectacle of all these reporters and minicams and photographers trailing after the president and shouting and jostling for position. And with some, I think, even if they don't articulate it, there's a feeling of "This is too big." It's always that way, of course—power and bigness alarm people and frighten people.

But there's a double standard at work here with respect to the press. I don't want to get paranoid. I've seen too many paranoid politicians. But nevertheless a double standard is being applied to the press, because elsewhere in the American society bigness is considered very, very good. It's considered a desirable thing. We used to have literally scores of automobile companies; now we have three. The entire trend of the American economy has been toward bigness. Bigness works and smallness is inefficient. Well, when the same thing happens with the news media, which are themselves big business, free enterprise—somehow something is wrong with it.

Now, I'm going to give you a little comment, if I may, on something that Helen said at the beginning of her very admirable presentation. She made a reference to the famous Herblock cartoon in early 1969, after Nixon had been inaugurated. Herblock, as Helen points out, had always pictured Nixon with a villanous five o'clock shadow. But now he drew a cartoon showing himself as a barber and offering Nixon a free shave, in other words, a fresh start. OK, the reporters remembered the McCarthy era, we remembered Jerry Voorhis, we remembered Helen Gahagan Douglas, we remembered the '62 gubernatorial election in California where they set up this phony Democrats-for-Nixon committee, using people's names without their permission or without even notifying them. Pat Brown took them to court, it was so flagrant. So we remembered all the demagoguery and all the dirty tricks, because the dirty tricks were operating even that early. There was nothing new about Watergate. As Victor Lasky said, it had happened before. Yes, it had happened before—under Nixon.

All right. We remembered all that, but what Herblock was doing was symbolizing the attitude that prevailed in the press corps. Nixon was now President of the United States, and as Lyndon Johnson said we only have one president at a time. If he succeeds, we succeed. If he fails, we fail. So there was going to be a honeymoon. The press was offering this man a honeymoon. That's what the Herblock cartoon symbolized. They were offering a fresh start in their relationship with him.

Now I want to give you Nixon's reaction, because it is not generally known what his reaction was. Jim Keogh, who was his speechwriter, attended Nixon's first cabinet meeting before the Inauguration. It took place on December 12, 1968. Nixon had been supported by 80 percent of America's newspapers, so the honeymoon spirit was in the air, and here was Nixon's reaction, as reported by Keogh:

> Always remember that the men and women of the news media approach this as an adversary relationship. The time will come when they will run lies about you. And the columnists and editorial writers will make you seem to be scoundrels or fools or both. And the cartoonists will depict you as ogres. Some of your wives will get up in the morning and look at the papers and start to cry. Now, don't let this get you down, don't let it defeat you and don't try to adjust your actions to what you think will please them. Do what you think is the right thing to do and let the criticism roll off your back. Don't think that the criticism you see or hear in one or two places is all that is getting through to the public.

It's that first sentence I want to draw to your attention. "Always remember the men and the women of the news media approach this as an adversary relationship." In other words, it didn't make any difference whether the press was offering this man a honeymoon or not. As far as he was concerned, there could not be a honeymoon. He wasn't going to have a honeymoon because he was absolutely convinced that the press was implacably opposed to him.

MS. THOMAS: And he had felt that way since 1940.

MR. DEAKIN: He had felt that way ever since he had discovered that the *Los Angeles Times* was not the only newspaper in America. As long as all he had to read was the *Los Angeles Times,* which was coddling him and giving no space to his opponents and playing him up as the great, young anti-Communist Congressman and so forth, he thought that's all the press was. Then all of a sudden he discovered there were other papers besides the *Times.*

MS. THOMAS: I think that the public reaction is understandable. They see us shouting at the president, in terms of the quicky so-called ten minute press conferences. It's very competitive, we're each shouting to get a question in, and the TV people are even more competitive because they have their cameras there and they have to make good for their bosses as well as imagewise. It's a real scramble, and ten minutes is certainly not enough to develop anything before Speakes panics and cuts it off. This is what they consider a feeding, and knowing that this would come across like a bunch of banshees to the public. We all get mail: How can you treat the president like this, you horrible person, and so forth. They'll never understand.

Also I think I resent quite a bit the columnists who do sit in their ivory towers after we scramble for one word from a president and I mean one. They can sit back and say: the president said this today. One day the president was walking out of the White House and I said, "Mr. President, is there a recession on?" As he stepped into his helicopter he said, "Yes." This is the kind of thing. Weeks could go by when you wouldn't have a press conference to ever ask him that. But you are there, you're there in the middle of the night, you're there at five o'clock in the morning or whatever time it's necessary to get one assessment.

MR. DEAKIN: I've got to tell you a story about Lyndon Johnson to add to that list. Helen is one of these reporters who lives for the honest answer that you occasionally get. During the Dominican crisis—you remember this, Helen—this was when twenty-five hundred people allegedly had their heads chopped off, the whole business. During the Dominican crisis, Johnson had this incredible walking press conference when he talked about our people being killed and the U.S. Ambassador telephoning from under his desk while the bullets were whistling by. And all of this was just absolutely untrue. Furthermore, two weeks had gone by and there had been plenty of time to check and Johnson was still giving out wrong information and declassifying secret reports from the CIA on the spot. That didn't seem to work. Sending the Marines to the Dominican Republic wasn't selling. So he came up with a new justification for it, and it was the standard justification—the Commies are behind it. The Dominican revolution is about to go Communist.

MS. THOMAS: First explanation for it was to protect the Americans.

MR. DEAKIN: Yes, first it was to protect the Americans. That didn't work. So then he switched to the Commie threat in the Dominican

Republic. He started saying the revolt had been taken over by the Communists. He doled out that line, the national security line. And then he held another walking press conference. John Chancellor was covering for NBC at that time, and John, not anticipating the kind of answer he was going to get, said, "Mr. President, at what point did you discover that the Dominican revolution was being taken over by the Communists?" He stopped and said, "At no time." It was the only time he told the truth in the whole crisis.

MR. CORMIER: I'd like to raise a point. I think that a lot of what Helen has been talking about is the necessity for the press to corner the president wherever they can, sometimes in a fashion that is a little unseemly, maybe. This really points back to a fundamental failure by Reagan to implement as promised the recommendations of the Miller Center Commission on presidential press conferences with respect to the frequency of holding these conferences.

If the man were available, as the Commission suggested and as he should be, this all would become quite unnecessary.

MR. DEAKIN: They may be sitting down for the press conference, Ken, in response to your report. But the other thing you called for was frequency of press conferences.

MR. JONES: In those statements the two characterizations that comes through to me most—both fascinating statements and descriptions of the relationship—are skepticism and cynicism, above all. Are these characteristics essential for doing a good job?

MR. DEAKIN: Yes on number one. If a reporter isn't skeptical of official statements, he is not a reporter. If a reporter is not skeptical of what not just the government but everyone tells him, what is the impetus for him to go on and try to find out what the truth is? If he just accepts it—oh, you say that black is white, all right I'll put it in my paper that black is white—what kind of reporting is that? Is that journalism? Is that communication, maintaining a conduit of information? Skepticism is absolutely vital.

Now cynicism depends. I spent twenty-five years covering the White House, and after it reached a certain point I had to guard against paralytic cynicism. Because I had seen so much human folly, so many mistakes, so many lies, that I had to pull myself up short all the time and say: yes, I understand. They are human beings, they are under pressure, they are lying because they wish to prevail, they want their policies and programs to prevail. I must understand why they are lying. I must not permit myself to become paralytically cynical, to the point that I cannot ever see a good motive or worthwhile motive in anything. I have to guard against that.

MS. THOMAS: I can see ourselves as believers. We have enough for a book on them in terms of skepticism, but we still are believers. Every day we go to the White House we expect to get the truth, we work to get the truth, and we put out what we can get.

MR. DEAKIN: You know what reporters at the White House are, or reporters covering city hall or the governor or anybody else? They're just like the American people in one respect. They all live by Dr. Johnson's dictum. Dr. Johnson said, "Mankind lives from hope to hope." The last hope is always disappointed but you live for that next one.

MS. THOMAS: I don't think you see cynics in the press corps.

MR. DEAKIN: Every time the president goes on television and makes *his* pitch and defends *his* programs, he has access to the American people to make his case, in that one-way communication we were talking about. And every time that happens, the press is saying implicitly: OK, we'll give you the benefit of the doubt. Tell us. We give you the facility, we give you time on the air waves, we give you the space in the newspaper, every time we print that State of the Union message, that budget message, that economic report—in all of it, we're saying we're giving you the benefit of the doubt. Tell us what you plan to do; tell us your reasons for it. We are not saying to you, no, no, we don't believe it from the beginning so we won't print it and we won't put it on TV.

I mean, what are we talking about here folks? There's one hell of a lot of cooperation and help, sheer help for the president from the press. We're not out there destroying this guy from the moment he gets in. We're giving him that time on TV to make his case. He may raise hell about the instant analysis that comes afterward. In the days when they were really attacking instant analysis, during the Nixon administration, people were saying, how come they let David Brinkley and Eric Sevareid and the other pundits come on right after the president and pick everything he says to pieces? It's a liberal conspiracy to destroy this man, to destroy the president, conveniently ignoring the fact that the president had just spent half an hour on national television making *his* case.

MS. THOMAS: And sometimes the analysis isn't picking it apart; it's simply saying, to sum up, this is what he's saying and what they'll do and so forth.

MR. JONES: Does the scepticism drive the determination of truth? In any one event there are a number of truths depending on how people see it.

MS. THOMAS: Neither Jim Deakin nor I really touched on the fact that there obviously is a handbook of cliché answers handed down from one press secretary to another to avoid telling you anything, to avoid telling you the truth sometimes but to avoid maybe outright lying: "I have no knowledge of that," "I'm not aware of that," etc. Then Larry Speakes has developed this. If you ask what you think is a telling question because he put something on the table—now, about the budget and so forth, Speakes came out and said we've narrowed the differences. He took the line that Baker had given him. Well, they had not narrowed the differences at all. And then when you challenge him the next day it goes on. On Friday when the unemployment figures came out, ten million unemployed, and so forth he stated the Reagan line because it's all the Democrats' fault. I claim that it's George Washington's fault.

MR. DEAKIN: Yes, because you can work every one of these all the way back.

MS. THOMAS: And so it was the Democrats' fault and so forth and Reagan has always said when the ten percent cut comes in on July 1 that's when his program will work. To Speakes I said, "Now you say that the Democrats are at fault but you are predicting an up-turn now. My question is, when does Reagan take responsibility for the economy, for the country, for whatever is happening? Can he say on July 1 that this is the date, this is the deadline?" He refused to answer. If you knew the frustration. Skepticism, we don't even have enough skepticism. You are constantly being defied on simple questions.

MR. DEAKIN: You know Lady Bird had to ask the Secret Service whether Lyndon Johnson was going to Texas. If you think we have trouble getting information—his own wife.

MR. CORMIER: On the question of scepticism versus possible truth, it seems to me that it is a truism that when the White House or the president says something it's much the same as Joe McCarthy the first time waving the list of alleged Communists. If what he says is wrong, it takes time for the press to catch up with the fact that he's wrong. His story is reported, more often than not, undiluted, first crack out of the box. Then reporters are skeptical, they start wondering, then you may get the follow-up stories that say, well maybe it isn't quite that way.

MS. THOMAS: That's the story of the disability, the man in the Virginia area. Reagan gave an interview for the *Oklahoma Daily,* they were very, very sympathetic. They said "You're right, Mr. President." He brought up that he's always being accused that these cuts in benefits are hurting people, he brought up this man who applied for disability, was offered a job and he wouldn't work, and how the government was really being taken. Well, his story stayed for a day or two. Then a few of us began to check into this question, the man was being interviewed, and he was sort of arbitrarily taken off of disability. The story is not unique. But they proceeded to show that this was—actually the cuts had come about through the Carter administration. They failed to say that Reagan had accelerated the program where there would be less inspection of anyone's right to have disability or not.

And then they read the social security regulations which will astound you. It seems that this man was a worker, a welder, and he had been hit on the head so he suffered from seizures and became progressively bad. The Social Security regulation said that he did not have enough seizures to merit payments! Then you say how many seizures does he have to have? Anyway, Frank's point is right, that the president can say something and then it takes you three days, if you have a reporter who wanted to follow it up, to see if it is true.

MR. DEAKIN: Only in recent years have people in Nevada and Utah, particularly Utah, begun filing suits against the government over atomic tests that the government said at the time were harmless. One-way communication, the government's version, the government's statement, the government's version of the truth. The press in this case didn't exercise skepticism. It accepted the official version. Now thirty years later we find that the leukemia rate among children in those Utah communities is scores of times higher than the national average, and people are dying off like flies. They're dying at forty instead of living to seventy. Only now, thirty years too late, are some reporters beginning to exercise skepticism, and even then it was only when the suits began to be filed. Often we can't find out. But if the skepticism wasn't there we would *never* find out.

MR. CORMIER: The hope is in the skepticism.

MR. YOUNG: I've read two articles recently, one by Tony Lewis and one by somebody, I forget who, out of the *New York Times* who was reporting on the Congress, on the mood of the Congress. And I would just like to have your comments about this in the context of your discussion. One of the points that Tony Lewis made in his article, it was on reportage, was about Reagan. You're undoubtedly familiar with it and I think I remember that one of the points he made was that, he was asking why the press was being so kind to Reagan when they know the truth about his state of mind, about his ability, and so on. It was rather striking and I didn't know quite what to make of it. It may have something to do with the honeymoon, maybe he's all off base—I would just like your comments about it.

The other thing I want to ask you about, the article on Congress, was a betrayal of the mood and mind-set of a certain group of newbreed congressmen, and one of them was quoted as saying, or words to this effect, that the President lies.

MS. THOMAS: Who says that?

MR. YOUNG: One of the congressmen quoted. And I wonder if that mood, if you'd encountered it. What do you do with that as a reporter?

MR. DEAKIN: If you say something in the newspaper or on television, and you can't document it, your editor will take that statement out, if he's on the ball. I get asked all the time, why didn't the press print anything about John F. Kennedy's sex life, the fact that he was chasing women all the time? How, since this always comes from the far right, I always answer: For the same reason we didn't print anything about Nixon's drinking. But the fact is if we couldn't document it we couldn't print it.

MR. YOUNG: I was struck by the fact that it was a reporter writing this statement.

MR. DEAKIN: Tony Lewis is very liberal. But Tony Lewis in this instance was forgetting the fact that if you can't document something, you can't print it. Look at the trouble the *Washington Post* got in when it printed something that its editors had let get by without demanding that the reporter document it; demanding to know who's your source when you say you've discovered this eight-year-old heroin addict named Jimmy. They didn't do it. They got themselves in terrible trouble.

MS. THOMAS: We don't write our personal opinions. Tony is absolutely wrong. His only perceptions of Reagan come through us. He's never there. He doesn't man the barricade. Far from it. He's off in the Middle East or somewhere else. What he knows about the President we have told him. And we have told him as factually as possible.

I believe in objective reporting. I believe there is certainly a place for it, and there's certainly a place for Tony. I love his writing, but I think he's absolutely wrong. In those euphoric moments after presidents become presidents, we may say, let him get his feet wet; but the question of judging him every day—we lay it down: this president has said this. And other reporters take off from there and see if it's so or not. But, "He said, he added," is still first.

MR. CORMIER: Let me get in something here. I know of only one instance where the White House press corps has semi-grappled with something that we did not want to write about on a president's trip. And that was when Jerry Ford was first in office. It sometimes seemed to us that he took a martini or two too many and we wondered how do we deal with this? Well, he went up to Boston and made a speech and *Newsweek*—I must say it was the only publication with the guts to do it—simply made an offhand reference to him slurring his words when he spoke. I never saw Jerry Ford approaching insobriety again.

MR. THOMPSON: You did draw a number of examples from foreign policy? Does that mean—maybe this is a "When did you stop beating your wife?" type question—that you would have doubts about the distinction between foreign policy matters and domestic policy matters? It is often argued that there are some issues where you, the reporter, can't expect to get to the heart of the issue when serious business is going on? It concerned Camp David, and presumably it concerns some of the negotiations going on now? Are there some constraints on what the reporters can find out, necessarily, about foreign policy, given its nature? Should there be a possibility for an administration, when highly sensitive issues and negotiations are in a make or break stage, to get away from reporters and get away from publicity?

MS. THOMAS: I believe in an almost total open society. I believe that we should know as much as possible about foreign policy, particularly when the President himself says you have seventeen minutes to get out of town before the bomb falls. I think the people should be alert as to what's happening. I think too much is suppressed. I would want no blocks in the legitimacy of the pursuit of trying to find out what they're doing in the foreign policy field. Perhaps there are some very legitimate military secrets and I don't think we ever really try to pull those. We try to find out what's going on. So much was suppressed and there was so much deception in Vietnam, for example. Those kind of things. The President has an NSC meeting, national security council meeting, maybe once a week, sometimes more. He will never say it's an emergency meeting and will never give you the topic. And once in a while you'll want to leak it, as three newspapers, for example, had on Thursday I think it was, that Reagan would propose a fifty-fifty equal deterrent and so forth. The story obviously came from the same source and had been placed with about three papers. My feeling is that we should try to find out as much as possible and that certainly foreign policy and national security should not be off-limits. I don't understand why the Americans will be hurt if they find out what's going on.

MR. DEAKIN: Well, skepticism as far as journalists are concerned, is based on experience. You know, there's a collective memory that journalists have when they have been in Washington for a long time, a greater memory of what's happened before than some people who are coming in for the first time to run the government, people who've never been in Washington before, which is usually the case with each new administration. So, reporters have a collective memory of these things that administrations usually don't have, unless they bring in a lot of old hands. And the collective memory that the journalists have is of time after time after time, instance after instance after instance, in which the government claimed that the security of the nation would be impaired or endangered if certain information were made public. Then the information was made public, did get into the press, and *nothing happened.* There was never the slightest evidence that it was of any aid to any adversary or enemy of the United States. Nobody took advantage of us in some negotiations or threatened us with any kind of military or nuclear blackmail. In other words, all the dangers that the government said would happen if certain information were made public did not materialize. They all turned out to be chimeras. So we get very skeptical about this claim of national security.

The classic instance, and I'm going to give you several, was the Pentagon Papers. The *New York Times* had obtained the Pentagon Papers. The Nixon administration wasn't even involved in the Pentagon Papers; they didn't cover the Nixon administration. Nevertheless, after an initial period of trying to figure out what to do, they went to court and got an injunction against the *New York Times* and subsequently other newspapers on the grounds that the publication of the Pentagon Papers would endanger the national security. It went all the way to the Supreme Court and it was very narrowly held that the *New York Times* and the other papers had the right to publish the Pentagon Papers. And so the rest of the Pentagon Papers came out and all this danger to national security didn't materialize. It wasn't there.

Let me give you two or three other examples. After Johnson left the presidency he was interviewed by Walter Cronkite. And Cronkite asked Johnson whether his last secretary of defense, Clark Clifford, had been responsible for the bombing pause in Vietnam. I don't know Johnson's motives, but apparently he didn't want Clifford to get the credit for having advocated and persuaded Johnson to stop the bombing of North Vietnam. So in an effort to show that it was not Clifford who had done this, Johnson pulled a document out of his pocket—and this was before a national television audience—and he read this paper which showed that on such and such a date he, Johnson, had ordered the study of possible alternatives to the bombing. And Johnson announced—he didn't imply it, he stated it explicitly—that this was a classified document, a national security document. And he wasn't even president at the time; he was a former president. He simply declassified this document on national television and read it to the American people. He did this constantly in press conferences, especially the press conferences he had on the lawn. He would pull out something and it was classified, a CIA report or a Pentagon report, and because it served his purpose to give out the information he declassified it on the spot. Other presidents have done similar things many times— leaking national security information. The Reagan administration has done it whenever it suited their purpose.

Now, the question that arises is this: If the information was such that it imperiled or might imperil the security of the United States, but the next moment it was no threat to the American people so it could be declassified, then what are we supposed to say national security is? And what we come down to, unfortunately, is that national security consists of what the president says it is at any given moment. But that is a very relative kind of definition. It's not a very absolute kind of definition. It's not something you can rely on very much.

MS. THOMAS: And it's also so that the people will not get in on the dialogue. They will not be able to say anything. It is a *fait accompli,* any time they want to make a decision, nobody else is able to get in on it and decide whether it's right or wrong.

MR. DEAKIN: Or if they do get in on it they only get in on the government's terms. It declassifies the information and gives it out. One-way communication. Let me give you another example. Johnson held a summit meeting with Premier Kosygin in Glassboro, New Jersey. It was all secret. The reporters weren't told anything. All we got was, you know, the length of the meeting. We weren't told what they talked about, what the results were or anything else because, of course, that would affect national security; that was a national security matter. So as soon as it was over Johnson flew to Texas and he invited Max Frankel, who was then covering the White House for the *New York Times,* out to the ranch. They take a swim together and Johnson is standing in the water and proceeds to give Frankel a one-hour report on everything that was discussed at the summit meeting. And Frankel is free to use it. So what is this national security stuff?

Here is another example. George Christian, who was Johnson's press secretary for the last two years, attended the so-called troika meeting that Johnson held every Friday morning with McNamara and Rostow, in which they made Vietnam policy. He was there every Friday for two years. But we never could get one word out of

Christian about what was said in those meetings until they were ready to announce something. If they had something to announce, they announced it. But we could never find out what the pros and cons were, what considerations they were weighing, what their thinking was, what they were doing. Not a word—couldn't get a word out of them for two solid years. Then Johnson leaves office and Christian writes a book. And Max Frankel talks about this book in his deposition in the Pentagon Papers case, and Frankel says there are seventy pages of that book that contain classified information. We couldn't be given it at the time, the American people couldn't be given it, but he could put it in a book.

MR. THOMPSON: Do you think there would have been a Camp David agreement if reporters had been allowed to mingle with the negotiators?

MS. THOMAS: Of course. It was just a question of Carter twisting Begin's arm off. We all knew it was going on. I don't understand why it had to be so secret. We were never allowed to even send one photographer there in—how long was it? More than a week. No, I don't see why all this had to be in total secrecy.

MR. DEAKIN: The American people have to pay for these decisions. They've got to pay for them, either in money or blood or loss of affluence or whatever it may be. They've got to pay for it. But they're not going to be told about it until, as Helen says, it is a *fait accompli.*

MS. THOMAS: Why should it be twenty-five years later in a White Paper. What good's that?

MR. THOMPSON: If my wife and I have any difficulties we have to work it out and the best chance for working it out is in private.

MS. THOMAS: Yes, but you don't control millions of people and their fates.

MR. THOMPSON: Well, the method is the same and we've learned that the open covenants openly arrived at works if the open arrived part isn't emphasized too much.

MS. THOMAS: I don't agree at all.

MR. CORMIER: I would throw in one thing here. Without defending the secrecy there, we were suddenly in a position of dealing with substance in the form of rumors that were appearing in the Israeli and the Arabian press. And oftentimes they were very well informed, much better informed than we were. We were getting it from the Middle East reporters. We knew nothing.

MR. DEAKIN: Do you know that practically every president we've had has been far more candid and far more frank and far more open with the foreign press than he is with the American press? Almost every one of them. They will talk to Henry Brandon and the British journalists and the French journalists and tell them things they'll never tell us. It's safe for the British and French to read about it, but it's not safe for the American people.

MS. THOMAS: In the bombing of Cambodia, for fourteen months the Cambodians knew they were being bombed, the Vietnamese knew that bombing was going on, the Russians knew the bombing was going on, the Chinese knew the bombing was going on. So why the secrecy? The secrecy was simply not to scare hell out of the American people and say that Nixon is widening this war while all the time he's saying he's pulling out.

MR. THOMPSON: What would you have said in the papers if you had known—maybe you did—that Hamilton Jordan was sitting up with the Panamanian head of state all hours of the night trying to get the last pieces of the Panama treaty worked out?

MS. THOMAS: Fine. What's wrong with that?

MR. DEAKIN: You think if we had said it, that would have stopped them from doing it? If they really wanted to do it?

MS. THOMAS: What's wrong with that?

MR. THOMPSON: First thing you would have said was that he didn't have any experience and that would have gotten flashed around the world. The second thing—

MS. THOMAS: Everybody knew he didn't have experience. Torrijos knew he didn't have any experience. I mean he came right out of Georgia and had no foreign policy background.

MR. THOMPSON: But they finally worked out the last—

MS. THOMAS: He was acting under Carter's orders. He was an emissary at the time.

MR. DEAKIN: The mere fact that the press says somebody is doing something has no legal force to prevent people from going right on and doing something. If they do stop, it's usually because they are doing something wrong.

MS. THOMAS: When this administration started making sounds like a little war in El Salvador might possibly occur, it gave the impression that they rule out nothing so they could send troops there. The administration, the White House was bombarded with letters from parents saying hell no, we won't go. They sent all these letters over to the State Department, I mean, the White House was not going to get this.

MR. THOMPSON: You would acknowledge there are some appropriate areas of quiet diplomacy?

MS. THOMAS: No. I like to know as much as possible and to be able to transmit as much as possible.

MR. DEAKIN: It depends on so many things. I think it's impossible to speak for the American press; it is not monolithic. We have conservative publications and liberal publications, conservative reporters and liberal reporters—you can't generalize. I suspect that if there was more candor from the administration about the factors that go into making decisions in foreign policy and so forth, national security matters, that it would ease some of the pressure and would actually permit them to do more of the quiet diplomacy. Because nothing disarms a reporter so much as feeling that he or she is being given some information. That's what they live for; that's what they exist for. Give them some information and go right back behind closed doors. It takes some of the heat off, and you can go on and do more of your quiet diplomacy without the press breathing down your neck. Because you're giving them something; you're giving them something to put in the paper or on the tube. I'm not saying that that is going to stop them. I'm not saying that they're not going to continue to go at you hammer and tongs for more; they'll always ask for more. So it's just a speculation on my part, that if they were more candid about things, and really, they could be candid about things without doing any real danger, they probably would take some of the heat off themselves. It is a matter of human nature. If you are absolutely told no, you can't do something, that increases your interest in doing it. And if reporters are told no, we won't tell you anything, they get that much more energetic in trying to find out something. But if they're given a little something, it takes the heat off. The analogy is with Bismarck. Otto was no liberal, but what he did with the Social Democratic party in Germany was to throw them a little bone here, a little bone there, a little bit of social welfare. Milk for nursing mothers. And what happened was that it quieted the Social Democrats in the Bundestag. It toned them down because he gave them a little something. If you do this with reporters, you'll get pretty much the same result.

MR. CORMIER: We're easily manipulated.

MR. JONES: In this national security area, I wonder if there are some limits. I watched the marvelous program on Oppenheimer. Is that a case, the development of a weapon during the kind of war that World War II was, is that a case where the press should not report, that we should insist on secrecy?

MS. THOMAS: I think it would have been much safer for the Japanese to know, that might have stopped a lot of killing.

MR. DEAKIN: The reason for it was because it was wartime and there was a censorship program. It was a voluntary censorship program that the press adhered to almost completely. There was the exception of the *Chicago Tribune* with the Japanese Purple Code. Otherwise this massive institution, the American press, adhered to the voluntary censorship program with practically one hundred percent compliance and the secret Manhattan project was kept secret throughout the entire war.

MR. CORMIER: But not by us. It was kept by the government.

MR. DEAKIN: Well, they also did a very good job of keeping the secret.

MS. THOMAS: Well, my point is maybe if it had been publicized that such a bomb existed finally and the U.S. was ready to use it maybe the Japanese could have saved themselves.

MR. DEAKIN: There's a problem with that, Helen, because if that had happened and it had got back to Hitler then we might have pushed Hitler into developing the atomic bomb.

MR. CORMIER: There is a sense of limits. I'm not quite sure what it is.

MR. DEAKIN: There have to be limits. But if the press is asked to exercise sound judgment and agree to limits, especially in wartime, then the government has to understand that there are limits on the limitation of information. Instead, we've come to the point now where everything is classified.

MR. JONES: Oftentimes one comes away from something like that Oppenheimer program with all of us saying that maybe there should have been more consideration—

MS. THOMAS: My feeling is that I have found out that any time a big secret has been revealed it has been more helpful to world knowledge and more important than the harm it does.

MR. BLACKFORD: Back in 1956 the CIA got Khrushchev's speech. And we still don't know how they got it. Does it make any difference?

MS. THOMAS: Out of Warsaw, huh?

MR. BLACKFORD: Does it make any difference how they got it out? The news is the speech, is it not?

MS. THOMAS: That's right. It's interesting in a replay of how it did happen but that wouldn't be the big part. The speech was the important thing and it really shocked the world.

MR. DEAKIN: But you can turn that one around and you can say ah, hah! Isn't that an obvious example where national security should have been maintained? Shouldn't that have been a closely held secret? We shouldn't have let the Russians know that we had that kind of intelligence, expertise, and facilities. But no, as soon as it suits the government's purpose to have it out, it comes out—and that's the point about national security. National security ceases to exist the moment the government decides that the information will be of some assistance to it.

We've seen this now with Reagan over and over and over again. Stuff that was absolutely secret classified information is suddenly released. Weinberger did it with the Soviet capability assessment. One moment something is top secret. The next moment they can use it, so they put it out.

MS. THOMAS: They flipped out when there was a report that we were helping the British [in the Falklands] with intelligence. They really flipped out. All kinds of running around finding the leakers

and stuff. I think that most Americans would assume we are
helping the British with intelligence. So I don't understand those
kinds of mentality.

V

Conclusion

Concluding Note

The power of the media has been demonstrated throughout the pages of this work. Its influence is manifested in every sector of American life. Yet voices continue to be raised asking what its impact will be for good or ill. What will observers looking back from the vantage point of the twenty-first century have to say about the media and what kind of balance sheet will they draw.

The authors of the separate essays in this book have proceeded empirically examining the media in relation to politics, the presidency and individual presidents. The conclusions to be drawn are implicit in the discussions. They bring us back to a recognition of the immense potential and power of the media. Only strong institutions and strong leaders can survive the brunt of the media's thrust. A Franklin D. Roosevelt harnessed the media to his ends, a Lyndon B. Johnson or Richard M. Nixon was destroyed. Those who would live in the television age must master it, not be ruled by it. This may be the foremost lesson from the pages of this book.

DATE DUE

SEP 1 0 1987		
MAY 1 9 1988		
APR 3 1989		
APR 1 2 1989		
APR 8 1991		
APR 1 4 1992		
APR 2 3 1993		
DEC 1 6 1994		
APR 2 1 1995		